KV-051-010

Chow Yun-fat and Territories of Hong Kong Stardom

Chow Yun-fat and Territories of Hong Kong Stardom

Lin Feng

EDINBURGH
University Press

Edinburgh University Press is one of the leading university presses
in the UK. We publish academic books and journals in our selected
subject areas across the humanities and social sciences, combining
cutting-edge scholarship with high editorial and production
values to produce academic works of lasting importance. For more
information visit our website: edinburghuniversitypress.com

Edinburgh University Press Ltd
The Tun – Holyrood Road
12 (2f) Jackson's Entry
Edinburgh EH8 8PJ

Typeset in 11/13 Monotype Ehrhardt by
Servis Filmsetting Ltd, Stockport, Cheshire,
and printed and bound in Great Britain by
CPI Group (UK) Ltd, Croydon CR0 4YY

A CIP record for this book is available from the British Library

ISBN 978 1 4744 0589 8 (hardback)
ISBN 978 1 4744 0590 4 (webready PDF)
ISBN 978 1 4744 0591 1 (epub)

Contents

Acknowledgements

I would like to dedicate this book to my dear family, especially to my parents, Shen Xuezhen and Feng Chengzhong. Without their tremendous encouragement and love, the completion of this book would not have been possible. I would like to express my sincere gratitude to all those who helped me along the way, including my PhD supervisors Dr Julian Stringer and Dr Mark Gallagher, whose comments, guidance and support have helped me to develop into an independent scholar. My sincere thanks also go to my editors, Gillian Leslie and Richard Strachan, whose patience and great support made this book possible. I appreciate the insightful comments, advice and suggestions given to me by Dr Gary Bettinson, Dr Luke Robinson and my friends regarding various sections of the manuscript. Last but not least, I would like to say thank you to David Thompson and his parents, Mary and Ron Thompson, whose love has given me enormous support during the period of writing.

Several sections of the book have been published previously in various journals and books. I am grateful to the publishers and editors who have allowed me to reproduce the content in this book. A short version of Chapter 1 was published as 'Chow Yun-fat: Hong Kong's modern TV *Xiaosheng*' in Yingjin Zhang and Mary Farquhar (eds) *Chinese Film Stars* (2010: 196–206). The article is reproduced here with permission of Routledge. A longer version of my article, 'Star endorsement and Hong Kong cinema: the social mobility of Chow Yun-fat 1986–1995', *Journal of Chinese Cinemas*, vol. 5, no. 3 (2011: 269–81) is included here as Chapter 3. Chapter 7 is derived in part from an article published as 'Glocalising Chinese stardom: Internet publicity and the construction of Chow Yun-fat's transnational stardom', *Journal of Transnational Cinemas*, vol. 2, no. 1 (2011: 77–91). Both chapters are reprinted here by permission of the publisher Taylor & Francis (http://www.tandfonline.com). A different version of Chapter 8 was published in Leung Wing-fai and Andy Willis' (eds) *East Asian Film Stars* (2014: 113–27), and is reproduced here with the permission of Palgrave Macmillan.

Figures and Tables

FIGURES

TABLES

Note on the Text

This book explores the construction and circulation of Chow's star image, both in regional and transnational cultural industries and markets. Therefore, I conducted a method of bilingual research by looking at materials from both English and Chinese sources. Accordingly, a translation was needed for the Chinese-language materials, either written (such as posters, magazine interviews and film reviews) or multimedia (such as film footage and songs). In this book, all films are referred to by their English title. The Chinese terms and phrases discussed in the book are also listed in the English–Chinese Glossary with a clear explanation of the original language. Unless otherwise specified, all Chinese-to-English translations are my own.

Another aspect of the translation is the romanisation of Chinese names. This book primarily adopts the *pinyin* system, which is the standard transliteration based on Mandarin pronunciation. However, this standard is not imposed on all the characters mentioned in this book, due to the different transliteration systems used in places like Hong Kong, Taiwan, and some other overseas Chinese communities (in which the romanisation of a name either follows the Wade–Giles system or is based on the Cantonese pronunciation). In such cases, the romanisation of many Hong Kong and Taiwan names retain their original or most popular spelling (such as 'Chow Yun-fat' rather than 'Zhou Runfa') in order to minimise confusion. In terms of the textual presentation of Chinese names, this book follows the Chinese tradition by displaying surnames first and given names last. In cases where an individual chooses to adopt a name in English or other Western language, the spelling follows Western convention, i.e. given name first and surname at the end (such as 'Andy Lau', not 'Lau Tak-wah'). In alphabetical listings, the family name appears before the given name, separated by a comma according to Western convention.

Finally, two more considerations regarding nomenclature need to be addressed. First, there are cases where two characters are generally known by their English names that are the same. For instance, there are two men called Tony Leung in the Hong Kong film industry, and both are well-known male stars of around the same age. Secondly, there is the issue of a person choosing to give the reader both his or her English and Chinese given names. In such cases, the name is presented in the order of English given name, Chinese surname and then Chinese given name (such as Tony Leung Chiu-wai, Tony Leung Ka-fai and Lawrence Ng Wai-kwok).

Introduction

In today's celebrity culture, stars' public images and their private lives are a popular topic of everyday discussion. From the newspapers, magazines and tabloids to the multimedia vehicles of film, television and the Internet, stars not only help to promote products and services, but also, as Christine Gledhill (1991: xiii) pointed out, signify various social and cultural values and personal desires. Since the mid-1980s, an increasing number of Hong Kong actors have entered the global film market and have transformed themselves from regional celebrities to transnational stars. Perhaps as a result of the success of Hong Kong action cinema in the global commercial film market, the majority of Hong Kong stars, such as Jackie Chan, Jet Li, and Michelle Yeoh, who have made their way into Hollywood and other major film markets outside East Asia, are those whose performances and images rely heavily on their control of their bodies and on their mastery of physical skills.

However, although these Hong Kong stars' screen images as action heroes or martial artists have helped to (re)define the Chinese image created by early Hollywood and even to impel the evolvement of the cinematic representation of Chinese people beyond East Asia in recent years, the prevalence of on-screen Chinese action heroes and martial artists has also established a new stereotypical image of Chinese men and women as constantly performing kicks, punches, jumps, spins and other spectacular action stunts. This in turn narrows the general public's perception of Chinese (including Hong Kong) stardom in the global film market, as well as limiting job opportunities for Chinese actors outside East Asia.

In response to these observations, this book investigates the construction and circulation of Hong Kong actor Chow Yun-fat's star image across various entertainment industries and cultural markets. As with the aforementioned stars, Chow captured Hollywood's attention through his performances in action films. However, he is also known in Asia as a versatile actor who has starred in films spanning a wide range of genres, including but not limited to melodrama, comedy, thrillers and Westerns. This raises a question concerning the way in which stardom permeates across various cultural borders. By following Chow's career path, this book examines how the different territories of Chow's star image are selected by the mass media as a way of articulating the social perceptions of Hong Kong's cultural identity in its specific historical, social and cultural contexts in relation to the discourse of gender, race, age, social mobility and political diversity.

By using the term 'territories', I refer not only to the different aspects or layers of Chow's star persona, but also to the specific industry and market conditions that have shaped his star image. As the book illustrates, star image shifts across various historical, geographic and cultural borders. In order to cater for, and sometimes to shape, the public's taste and expectations, different media highlight certain dimensions of star image, while at the same time downplaying or even neglecting others. As a result, the star image we encounter is always temporary, fragmented and partially presented. An emphasis on the territories of stardom, however, does not imply treating different aspects of Chow's star image as unrelated pieces separated by various borders; by contrast, it stresses the complex interfaces across boundaries. As such, this book argues that an understanding of star image should always be intertextual and multidimensional.

Yvonne Tasker (1995: 76) argued that 'the territory of the star image is also the territory of identity'. It is important to note that the film industry and its market conditions are determined by their own specific social and cultural locations of the time. In light of Tasker's observation, this book's discussion of the plural territories of Chow's star image not only suggests the hybridity of Chow's star image, but also reveals the tension among the different social forces that shape the public's perception of Chow's popularity in various cultural spaces, both within and beyond Hong Kong's regional borders. Following the trajectory of Chow's career moves, this book engages with the debates on glocalisation - the complex interaction between global and local – and aims to investigate the precise role of a star in modern global cultural industries.

WHY CHOW YUN-FAT? A SHORT BIOGRAPHY IN CONTEXT

Born in 1955 on Lamma Island, Hong Kong, Chow was the youngest son of a working-class family. After dropping out of school at the age of seventeen, Chow had worked in a variety of odd jobs, including as a hotel bellboy, a shop assistant and a postman. In 1973, he was recruited for an acting course organised by Television Broadcast Ltd (hereafter referred to as TVB). After finishing his training, Chow became a TVB-contracted actor and gradually attained his TV stardom. In 1986, Chow starred in John Woo's *A Better Tomorrow* (1986). The instant success of the film made Chow one of the most popular stars in Hong Kong in the subsequent decade. During this period of his Hong Kong career, Chow starred in over seventy films. Chow's performance not only generated a huge profit for the studios, but also earned him numerous awards, including two Best Actor awards from the Asia-Pacific Film Festival and Golden Horse Awards for his role as Yip Kim-fay in *Hong Kong 1941* (1984), an additional Best Actor award from Golden Horse Awards for his portrayal of Boat-head in *An Autumn's Tale* (1987), and three Best Actor awards from the Hong Kong Film Awards for his performances in *A Better Tomorrow*, *City on Fire* (1987) and *All about Ah-Long* (1989) in 1987, 1988 and 1990, respectively.

To understand Chow's career success in Hong Kong, we need to consider the social changes that occurred in the city. During the early history of the Hong Kong film industry, many filmmakers and stars were migrants from mainland China. However, the border between Hong Kong and mainland China was closed in the early 1950s and the travelling to Hong Kong from the north became more difficult.[1] The stringent border control saw gradually widening differences between mainland Chinese and Hong Kong societies during the next three decades in terms of their political systems, taste in cultural products, economic infrastructure and many other aspects. In mainland China, the Communist Party emphasised a centralised government and encouraged personal worship of the party's paramount leader, Chairman Mao Zedong, from the 1950s to the 1970s. The national chaos caused by a number of political movements instituted by the party, such as the Anti-rightist Movement (1957–9), The Great Leap Forward (1958–61), the Cultural Revolution (1966–76), and the Up to the Mountains and Down to the Countryside Movement (1968–78), not only damaged the country's economy severely, but also disrupted the education system in mainland China during this period.

In the meantime, in Hong Kong, the non-interventionist policy promoted by Hong Kong's Financial Secretary at the time, Sir John James Cowperthwaite, saw the rapid growth of the city's economy, which gradually transformed Hong Kong into one of the four 'Asian Tigers', together with Singapore, Taiwan and South Korea.[2] In 1971, the Hong Kong government introduced six years' free compulsory education, and this was expanded to nine years in 1978. The booming economy and improved educational infrastructure saw an expanding middle-class society characterised by an increasing number of locally born Hong Kongers moving up the social ladder since the 1970s. Given this social context, local citizens started to question their self-identity as Hong Kongers.

As such, a divergence between mainland Chinese and Hong Kong cinema emerged. Unlike mainland Chinese cinema, in which propaganda promoting communism dominated the country's big screen from the 1950s to the 1970s, Hong Kong cinema prioritised commercialisation. Although Hong Kong's colonial government also adopted censorship to control criticism of the government,[3] it did not interfere overly in other aspects of filmmaking and narrative morality, such as choices of genre, dress codes and make-up, and jokes about religion, gender, race, disability and so on. As a result of the relatively relaxed censorship, Hong Kong cinema not only had the freedom to adapt traditional Chinese folk stories, theatre dramas, and classic and popular literature for its big screens, but could also borrow ideas vigorously from other screen cultures, such as those of Japan and Hollywood.

However, simply borrowing stories or ideas from elsewhere could not satisfy the growing demands of Hong Kong audiences. The rapid urbanisation and industrialisation of Hong Kong in the 1960s and the 1970s urged local entertainment industries to produce cultural products, such as films, TV programmes and music, specifically telling local stories and addressing local social concerns. Along with the colonial government's further loosening of control over film content since the 1970s, Hong Kong cinema gained more creative freedom (Liang 1992: 63). It is in this context that a new generation of filmmakers was coming of age. The presence of those locally born and locally educated talents brought 'an all-new façade' to local (Cantonese) cinema by following the track of modernisation while remaining sensitive to local and regional differences, as Hong Kong film critic Sek Kei (1999a: 54–5) pointed out.

It was during such a period that Chow began his career as an actor and gradually attained his stardom in Hong Kong. One may note that many Hong Kong actors, such as Andy Lau, Tony Leung Chiu-wai, Stephen Chow and Maggie Cheung, took a similar career path to Chow, starting their careers and achieving initial fame via the local TV industry before moving to the big screen. Chow was at the forefront of this trend, and can thus be identified as an ideal candidate for studying the system of stardom in Hong Kong. In this regard, the diversity of Chow's star personae and his career moves across different industries enable this book to examine Hong Kong's shifting cultural landscape.

In addition, Chow's career move from Hong Kong to Hollywood and then back to Chinese cinema provides an exceptional case to investigate a Hong Kong star's role in mediating different social, political and cultural discourses in relation to Hong Kong's relationship with China. The boom in the local film industry made Hong Kong one of the most important cities for film production in East Asia during the 1980s and early 1990s, and this resulted in the introduction of many local stars, including Chow, to the global film market. However, after more than a decade of prosperity, Hong Kong cinema went into a long period of recession. Annual film production in Hong Kong dropped by nearly 40 per cent, from 242 films in 1993 to 150 in 2000, and its revenue was almost cut in half, from HK$1 billion in 1993 to HK$0.45 billion in 2001 (Mo 2002). Chow, despite his commercial and critical success in local cinema, was not immune to the crisis in the Hong Kong film industry. As cited in Yang (1995: 26) he criticised the deteriorated condition of the Hong Kong film industry and market, which became flooded with low-quality films that were distinctive only in their derivativeness, inattention to original storytelling, and general lack of creativity. As a result, Chow appeared in significantly fewer films in the first half of the 1990s than he did in the second half of the 1980s.[4]

Many factors contributed to Chow's popularity in local cinema (especially in action cinema), as well as to the rise and decline of the Hong Kong film industry during the 1980s and 1990s. One of the most popular explanations refers to the city's uncertain political prospects for 1997, or what Stephen Teo (1997: 207) called the 'China syndrome'. As Chris Berry and Mary Farquhar (2006: 158) noted, the star personae of many Hong Kong stars, such as Jackie Chan, Ti Lung, Danny Lee and Jet Li are often related to their screen images as national heroes or upright police officers who either fight for national pride or defend social justice. In comparison, many of Chow's acclaimed screen roles frequently step across the boundary of legal society and the illegal underworld, such as his roles as Mark Gor in *A Better Tomorrow* (1986), Chung Tin-ching in *Prison on Fire* (1987), Joe in *Once a Thief* (1991), and Ah Jong in *The Killer* (1989). Julian Stringer (2004: 450) argued that the instability of Chow's star image between being in and out of control helps us understand the narratives in *A Better Tomorrow* and *The Killer* as positioned within a historical situation identified in terms of the social mechanisms of paternity and survival. Similarly, Jillian Sandell (2001: n.p.) argued that male heroes in John Woo's action films, particularly those played by Chow, 'locate the fear, uncertainty, and moral confusion about Hong Kong's future'. In these scholars' readings of Hong Kong action cinema, Chow and his screen heroes represent Hong Kong's rampant social anxieties created in the popular imagination by the city's reunification with China in 1997.

In a similar vein, some film scholars have deemed the social fears concerning Hong Kong's return to Chinese rule to have contributed to the growth of Hong Kong's emigrant population, an issue closely related to the Hong Kong film industry's crisis because of the reduction of the number of film industry professionals, investors and local filmgoers. From the film production perspective, Liang Liang (1992: 62–65) argued that investors were seeking quick returns on their capital investment before 1997; as a result, many studios and filmmakers ceased to make long-term schedules for filmmaking. In this regard, Chow's comment on the market condition of Hong Kong cinema, as mentioned earlier, suggested that the star sensed a career crisis as a result of being a professional actor under the reductive way of filmmaking in Hong Kong. It was under these circumstances that Chow decided to relocate his career to Hollywood in 1995.

According to Steve Fore (1997: 239) Chow's career move to Hollywood was just one of the examples that confirmed Hong Kong's social anxieties and the local film industry's concerns over the city's political shift after the Chinese takeover.

However, focusing primarily on the negative side of the crisis, namely the danger and threat associated with the approach of 1997, the interpretation of Chow's star image as a man in crisis is only one side of the coin. In the Chinese language the word 'crisis' combines two characters, *wei* and *ji*. Whereas the former part of the word means danger and threat, the latter part refers to chance and opportunity. As Ronald Skeldon (1994: 37) argued, although emigration from Hong Kong at the time was high, the feeling of panic determining people's desire to leave the city at any cost by seeking foreign passports was not widespread prior to 1997. Decisions concerning applications for emigration were, by contrast, often made after careful calculation and pragmatic consideration of such factors as social welfare, the education system and business opportunities.

In addition, the deregulation of immigration since the 1980s by several Western countries has encouraged Hong Kong citizens' global mobility by making it much easier for Hong Kongers moving abroad to seek new opportunities, as the Chief Secretary of Hong Kong at the time, David Robert Ford (cited in *Ming Pao Weekly* 1987: 87) noted.[5] While I agree that *wei* played an important part in shaping a sense of self and local identity in Hong Kong's citizens at the time, my study of Chow's stardom beyond action cinema also suggests that *ji* is equally important to an understanding of Chow's popularity in Hong Kong, as well as an understanding of the complex relationship between Hong Kong and mainland China prior to 1997 – a point I will discuss in various chapters in the first half of the book.

As a result of the more favourable conditions resulting from the simplified immigration and international travelling procedures granted by these host countries, the emigration exodus that took place from Hong Kong during the late 1980s and 1990s was very much, as Skeldon (1994: 48) argued, 'part of a regional system of migration, with Chinese peoples throughout that region responding in similar ways to global economic conditions'. Skeldon's observations could be demonstrated by the situation in the contemporary Chinese-language film industries (including those in Hong Kong). While the prosperity of Hong Kong's commercial cinema during the 1980s gradually gained the attention of Hollywood, the emergence of the so-called 'fifth-generation' filmmakers also saw mainland Chinese films re-entering international film distribution after nearly two decades of absence from the global film market following the outbreak of the Cultural Revolution in the mid-1960s.[6] The rise of both Hong Kong's commercial cinema and the fifth-generation filmmakers in mainland China not only prompted widespread interest in Chinese-language films, but also initiated an increasing amount of contact between filmmakers working within and beyond Chinese-language film industries.

During the 1980s and 1990s, a great number of Chinese filmmakers and actors migrated to America, Britain, France and other Western countries in order to learn different techniques and skills. In addition to Hong Kong stars like Jackie Chan, Jet Li, Sammo Hung and Chow, the list of emigrating Chinese filmmakers and actors also includes mainland director Chen Kaige, director and cinematographer Gu Changwei, and actors Joan Chen, Vivian Wu, Zhang Yu, Cong Shan, Zhang Tielin, Wang Ji and many more. Although few actors from mainland China have succeeded in building their stardom in the global film industry as some Hong Kong stars have managed to do, their emigration demonstrates that the outflow of film talent did not take place in Hong Kong alone.

As Chu Yiu-wai (2004a: 46) pointed out, the 'Hong Kong film industry has been long in pursuit of the Hollywood dream'. In an interview, Chow (cited in Yang 1995: 26) similarly stated that his intention in going to Hollywood was 'to learn . . . to learn the language . . . and . . . to know local producers and production modes'. By describing working in Hollywood as an opportunity to learn new skills and to extend his professional network, Chow demonstrated how his emigration could be seen as revealing similar motivations to the mainland Chinese filmmakers and actors mentioned above. In considering his career prospects and personal development as a film professional, Chow's decision to move from Asia to America was thus made because of his intention to seek new career opportunities on the global stage, rather than purely because of the fear of political and social uncertainty.

It is important to note here that Chow did not experience any acclimation period before he was cast as a leading man in a Hollywood production. Unlike Jackie Chan, who re-entered the American mass market through his dubbed Hong Kong-produced *Rumble in the Bronx* (1995),[7] or Jet Li who played a supporting role as the villain Wah Sing Ku in *Lethal Weapon 4* (1998) before becoming a leading man in Hollywood cinema, Chow bypassed these processes. In fact, although Chow's Hong Kong films were circulated in Chinatown's video shops, his star presence was somewhat limited to the cult circle in the American market before the mid-1990s. As possibly the first Hong Kong star to be introduced directly to the American public as a Chinese leading man by Hollywood (without any of his old films being released in American mainstream theatres, or himself appearing in a supporting role in a Hollywood film), Chow's career transition across the Pacific thus also provides a compelling case for studying transnational Chinese stardom.

In the meantime, filmmakers and actors from three Chinese-language film industries (those of mainland China, Taiwan and Hong Kong) have increasingly worked together to produce *huayu dapian* (Chinese-language blockbusters), which subsequently saw the formation of what has become known as *huayu dianying* (Chinese-language cinema) – a concept that has been adopted by many film scholars since the 2000s to 'bypass a geopolitical impasse caused by the idea of the nation-state' (Lu 2014: 18–19) as a result of the integrated market and vigorous mobility of talent across the different Chinese film industries. As Sek (1999a: 54) noted, the combination of Chinese cultural traditions and Western influences imported during its rapid modernisation since the 1970s made Hong Kong the richest and most dynamic production centre of Chinese cinema. However, this unique feature of Hong Kong cinema started to fade when the industry was confronted by the rise of mainland Chinese cinema beginning in the late 1980s and China's increasing interaction with the rest of the world. In this context, the Hong Kong film industry needed to rethink its production practices and to seek different solutions for improving the quality of locally made films and regenerating local film businesses when faced with confronting both the powerful Hollywood industry and the increasingly ambitious mainland Chinese cinema industry.

As the (mainland) Chinese film market has continued to grow strongly, many of the émigré filmmakers and stars, including John Woo, Hark Tsui, Terence Chang, Jackie Chan, Jet Li, Sammo Hung and Chow, have gradually returned to the Chinese-language film industry since 2000. Although, strictly speaking, Chow has starred in only a limited number of Hollywood films up to the present day, he managed to become probably 'the first Asian film star to play a complex, romantic leading man in a serious, big-budget Hollywood movie', as Dorinda Elliott (1999: n.p.) pointed out. Elliott's observation is important, as she not only noted the dilemma that Asian stars face throughout the entire Hollywood film history, but also pointed out the significance of Chow's casting in *Anna and the King* (1999). Although the film remains to this day the only Hollywood production to cast Chow as a romantic lead, Chow's experience was highly valued by the Chinese-language cinema, which clearly has a vision of entering the global commercial film market. Placed within this larger context, Chow's post-1997 career not only illustrates how a Hong Kong star has become an agent for mediating social perceptions of Asian men's cultural identities in America's film industry, but also maps the emergence of transnational Chinese-language cinema in terms of the star presence – a point I will discuss in detail in the second half of the book.

UNDERSTANDING THE STAR IMAGE: PREFIGURATIVE MATERIALS, SOCIAL CONTEXT AND INTERTEXTUAL ANALYSIS

The significance of the study of stardom as an academic discipline is not limited to merely understanding an individual star's career achievement or revealing the 'secret' of a star's private life, in the way that biography does.

Instead, star studies aims to explore the social and cultural implications articulated through public discourse about a star. The cross-disciplinary value of the study of stardom is well reflected in Christine Gledhill's observations:

> The star challenges analysis in the way it crosses disciplinary boundaries: a product of mass culture, but retaining theatrical concerns with acting, performance and art; an industrial marketing device, but a signifying element in films; a social sign, carrying cultural meanings and ideological values, which expresses the intimacies of individual personality, inviting desire and identification; an emblem of national celebrity, founded on the body, fashion and personal style; a product of capitalism and the ideology of individualism, yet a site of contest by marginalised groups; a figure consumed for his or her personal life, who competes for allegiance with statesmen and politicians. (1991: viii)

It is according to this understanding that stars and their public images are identified as a valuable conduit through which a wide range of social and cultural values become interconnected. Similarly, rather than seeing star image as coherent and singular, Andy Willis (2004a: 1–2) pointed out that a star's public images vary across different media texts in their specific social contexts, and that a star's plural and even contradictory images offer the film studios a vital ground through which different tastes in the film market are mediated.

In line with Gledhill's and Willis' observations, this book pays particular attention to the construction and circulation of Chow's star image in what Martin Barker (2006: n.p.) terms 'prefigurative materials' (also variously termed secondary, ancillary or satellite texts), such as press releases, posters, trailers, 'The making of . . .' programmes, critics' columns and reviews, Internet forums and even rumours. The construction of a star's image is derived not only from the films in which he or she appears, but also from other media texts that can either be under, or beyond, their control. An acknowledgement of the importance of these prefigurative texts thus reminds us that these texts may not fit easily with critical approaches that focus on serious critical reviews or primarily text-interpretative approaches to film content. In his article about the promotion, exhibition and distribution of films, Barker (2006: n.p.) argued that extra-cinematic media texts, while appearing in the form of an accompaniment and a discursive address to a film, 'guide and help construct the manner we attend to, and indeed often concentrate on, the films we watch'. By helping to build and connect these interests before, during, and even after the film is released at cinemas, prefigurative texts mediate distribution practices as well as film interpretation.

Although Barker's study is concerned with film distribution, his definition of prefigurative materials is useful for the examination of star image. This is not only because stars often occupy a remarkable position within these pre-figurative texts, but also because such media texts build a bridge between the production and consumption of star images in specific market sections. By guiding public attention to certain aspects of a star's image or lifestyle, the prefigurative materials reflect, promote or, in some cases, denigrate particular social types. While the different cultural messages focused on in the prefigu-rative materials exhibit the hybrid nature of a star image, they also construct the star as a confluent site at which various perceptions and social values can interact. Thus, these media texts should not be seen as secondary or ancillary to, or as satellites of film texts or audience responses in the way that many rep-resentation and reception studies do. Instead, I argue that these media texts are essential to our understanding of the articulation of star image and its various social identifications within specific historical and cultural contexts.

The scope of prefigurative materials is wide, and the materials analysed in this book can be divided roughly into four categories, although some of these prefigurative texts could be included in different groups or transmit their message from one group to another. The first category is that of industry-produced promotion materials: including posters, trailers, 'the making of . . .' programmes, press conferences, the film's official website and so on. As a type of text directly related to the star's appearance in the films, the promotional materials are probably 'the most straightforward of all the texts which con-struct a star image, in that [they are] the most deliberate, direct, intentioned and self-conscious' (Dyer 1998: 60). In order to target the right market section and to maximise the audience's interests in a film, the marketing department of a film studio often conducts extensive market research, for example by holding interviews with selected audiences and focus groups, before the release of the film. As Andy Willis (2004b: 178) argued, a film's marketing and promotional materials often demand 'a certain level of mutual knowledge on behalf of the filmmakers and their audience'. Since audiences' expectations and viewing practices vary in different contexts, marketing experts are well aware that they need to select and highlight different features of star image to cater for dif-ferent tastes across the different film markets. Therefore, these promotional materials are useful for disclosing the dialogue between the production and consumption of a star's image in specific film markets. Thus, this book pays particular attention to the sources of these types of prefigurative materials, all of which are targeted at or circulated in a specific market.

The second category of prefigurative materials relates to a star's appearances and performances beyond cinema. In Chow's case, this includes commercial advertisements, music albums and TV dramas. As I will explore throughout this book, Hong Kong stars rarely restrict their performances to cinema alone, and their career development and management is frequently enacted across media industries. Although these types of materials are perhaps the most neglected texts in the study of film stardom, I argue that such extra-cinematic appearances play a vital role in shaping the star's public image. Not only does the distribution of such material reveal the development of the stars through-out their careers, but it also helps to uncover different dimensions of the stars' public image, which may or may not be consistent with their screen images as created by the film industry. Therefore, this type of material helps to shape and reshape the public's perception of star image through reinforcement, contestation and contradiction.

The third category of prefigurative materials is media publicity. Rather than appearing as a promotional tool, this type of prefigurative material reaches the public in the forms of news reports, 'leaked' information, tabloid photographs, rumours and even scandals. As both Paul McDonald (2000: 5) and P. David Marshall (2006a: 5) noted, studios often assign a unit publicist to create and manage the publicity surrounding an individual production; and during the period leading up to the release of a film, the publicity department prepares stories about the production and its stars, which are then positioned by 'planters' in the trade and news media to maximise exposure. Although distinct from a film's promotional materials, this strand of media publicity has a similar function to that of the first category of prefigurative materials mentioned earlier: Both types of extra-cinematic promotion to the public are heavily manipulated by the industry. However, this type of media publicity is conducted by channels operating independently of the star or film studios. Thus it serves to provoke debate regarding the star's public and private images, which is crucial to the star's fame and popularity.

The last category of prefigurative materials analysed in this book is the film reviews, written either by professional film critics or by Chow's fans during the period with which I am concerned. Although this type of material has con-ventionally been categorised as a reception text, it also constitutes, as Barker (2006: n.p.) argued, a 'more or less patterned discursive preparation for the act of viewing', which reveals the reviewer's personal tastes and interests concern-ing a certain topic. Since film reviews always rely on information from other media, such as a reviewer's knowledge of the star, genre and even the develop-ment of film technology, these texts offer valuable feedback concerning how an individual viewer interprets a star's performance in a film, in association with his or her own engagement within particular social and cultural contexts.

Despite the different producers, media channels, functions, and formats of these prefigurative materials, the texts analysed in this book share some common features. One such common feature is the mass distribution enacted in the public domain. As Chris Rojeck (2001: 13) argued, the representations of the mass media are crucial to the formation of celebrity culture, and a star's presence in the public eye is essential to his or her status. The circulation of these prefigurative materials thus encourages public participation in the exchange of ideas and experiences in this process whereby audiences access and engage with a star's image.

The distribution of these prefigurative materials is not infinite or aimless. Instead, the production and circulation of these texts are confined to a specific market, society or community. In other words, prefigurative materials are subject to their own social, cultural and historical contexts. This leads to another feature of prefigurative materials: that of their strong performativeness. As detailed earlier, the content and delivery of many prefigurative materials are not random. They intend to raise the public's interest by catering for, confirming, disavowing or providing alternative options to existing ideas and perceptions about the star in a specific market. Therefore, the content of prefigurative materials is well planned and manipulated in accordance with the interests of particular readers or audiences. The performative features of prefigurative texts suggest that the presentation and discussion of star image in these prefigurative materials is highly selective and fragmented. To some degree, this confirms Dyer's observation that a star's image is a structure of social and cultural polysemy, and is open to contradiction (1998: 2–3).

It is important to note here that, although these prefigurative materials exist as different forms of media texts, they are also intertextually connected. This is not only because their meanings are mutually determined but also, as Sean Redmond and Su Holmes (2007a: 6) pointed out, because together they reveal that star image cannot be restricted to a single form of media. As both Frances Bonner (2005: 59) and P. David Marshall (2006b: 179) argued, media texts are not merely created as isolated, finished products for consumers, but are constructed as a direct response to consumers' tastes and experiences within a historically and culturally specific context. Therefore, the critical interaction between different media texts and the intertextual analysis thereof helps to reveal the complexity of social meanings and values associated with the star image of an actor like Chow.

By rejecting the rigid division between representation and reception in studies of stardom, this intertextual approach encourages the consideration of how the public encounters the star image through different forms of media contact. This approach thus places the investigation of Chow's star image within academic studies of contemporary celebrity culture, which is defined by Jessica Evans (2005: 1), Su Holmes and Sean Redmond (2010: 5) and Graeme Turner (2004: 26) as a multimedia and multi-textual phenomenon. In order to relocate the media construction of Chow's star image in its specific social, cultural and historical context, many prefigurative materials analysed in this book are drawn from the same historical period as the production and release of Chow's screen works. This means that Chow's screen works and acting career constitute a reference point from which different prefigurative materials communicate with each other. By so doing, this book recognises that the encounter between the star image and the public is not a straightforward process, and that the construction and circulation of Chow's star image involves constant exchange, negotiation and a compromise among different social perceptions of Hong Kong citizenship and Chinese cultural identity.

OUTLINE OF THE CHAPTERS

As this book argues, a star's image often contains different territories simultaneously, and these do not always cohere with each other. Such territorially defined star images cannot be understood without considering their specific social and cultural contexts. In order to delineate a clear picture of the context in which Chow's star image is constructed, this book is organised in chronological order. It is roughly divided into two parts, each part containing four chapters. Part I examines Chow's star images across different media forms and entertainment industries in connection with the formation of Hong Kong's urban culture since the 1970s. I argue that the transformation of Chow from an ordinary young man to a new local icon is deeply imbedded in Hong Kong citizens' growing awareness of being Hong Kongers. The cross-media construction of Chow's star image as a local icon conveys the complexity of social mobility in Hong Kong during the period, in which the city experienced a rapid change in its politics, economy and culture. Chapter 1 examines Chow's TV stardom during the 1970s and early 1980s. This chapter discusses Chow's early TV persona as a modern *xiaosheng* (a type of young male character developed from traditional Chinese literature and theatre). I argue that the medium of TV played a significant role in contributing to Chow's popularity in Hong Kong and to shaping audiences' readings of Chow's Hong Kong film stardom.

Chapter 2 maps out the transition of Chow's public image from a TV star to a film actor during the early 1980s. This chapter makes a strong case for a connection between Chow's star image as a film actor and the shifting culture and aesthetics of Hong Kong's Cantonese cinema during the late 1970s and early 1980s. This chapter recognises that an actor's professional reputation is located in a specific cinematic vogue within Hong Kong's film industry and market, and that the transformation of Chow's status from a TV star to a film actor offers a new perspective for investigating the shifting landscape of Hong Kong (Cantonese) cinema in relation to the social changes taking place in Hong Kong during the period in question.

Chapter 3 tackles two key issues that have been overlooked in both star studies and film studies, namely a male film star's image as a fashion and lifestyle icon, and the social implications of star endorsement beyond Western consumer culture. This chapter argues that the interaction between Chow's on-screen images and his presence in consumer commercials creates a specific public space for Hong Kong's new middle-class citizens to articulate the rise of their political and economic power. The fourth chapter focuses on the cross-media construction of Chow's star image as a comedic actor in relation to the discussion of Hong Kong's metropolitan history. This chapter explores the ways in which Chow's comedic images updated Hong Kong comedies fundamentally by replacing an account of modernity based on technological mastery with one of spatial mastery.

The second half of the book focuses on Chow's star presence in American and transnational film markets, questioning an Asian star's encounter with cultural barriers in global star promotion, as well as proposing an original investigation of a Hong Kong star's negotiation of Chinese racial and politic identification in the global and local film markets. Chapter 5 investigates Chow's career move from Hong Kong to America. This chapter investigates how Chow's star image as an ethnic professional, as opposed to a merely exotic supplement, has problematised the formation of Asian subjectivity and Oriental objectivity in Hollywood. Chapter 6 considers the issue of ageing as it affects a star's screen career, by interrogating Chow's screen image as a master of martial arts in both Chinese-language and English-language films. This chapter investigates the complex and dynamic interactions between the industry's practices of star employment, wider social understandings of ageing, and body traditions of martial arts cinema, which is arguably the most successful Chinese film genre in the global commercial film market. This chapter argues that, although ageing has become a challenge regarding Chow's screen performances and film career in both American and Chinese film markets, it occurs in different ways as a result of the different social attitudes towards ageing and the different representations of the body in Western and Asian cultures.

The rise of Chinese stars in the global film market has raised the question of how stars' public appearances are used to sell films in different markets, and how their cross-border stardom should be understood in local contexts. Chapter 7 addresses these two questions by comparing the Internet discourses surrounding Chow's star image on both English- and Chinese-language websites. Rather than seeing such cross-border stardom as homogeneously applied to the star's public status in different film markets, this chapter argues that, in many cases, the perception of a star's global status is often restricted to a certain regional and cultural space, and the recognition of Chow's global value is fragmented and plural across different market sectors. Chapter 8 discusses how Chow's star image is incorporated with the transnational Chinese cinema's narrative of intergenerational relationships during a period in which China has been recognised as a key player in global affairs and international trade. Through the discursive discussion of the shifting of Chow's star image, this chapter also illustrates how expatriate Hong Kong stardom is deployed as a site where a Hong Konger's local identity is imagined and interrogated beyond the city's territory.

I need to point out here that, although this book is organised in chronological order by following Chow's career moves, it does not mean that the arrangement of individual chapters is entirely linear. In fact, some of the specific dimensions of Chow's star images discussed in different chapters are actually taken from the same period, which already demonstrates a case of multi-territorial stardom. Through a careful perusal of Chow's media presence (including the star's films, television programmes, music albums, commercial advertisements) and accompanying prefigurative materials in both English- and Chinese-language sources, this book attempts to break down the rigid distinctions between the production and consumption of the star image. Finally, as mentioned earlier, this book looks at the construction and circulation of Chow's star image, both in regional and in transnational film industries and markets. Accordingly, it explores star agency in the translocal imagination of Hong Kong's cultural identity. However, this book deliberately chooses Chow's images in the films and media vehicles beyond such popular action films as *A Better Tomorrow*, *The Killer* and *Hard Boiled* (1992), as these have already been studied extensively. The intention here is not to undermine or deny the current interpretation of Chow's action stardom. Instead, I argue that identifying different aspects of Chow's star image helps us to understand the complexity of Hong Kong cultural identity, and the necessity for careful consideration when exploring Chow's star vehicle.

NOTES

1. In 1951, the Crown Colony Government of Hong Kong set up Frontier Closed Areas along the border of northern Hong Kong, and officially adopted policies to control migration. The controlled borders were extended further in 1962. For details see, Hong Kong Legislative Council Police Tactical Unit (2002) and Salaff and Wong (1997: 203).
2. The 'four Asian tigers', 'East Asian tigers' and 'Asia's four little dragons' are terms referring to the four regions that were experiencing high economic growth rates and rapid industrialisation between the early 1960s and the 1990s.
3. Hong Kong's colonial government required every locally produced film to submit a synopsis in both Chinese and English before production, as well as requesting all films to be subtitled in English. This requirement, however, ironically helped the Hong Kong cinema to promote and distribute its films overseas.
4. From 1986 to 1989, Chow starred in between six and eleven films every single year, while from 1990 to 1995, the maximum amount of films in which he starred in a single year was three. For a full list, see Appendix II.
5. During the 1960s, many Western countries issued a limited number of visas to Chinese applicants (including those from Hong Kong) under the family reunification scheme. For example, in 1965, the United States reserved 74 per cent of the quota for applicants

applying to be reunited with family members (Kwong 2002: 27), even though the Chinese Exclusion Act implemented from 1882 to 1943 suggested that only a very small number of Chinese applicants fulfilled the criteria by having close relatives who had already obtained American citizenship by the time of their application. In Canada, a heavy Chinese head tax was introduced at the turn of the 20th century to reduce the number of Chinese migrants (Chinese Canadian Military Museum n.d.; Poy and Cao 2011). Between 1923 and 1947, Canada also adopted a Chinese exclusion act, known as the Chinese Immigration Act (1923), to bar Chinese immigrants (Price 2012). It was not until the 1970s that the new immigration rules and policies in the United States and Canada allowed more Chinese people, especially those from Hong Kong and Macau, to enter North America as travellers, skilled workers and businessmen. For details of the Chinese Exclusion Act, see Law (2010) and Soennichsen (2011).

6. The 'fifth generation' refers to a group of Chinese filmmakers who achieved international fame during the 1980s and 1990s. The majority of these filmmakers graduated from the Beijing Film Academy in the early 1980s. They won many top awards at global film festivals and rejuvenated the popularity of Chinese cinema abroad. Examples include Zhang Yimou's *Red Sorghum* (1988), which won the Golden Bear at the Berlin International Film Festival, while his *The Story of Qiu Ju* (1992) won the Golden Lion at the Venice Film Festival; Chen Kaige's *Farewell My Concubine* (1993) was awarded a Golden Palm at the Cannes Film Festival; Tian Zhuangzhuang's *The Blue Kite* (1993) won the Tokyo Grand Prix at the Tokyo International Film Festival; and Wu Ziniu's *Evening Bell* (1989) was awarded a Silver Bear at the Berlin International Film Festival. Many of these films were produced with investment from Hong Kong. The Hong Kong film industry has been heavily involved in the global distribution of these films made by fifth-generation directors in mainland China.

7. In the early 1980s, Golden Harvest tried to introduce Jackie Chan, already a big star in Hong Kong, to the American market. Casting Chan as a young fighter in two English-language films *The Big Brawl* (1980) and *The Cannonball Run* (1981), Golden Harvest's intention to promote Chan as a new male Chinese icon in the American market turned out to be a failure. Chan returned to Hong Kong without achieving any success, and subsequently concentrated on developing his own style of Kung Fu comedy.

PART I

From a Hong Kong Citizen to a Cosmopolitan Resident: A Face of Social Mobility in Hong Kong between 1973 and 1995

CHAPTER I

The Birth of a TV Star:
A Modern Hong Kong *Xiaosheng*

In the 1970s, the Hong Kong film industry, especially Cantonese film production, was largely stagnant due to the cheap production and the oversupply of films in genres such as comedy and opera throughout the 1950s and 1960s. The production of Hong Kong films was also hindered by import taxes and quota systems affecting films that were introduced in the 1970s in many Southeast Asian countries, such as Thailand, Indonesia, Malaysia and Singapore, which used to be major overseas markets for Hong Kong films.[1] By contrast, Hong Kong's local TV industry experienced rapid growth. As Zhong Baoxian (2004: 240) observed, while the Hong Kong TV industry provided an alternative site for established filmmakers to continue to work when the Cantonese cinema experienced a downturn in the 1960s and early 1970s, it also cultivated many new talents who later became the key workforce of the Hong Kong cinema in the 1980s. To a great extent, the 1970s' Hong Kong TV industry can be seen as an indispensable linkage connecting the Hong Kong cinema of the 1960s and the 1980s, not only because the operational correlation between Hong Kong's TV and film studios in this period was too close to be ignored, but also because local stars and creative talents frequently traversed the two industries.[2] Thus, it is important to look at these stars' TV images if we are to develop an adequate understating of Hong Kong film stardom.

In the 1970s, Hong Kong TV studios adopted a similar star system to 1960s' film studios. Backed by strong financial input and a vast pool of viewers, TVB was known as the 'cradle of stars' and as a 'dream factory of stars' (Zhong 2004: 318; Pang and Zheng 2005). Following the example of the Shaw Brothers, Hong Kong's biggest film studio in the 1960s and 1970s, TVB also tried to control its stars and their images.[3] As one of these studio-trained actors, Chow spent nearly fourteen years at TVB before moving exclusively to the film industry. During this period, Chow acted in nearly a thousand episodes of TV dramas, which earned him the reputation of the 'king of TVB drama' by the start of the 1980s (Pang and Zheng 2005). As the starting point of his acting career, Chow's experience in the local TV industry and the circulation of his image in and around local TV dramas was crucial for establishing his stardom and popularity with the local public.

The principal paradox of stardom is its combination of the ordinary and the extraordinary. As John Ellis (1991: 313) argued, television only presents a personality or celebrity because it 'reduce[s] the star phenomenon by reducing the extraordinariness of its performers'. Placing the 'presence–absence' binary at the centre of his argument, Ellis emphasised that a star's charisma comes from his or her absence from the daily lives of ordinary people, and only film's photo effects could impute a 'rarity value' to a star's image. This rarity value, according to Ellis (1991: 313), is the source of a star's extraordinary glamour. As in Roger Silverstone's (1994) study on television, Ellis (1991: 313) also regarded television as a medium that derives power and significance from everyday life. While agreeing with David Lusted's (1991: 256) argument that television connects the popularity of these personalities with their audience by offering a crucial form of recognition and expression, Ellis further claimed that television performers do not activate any conflict of meaning or real enigma because of their frequent contact with the audience. Based on this observation, Ellis (1991: 314) argued that television performers 'bear a fairly minimal relationship to the desire of the spectator', because they are known by the audience for their familiarity rather than for their remoteness.

However, while Ellis' extraordinary–ordinary framework is a valuable tool in helping us to understand the differentiation between a celebrity/personality and a star, his rejection of TV stardom is questionable. In her study of cult television stardom, Roberta E. Pearson (2004: 67) argued convincingly that the domestic nature of television viewing, the close affinity of the celebrity with the consumers of their images, and the continuity and integrity of character and actor, do not necessarily expel star charisma from TV performers. In a similar vein to Pearson, this chapter demonstrates how, under the circumstances in Hong Kong in the 1970s and early 1980s, the closeness and familiarity between a TV actor and the audience created a sense of intimate reality which, instead of diminishing the desire of spectators, enhanced such desires in tandem with the star's extraordinariness.

MODERN *XIAOSHENG*: A ROMANTIC, GOOD-LOOKING YOUNG MAN

In 1957, Rediffusion Television (hereafter referred to as RTV; later restructured as Asia Television Limited in 1982 – hereafter referred to as ATV) aired the first TV programme in Hong Kong. Ten years later, TVB was established, launching free channels for the public. However, during the early period of Hong Kong's TV history, the majority of programmes were imported from foreign countries, such as the United States, Japan and Britain. There was only a handful of locally produced programmes, which were hosted by, or starred, actors from early Cantonese cinema and Cantonese operatic theatre, such as Ng Cho-fan, Cheung Ying, Mark Sin-sing/Heung-kam Lee and Lydia Shum. To meet the public demand for local programmes, TV studios had to broadcast old Cantonese films, many of which were already adaptations of theatrical performances from classical Cantonese opera. With the depreciation of television prices, more working-class families have been to afford their own television sets since the 1970s. The rate of domestic TV-set ownership soared from 3 per cent in 1957 to 90 per cent in 1976 (Wong and Yu 1978: 3). The popularity of television not only led to a demand for TV companies to provide more Chinese-language programmes, but also required studios to produce more programmes concerning local life. To attract more viewers and to compete with each other, both RTV and TVB started to expand production of their own TV dramas and entertainment shows in the early 1970s. In order to secure talent resources for such productions, both studios started to organise training classes for in-house actors.

In 1971, TVB and Shaw Brothers co-organised the TV studio's first training class for actors. Two years later, Chow Yun-fat was recruited by TVB and became a trainee actor. After his graduation, Chow became a contracted actor with the studio. As a new actor at the studio, Chow was only given some walk-on parts and undemanding supporting roles during his first two years with the studio. In 1976, Chow was cast as a leading character for the first time, as Shao Huashan in TVB's first long-length *shizhuang ju* (drama in modern dress) *Hotel* (1976, 128 episodes). Thereafter, Chow gradually attained TV stardom, finally becoming a household name through his performance in *The Good, the Bad, and the Ugly* in 1979 (Zhong 2004: 253).

Described by Leslie Fong (1980: n.p.) as 'tall, elegant and with dark eyes so smouldering they can melt a girl's heart at 20 paces', the studio promoted Chow as a typical *xiaosheng*.[4] In addition to his performance on the TV screen, Chow's appearance and heterosexual attractiveness were frequently emphasised in his dramas' promotion booklets, which were designed to inform and attract local audiences to watch the new drama. The booklet for *The Fate* (1981), for example, presented a pseudo interview between Ngai Chun, the character played by Chow, and a journalist. The pseudo interview script started with a short opening comment by the journalist, 'You are strikingly handsome and generous, and it is widely known that you have many female fans in the public' (TVB 1981a, n.p.). Similarly, the promotion booklet for *The Good Old Times* (1981) introduced Chow's character Ouyang Han as a 'handsome and charming young man who attracted many females' (TVB 1981b, n.p.). Instead of emphasising the actor's acting skill and his personification of the character, TVB's emphasis on Chow's conspicuously good looks not only emphasised the extraordinariness of the TV star's physical attributes, which distinguished Chow from ordinary people but, more importantly, reinforced the myth of a 'star look', propagating the notion that only a few handsome actors have the potential to become *xiaosheng*-type stars.

It is interesting that, while Chow was generally considered to be a good-looking young man in *shizhuang ju*, his appearance was often criticised as being unsuitable for playing pre-modern characters. Not only was the mention of Chow's looks generally omitted in the promotion booklets for his TV dramas that were set in ancient times, but his pre-modern images, such as Liu Chi in *The Lone Ranger* (1982) and Linghu Chong in *The Smiling Proud Wanderer* (1984), were also frequently criticised by local critics as being improper and unsuitable compared to classical *xiaosheng* images promoted by early martial arts cinema and TV dramas (Zhong 2004: 253; Qiao 1991: 23). From texts concerning Chow's appearance, the conclusion that Chow's *xiaosheng* stardom was only acclaimed when set in a contemporary urban background could conceivably be drawn. The question raised is then what is it that makes Chow look good only as a modern character?

Responding to just this issue, one of Chow's fans, Zhou Chengzhen, questioned the legitimacy of differentiating between a man's modern and pre-modern looks in his letter to the local film magazine *City Entertainment*.[5] In the letter, Zhou (1982: 38) argued:

> What is the legitimacy for saying Chow's image is not suitable for pre-modern characters? ... Is there any evidence that all ancient men looked like the model promoted by those critics who argued that Chow does not look like a pre-modern *xiaosheng*?... Those critics' perception about 'classical image' is actually from the traditional Cantonese opera. Using such criteria to judge whether an actor is suitable for playing an ancient *xiaosheng* or not is inappropriate ... Those *xiaosheng* images in Cantonese opera were stereotyped ... That is why while Adam Cheng is deemed to have a 'classical' look, Chow is seen as 'too modern' with 'no classical feeling'.

Zhou's argument is important here, as it not only highlights that the portrayal of *xiaosheng* characters in local TV was often stereotyped, but more importantly it notes that local perceptions of this pre-modern look were largely shaped by, and even derived from, the tradition of Chinese operatic theatre. It is undeniable that the emphasis on appearance is a typical discourse in the traditional Chinese theatre, and it often functions as a visual indicator of a character's personality or even sexual appeal. Borrowed from traditional Chinese operatic theatre, the concept of *xiaosheng* suggests that youth, good looks and heterosexual attraction are included in the criteria for casting a leading man. However, everyone has a different appreciation of beauty. Since there is no supplementary make-up to help to formulate the character's appearance, the depiction of TV and film *xiaosheng*'s appearance relies, to a greater extent, on the actor's own features. Zhou's observation, therefore, is not sufficient to explain the reason that Chow's pre-modern look became problematic in the eyes of local critics and audiences when the star was generally seen as being simultaneously a good-looking young man and a *xiaosheng*-type actor.

While I agree with Zhou's argument that there are no specific criteria for judging a man's modern or pre-modern looks, I would like to further question why a fictional character's historical background impacts on the local Hong Kong audience's perceptions of the actor's appearance. Unlike his counterparts in traditional Chinese operatic theatre, a *xiaosheng* on TV or on film does not need face painting to make his countenance more dramatic. However, his appearance still functions as a visual sign of social and cultural identity. Often adapted from characters in classic Chinese novels and folk stories, a premodern *xiaosheng* is therefore a fictional figure representing the double imagery of a man's extraordinariness and a remote space in China's historical past. By contrast, the modern *xiaosheng* featured in TVB dramas was more often seen in original productions. Many of TVB's *shizhuang ju* were set in contemporary spaces with which Hong Kong audiences would have been familiar, telling stories of local people and local life. As ideas of a Western lifestyle and ideals of beauty became more popular in Hong Kong after the Chinese civil war, the portrayal of a modern *xiaosheng* often emphasised that the character belonged to an urban society and had a Westernised image. Accordingly, judgements of a modern *xiaosheng*'s appearance would refer increasingly to contemporary cultural ideals of manliness, in which the image of a local young man and a screen image drawn from the romantic lead in Western films and TV dramas were often integrated. Therefore, a modern *xiaosheng* often possessed two ambivalent features. On one hand, in conjunction with pre-modern *xiaosheng* and many glamorous film stars, he was considered to be an extraordinary man in terms of his charisma and sexual appeal. On the other hand, he represented an ordinary, local young man. Accordingly, the physical attributes of a modern *xiaosheng* often indicate both extraordinariness/ordinariness and remoteness/closeness.

As Pamela Robertson Wojcik (2004a: 166) argued, 'Typecasting contributes to narrative economy, allowing audiences to quickly and easily recognize a character by associating him or her with an actor's previous roles'. As mentioned earlier, local TV studios recruited many film and Cantonese opera actors in the late 1960s and early 1970s. Many of these actors, such as Adam

Cheng, had already established their images as pre-modern *xiaosheng* before they moved to the TV industry. Even those actors who graduated from TVB's early actor training classes, such as Wong Wan-choi and Lawrence Ng Wai-kwok, built up their star images as pre-modern *xiaosheng* through their performances in historical dramas and martial arts serials; two dominant genres on local TV screens during the early period of Hong Kong's TV history. By contrast, far fewer actors were known by local audiences primarily for their modern images before the mid-1970s. It might be noted that, except for a few walk-on parts and minor characters, Chow did not play any important pre-modern characters before he starred in his first long TV drama – *Hotel*. Thus, at the time playing his first memorable character, any deep inscription of a pre-modern image simply did not exist.

In addition, the success of *Hotel* led to an increase in the production of *shizhuang ju*, dealing with local young people's dilemmas about personal growth (such as career development), interpersonal relationships (such as friendship, romance and family) and social problems (such as corruption and the wealth gap). After Chow achieved initial popularity through his urbanised and Westernised role in *Hotel*, TVB recognised the appeal of this specific type of *xiaosheng* image for local audiences. Chow was thus subsequently and frequently cast as a modern young man in TVB dramas, such as *The Good, the Bad, and the Ugly* and *The Fate*.

Even in period dramas set in the 1930s and 1940s, Chow was always cast as a man who dressed in a Western suit, such as Hui Man-keung in *The Bund* (1980) and Ouyang Han in *The Good Old Times* (1981), in contrast to other characters who still wore *changshan* – a kind of traditional Chinese costume. These early TV works thus served to integrate an urbanised and Westernised image into Chow's star persona. As a result, when Chow was cast in a pre-modern role in *The Lone Ranger* in 1982, his strongly established modern persona disrupted the association of his pre-modern look via his modern star image. In this sense, the criticism of Chow's pre-modern looks indicates local audiences' refusal to accept the movement of Chow's image from closeness to remoteness.

The relationship between *xiaosheng* and *huadan*[6] should not be overlooked either. As another typical feature of the two types of roles, heterosexual appeal often suggests that the discourse of romance is a popular narrative in the Hong Kong media. For instance, the cover page of *Family Feelings* (1980) booklet features a photograph of Chow standing behind his female co-star Carol Cheng, cuddling her with their faces close together, which suggests the intimacy between the two. Furthermore, the booklet not only delineates the romantic story between the two stars' on-screen characters, but also highlights the image of the two stars as screen lovers. Since it was the second time that Chow and Cheng had starred together in a drama involving a romantic relationship, the booklet explicitly raised the question of whether Chow and

Figure 1.1: Hui Man-keung (Chow Yun-fat) [in the middle] and local gangsters in *The Bund*, TV, Hong Kong: TVB, 1980.

Cheng might become a couple in their real, off-screen lives. In this regard, TVB's promotion of Chow as a new screen icon not only closely followed the tradition of delineating a romantic relationship between a *xiaosheng* and a *huadan*, but also responded to the public's curiosity about the stars' private romantic lives.

It was through these TV dramas, as well as through the discourse in the promotion booklets, that Chow became a star with extraordinary heterosexual attraction. Although the romance narrative in these TVB dramas does not entirely challenge traditional gender relations with their emphasis on male social power, one difference between Chow's modern *xiaosheng* and a pre-modern *xiaosheng* in terms of 'whom he loves' can be identified. Unlike the typical narration of a pre-modern *xiaosheng*'s romance, in which the *huadan* is often depicted as a dependent, passive woman whose physical beauty is often highlighted, Chow's *xiaosheng* often falls in love with the 'new women' who are 'smart' and 'intelligent' (TVB 1981a, n.p.), 'independent' and 'brave' (TVB 1980, n.p.), and 'rebellious' (TVB 1981b, n.p.). This is in contrast to the pre-modern *xiaosheng*, who often found females who shared their traditional patriarchal perceptions of gender roles attractive; an example would be that a woman's domain should be confined to the family. Chow's modern *xiaosheng* is more likely to devote his love to career women who challenge traditionally male-dominated public and professional domains, such as the magazine editor and business woman Fong Hei-man in *The Good, the Bad, and the Ugly*, the solicitor Dung Shun-wah in *The Fate*, factory worker Chow Tong in *Family Feelings* and so forth. Selecting these females as his ideal partners, Chow's modern *xiaosheng* displays his appreciation of female talent rather than of physical beauty.

It should be noted here that the portrayal of Chow's romantic image was informed by rapid social changes in gender roles. Along with industrialisation in Hong Kong, perceptions of gender and gender relationships started to shift in the 1960s as more women joined the workforce and even became their family's breadwinners. Song Lin (2004) revealed that TVB, under public pressure, rewrote the ending of *The Good, the Bad, and the Ugly* to reunite Chow's Ching Wai and Cheng's Fong Hei-man. Similarly, the initial plot of *Family Feelings*, in which Chow's Shi Hui and Cheng's Chow Tong were separated, dissatisfied the public, causing complaint letters to pile up at TVB. As a result, TVB re-shot the ending and added a scene in which Shi Hui confessed his love for Chow Tong in front of her grave. The collective creation of these characters and the popularity of Chow's modern *xiaosheng* image in Hong Kong thus indicated that local audiences not only celebrated those female stars, such as Carol Cheng, who represented the rise of the new career woman, but also called for a male icon who valued career women and shared their perception of new gender relations.

LOCAL *XIAOSHENG*: A ROLE MODEL OF HONG KONG SUCCESS

Beginning in the 1950s, the rapidly growing economy turned Hong Kong into one of the four Asian Tigers in the 1970s. As Liang Kuan (2002: 123) and Yao Yao (2002: 16) pointed out, respectively, the urbanisation and modernisation of the city changed public taste in media content quickly, and national glory and heroic behaviour were no longer key concerns in Hong Kong's TV programmes of the 1970s. Instead, local audiences started to show a preference for stories of individual struggles for upward social mobility, a narrative that is evident in many of Chow's TV dramas. Indeed, this changing taste was underpinned by a growing sense of self. Michael Curtin (2003: 250–1), in his study of Hong Kong's TV drama, pointed out that Chow's Ching Wai in *The Good, the Bad, and the Ugly* achieves success through meritorious labour rather than through favours or privileged advantages from friends or family; thus, the character was designed to represent a positive image of a local young man who provided the opportunity for local people to see themselves portrayed as 'diligent, educated, and law-abiding citizens' (Curtin 2003: 250–1). By contrast, Ching Wai's younger brother Ah Chian,[7] a *chou*-type character,[8] was designed to represent an illegal immigrant from mainland China, embodying all that is poor, rural, lazy, uncivilised and law-breaking. Unlike an ancient *xiaosheng*, whose citizenship is often de-emphasised, vague or even absent from discourse, Chow's TV characters often (though not always) have a clear Hong Kong citizenship, which facilitates local citizens' pride in the rapid growth of the economy. Consequently, Chow, as the star who portrays Ching Wai and many other similar roles, was recognised as providing a role model for local young men.

Chow's image as a Hong Kong role model was created not only via the characters he played, but also through his own experiences in both the TV and the film industries. With the boss of Shaw Brothers, Run Run Shaw, taking over the chair of TVB's board of directors in 1980 and gradually moving his core business from Shaw Brothers to TVB, the old studio system was gradually approaching its end in the local film industry. Meanwhile, Hong Kong's film industry became more open to young talent. With increasing investment from the nouveau riche, Hong Kong's film industry gradually revived and began to witness the growth of independent productions. Towards the end of the 1970s, there was an outflow of talent (including many of the later so-called New Wave directors, as well as actors like Chow) from the TV industry to the film industry.

It should be noted that Chow started working in local cinema as early as 1976 – the year he gained his initial stardom through his performance in *Hotel*. However, Chow's early attempts in the film industry did not attract much attention (I will discuss Chow's early film career in more detail in the next chapter). As a result, Chow decided to concentrate on developing his TV career. However, Chow was not entirely satisfied with his personal development at TVB, despite having achieved the top rank of stardom in the TV studio following the broadcast of *The Good, the Bad, and the Ugly*. As Chow (cited in Ma 1985: 20) recalled in an interview,

> I did not have time to study the characters, especially in the TV industry. Each day I got the script for the next day's scenes. Quite often we just had a brief meeting before the shooting, and the producer then told us what we needed to do in that scene. How could I get time to understand a character? Film is better – at least I get the script before filming; at least I know what I am doing.

Dissatisfied with the fast, streamlined production of the TV industry, Chow clearly expressed his concern that the production mode at TVB, which inhibited his understanding of his characters, would affect his acting career negatively. Therefore, in 1980, as New Wave cinema came into force in the local film industry, Chow decided to re-enter the film industry.

In 1981, Chow was offered a leading role in Ann Hui's *The Story of Woo Viet*. However, his decision to star in the film encountered a resistance from TVB. With Adam Cheng leaving for Taiwan, Wong Yuen-san and Damian Lau Chung-yan moving to RTV, and Patrick Tse reaching middle age, TVB foresaw a shortage of *xiaosheng*-type stars available for roles as leading men in its programmes and dramas. In the meantime, local audiences had gradually changed their preferences from long TV dramas to medium-length serials of around fifteen to twenty-five episodes, and such a change increased the demand for leading stars in different shows (Zhong 2004: 253; Qiao 1991: 23). TVB's competition with its rivals RTV and CTV (Commercial Television) further required the studio to produce more original TV dramas in a speedy way, which again increased the demand for actors. Accordingly, TVB was trying to prevent Chow from acting in Ann Hui's film.

However, Chow was determined to accept the role regardless of TVB's objections. Threatening to sue TVB over his contract, Chow finally obtained the chance to star in *The Story of Woo Viet*. However, the issue ultimately brought the star to a crisis in this career during the first half of the 1980s. As Chow (cited in Yang 1994: 49) confessed in 1994, 'the relationship between TVB and me turned hostile when I was leaving. It meant that an actor's career could be ruined.' It is believed that Chow's contract dissension with TVB caused him a few years of 'frozen time' shortly after TVB decided to promote more new in-house actors.[9] As a kind of punishment, being 'frozen' meant that an actor would not be promoted by the studio, or might not even appear in any of the studio-produced programmes. Since an exclusive contract stops or restricts actors working for other studios during their contracted term, this practice often creates difficult times for the actors regardless of whether or not they are stars. Receiving only a notoriously low basic salary, the 'frozen' actors not only have to cope with financial pressure, but also have to face the possibility that their long-term absence from public appearance will lead to their being forgotten by the audience – a risk that could jeopardise their future screen careers.

Although Chow was still allowed to appear in some TVB programmes after the contract dispute, Chow's status as a top *xiaosheng* in the studio was quickly replaced by new actors (the 'TVB Five Tigers'[10] in particular) in the mid-1980s, as Zhong (2004: 320) noted. In comparison to his early TV characters, Chow not only appeared in far fewer TV dramas, but also was more likely to be cast as a middle-aged man or as a supporting character during his last few years at TVB. For example, Chow dyed his hair grey and played a middle-aged triad leader, Lok Chong-hing, in the 1985 TV drama *The Battle among the Clans*. In another TVB drama, *Police Cadet '85* (1985), Chow was cast as a supporting character, Ging Shing, the uncle of the leading *xiaosheng*, Cheung Wai-kit (Tony Leung Chiu-wai). In his last TVB serial, *The Yang's Saga* (which starred the 'TVB Five Tigers'), Chow played a minor role, Lü Dongbin, a middle-aged character who is one of the Eight Immortals in Chinese Taoist mythology. These middle-aged supporting characters all seemed to indicate the fading of Chow's *xiaosheng* persona.

By then, however, Chow was increasingly being accepted as a serious film actor, after winning the Best Actor award twice—at Taiwan's Golden Horse Awards and at the Asian Pacific Film Festival—for his performance in the film *Hong Kong 1941* (1984). Together with Chow's move to the film industry and his eventual achievement on the big screen, Chow was also increasingly being recognised by the local audience as a man who managed to achieve success through his personal qualities of industriousness and a sense of self-improvement, just as Ma Hui (1985: 19) observed. Qiao Chu (1991: 22) pointed out that Hong Kong citizens in the 1970s did not want an imaginary hero; what they wanted was a real model whose success could also be theirs. Chow's experience in the TV industry and his cross-media career exemplified, in some sense, an aura of credibility and reality: the message that extraordinariness is achievable. According to Qiao (1991: 22), Chow was seen by many of his local audience as an 'aspiration' rather than as an 'imagination' of achievable success. Qiao's observation is illustrated well by local film critic Shu Kei's comments in 1987 (cited in Sek et al. 2000: 108–9):

> The strongest attraction of Chow is that he belongs totally to Hong Kong. He is a star but he has at the same time a down-to-earth quality that enables the audience to identify with him. Few other stars have this rapport with the audience. The closeness we feel towards him comes in part from his television career and in part from his total accessibility. We know about his history . . . He started from the lowest rung in the ladder [TVB actors' training class] and as he worked his way up step by step, we were there to witness the process. Although Jackie Chan is also a box-office guarantee, we cannot feel the same intimacy towards him. First, we know little about his history; secondly, he rose to fame overseas and not in Hong Kong, returning home to develop his career only after achieving success in Japan. His physical prowess elevates him to more of a hero figure than an actor. With Chow Yun-fat, it is the opposite

It is clear from Sek's comments that Chow's TV experiences, particularly his small-screen characters, facilitated a sense of closeness between the star and the local community. In contrast to Jackie Chan, who was celebrated as a larger-than-life hero, Chow showed local audiences the process and possibility of an ordinary, local young man who not only managed to cope with difficulties and career uncertainty, but who also transformed himself successfully into an extraordinarily glamorous star.

As Silverstone (1994: 22 and 175) argued, television is 'part of the grain of everyday life', and the consumption of television programmes is incorporated into our private spaces, times and practices. Seeing television as a domestic medium, Silverstone claimed that television is a member of the family in a metaphorical sense, as well as in a literal sense, 'insofar as it is integrated into the daily pattern of domestic social relations' (Silverstone 1994: 40). Since other entertainment methods, such as karaoke and video games, did not become popular pastimes until the late 1980s, watching television was one of the most popular forms of entertainment for Hong Kongers in the 1970s and 1980s, as Qiao observed (1991: 21).

As a pre-eminent TV star during that period, Chow appeared frequently on this domestic medium. The contact between the audience and the star's TV characters thus took place in a more intimate, friendly and relaxed environment because TV screens decreased the distance between the actor and the local audience. Chow (cited in Xiao 1987: 3) once stated in an interview:

> I feel the Hong Kong audience takes me as a friend rather than an icon. Probably starting with TV, I became a son, a friend . . . I am not that kind of hero or *xiake* [martial arts errant-knight] . . . and I do not have that kind of mysteriousness or arrogance. Audiences see me every day. I have nothing to hide, so they take me as a friend.

Chow's understanding of his relationship with local audiences is well confirmed by Qiao's (1991: 24) statement that 'probably no [local] girls or boys took Chow as an icon as Leslie Cheung or Anita Mui . . . It is because Chow lives in their real life and no one would take their neighbour's son as a bigger-than-life icon.' From both Chow's and Qiao's comments, we may infer that Chow's star charisma is closely related to the perception of his proximity to local citizens' daily lives. Therefore, unlike watching an actor playing an idealised *xiaosheng* character on the screen, local citizens were witnessing the growth of a local young man who was part of their own community.

This was particularly important during a period in which Hong Kong citizens began to question their own identities more than ever. Rapid economic progress had transformed Hong Kong into a metropolis by the 1970s, but mainland China still suffered from poor infrastructure, lack of public services and a chaotic financial system in the wake of ten years of the Cultural Revolution. Living conditions and material life in Hong Kong were far more advanced than they were in mainland China, despite the economic reforms in mainland China that began in 1978. In this context, Hong Kongers began to question their Chinese identity. The divergent political ideologies of capitalist Hong Kong and communist mainland China also challenged locals' perceptions of Hong Kong as 'Chinese', especially when rumours of negotiations between the Chinese and British governments regarding the return of Hong Kong's sovereignty became public in the late 1970s. In the meantime, the discussion about the return of sovereignty also reminded Hong Kong's citizens of their colonial identity. When the people of Hong Kong discovered they were unable to join in the Sino–British negotiations that had started in 1982, this was a wake-up call for local citizens to rethink their political voices as Hong Kongers. The city's distinctive political status, remarkable economic achievement, and the public's concern about Hong Kong's future all increased local citizens' desires to take control of their local communities. As a local young man who had managed his acting career successfully across media industries, Chow and his *xiaosheng* image thus allowed local audiences to hope that a local young man could manage to take control of his own fate.

CONCLUSION

Chow's popularity in Hong Kong is inseparable from his early TV career and from Hong Kongers' growing awareness of their identity. The popularity of television during the mid-1970s created a large audience and fan base for Hong Kong's local TV star. As a leading *xiaosheng*-type star at TVB, Chow starred in many long- and medium-length dramas broadcast on prime-time slots. As such, watching Chow on the small screen became ubiquitous entertainment consumed on a daily basis. Chow's modern *xiaosheng* image not only helped him to achieve his initial stardom, but also satisfied the public's demand for a local TV programme that portrayed the lives of ordinary local people. Unlike the pre-modern *xiaosheng*, whose image embodied imaginative associations with the past and remoteness, Chow's modern *xiaosheng* image tended towards the present and an intimate proximity.

Although Chow's TV stardom was controlled well by the studio's star system, his image as a romantic, urban young man was also the result of negotiation between his Hong Kong audience, his fans' perceptions of local social changes and the studio's conventional typecasting practice. Along with the rapid economic growth in Hong Kong's society, local audiences began to call for a new local icon who could represent Hong Kong's modern and metropolitan identity. While typecasting in the Hong Kong TV industry still emphasised a leading man's appearance and heterosexual attraction, the shifting features of Chow's *xiaosheng* images indicate the social changes underway during a period in which Hong Kong experienced rapid economic growth and an increasing awareness of political change. While Chow's TV experiences de-glorified his star image as an extraordinary public icon, his career move provided local citizens with a window through which to view the process of a young man changing and controlling his own fate. The popularity of Chow's *xiaosheng* image thus not only met local people's desire for success but, more importantly, also fulfilled local citizens' perceptions of themselves and of their society.

NOTES

1. In the 1970s, the Indonesian and Malaysian governments introduced a film quota system. For instance, in Indonesia, the number of films imported from Hong Kong decreased from 766 in 1972 to 100 in 1978. Singapore and Thailand also substantially raised its film import and income tax on overseas films since 1976. In Singapore, the import tax on films reached nearly one-third of their price, and in Thailand the import tax increased by fourteen times. Meanwhile, Singapore and Malaysia imposed strict censorship on imported films. For more details, see Zhong (2004: 234–6).

2. In the Hong Kong TV industry, actors and actresses are generally referred to as *yiren* (entertainers) than as actors. One of the reasons is that actors also need to do additional jobs for the TV studios, such as hosting talk shows or children's programmes, or singing and dancing in entertainment programmes and variety shows. Since this chapter is mainly concerned with Chow's star image in TV dramas, I will use the word actor or star when I discuss Chow's role in TVB.

3. Run Run Shaw, the owner of Shaw Brothers, was one of the major stakeholders at the time that TVB was established. He continued to increase his shares and became the largest stakeholder after Harold Lee Hsiao-wo passed away in 1980. Shaw was the chairman of TVB from 1980 to 2011. For details, see Zhong (2004: 247, 262–7).

4. The terms *sheng, dan, jing, mo* and *chou* refer to different character types in traditional Chinese opera. The characters are divided into these categories mainly according to their ages, genders and appearances. *Sheng* is a term for a male character, and *xiaosheng* refers to a good-looking young man who often has a romance with a *huadan*, the young and pretty female character.

5. Most of the critics' comments and interview scripts analysed in this chapter were published in *City Entertainment*, a local influential, semi-professional and semi-commercial film journal in Hong Kong. It was also the founder of the Hong Kong Film Awards.

6. See note 4.

7. Ah Chian was the name of a character in *The Good, the Bad, and the Ugly*. Due to the popularity of the drama, this name became a popular term to refer to other mainland Chinese characters on Hong Kong TV and in film, who are portrayed as uncivilised, dirty, foolish and trouble-making. For a detailed study of the image of Ah Chian, see Cheng (2002: 181–6).

8. *Chou* is another term from the typecasting in traditional Chinese opera. It often refers to funny or ugly characters, such as clowns.

9. Although TVB has never officially admitted to the practice, rumours about TVB 'freezing' its contracts with actors who brought 'trouble' to the studio are widespread. As a TV studio greatly influenced by the studio system, TVB adopted similar strategies to those of the Shaw Brothers in the 1950s and 1960s when controlling its contracted stars' public images and careers.

10. 'Five Tigers' was a term used in a programme in an annual TVB jamboree show – the TVB All Star Challenge in 1983. Thereafter, it became a popular term to refer to five TVB contracted actors who attended this show. These five actors were Andy Lau, Tony Leung Chiu-wai, Felix Wong Yat-wa, Michael Miu Kiu-wai and Kent Tong, who were all selected and promoted as *xiaosheng*-type actors by the studio in the 1980s.

CHAPTER 2

From TV Star to Film Actor: Star Performance in Hong Kong Cinema

Chow Yun-Fat is a very good actor.

Ann Hui, director (cited in Berry 2005: 428)

As a professional actor, Chow Yun-fat is distinctive.

Ringo Lam, director (cited in Yang 1995: 26)

Chow's appeal is at its strongest as an actor.

Li Cheuk-to, film critic (cited in Sek et al. 2000:108)

Chow is an enormously versatile actor, probably the finest working in Hong Kong in the 1980s.

David Bordwell, film scholar (2000: 159)

As the above quotations demonstrate, Chow Yun-fat's image as a good actor is widely acknowledged by film professionals, both inside and outside the Hong Kong film industry. This can also be confirmed by the list of numerous acting awards that Chow won, as mentioned briefly in the Introduction. To elaborate on this point, we could take a look at the Hong Kong Film Awards nomination list. Between 1985 and 1996, Chow was nominated almost every year, and in some years he even received two or three nominations. In 1987, for instance, in addition to winning Best Actor for playing Mark Gor in *A Better Tomorrow* (1986), Chow was also nominated for Best Supporting Actor for his role as Detective Lan in *Love unto Waste* (1986). In 1988 he had three Best Actor nominations for playing Boat-head in *An Autumn's Tale* (1987), Chung Tin-ching in *Prison on Fire* (1987) and Ko Chow in *City on Fire* (1987), the last role winning him the title. Acting in a wide range of film genres, including melodrama, action, comedy, romance, thrillers, biopics and Westerns, Chow is indeed one of the most versatile and acclaimed actors in the local film industry.

As a leading TV star in the late 1970s and early 1980s, Chow's TV stardom opened the film industry's door for him. However, many of his early films, such as *Massage Girls* (1976), *Bed for Day, Bed for Night* (1977) and *Miss O* (1978) only earned Chow a reputation as 'box-office poison' (Pan 1987: 23). It was not until 1986 that Chow achieved both commercial and critical success for his performance in *A Better Tomorrow*. Since then, Chow's image as a mega film star and as a fine actor has been widely acclaimed in the media. Therefore, the late 1970s and first half of the 1980s can be identified as the critical period in which Chow's star image was (re)fashioned from that of a TV star to that of a film star. In order to explore Chow's actor image in detail, it is important to consider it within the broader social and historical context of Hong Kong cinema in relation to performance. In so doing, this chapter moves beyond the question of an individual's acting skills or performance styles to recognise that an actor's professional reputation is located within a specific cinematic vogue in the Hong Kong film industry and market.

FROM MR PHYSICALLY CHARMING TO MR EMOTION: PERFORMING IN HONG KONG CINEMA

Film actors' performances and their creation of screen characters cannot be understood in isolation from an understanding of film industry practices and audience demands within a specific film market. On one level, an actor's deployment of body language and other sign systems such as gestures, language and mannerisms, according to Pamela Robertson Wojcik (2004b: 7–8), contribute to an individual actor's idiolect. Performance and acting skills often determine the actor's on-screen charisma and, to a great extent, impact on the actor's career as a whole. On another level, screen performance is 'the work of the entire apparatus of film or television (the coded conventions of editing, lighting, sound, and so on)' (Butler 1991: 9). In this sense, the transformation of Chow's public image from a TV star to that of a film star and the public discourse of his performance offer a new perspective for investigating the shifting landscape of Hong Kong (Cantonese) cinema in relation to the social changes taking place in the city in the early 1980s.

Then what was it exactly that gave Chow a reputation as a good actor? To answer this question, we need to go a bit further back into the history of Hong Kong cinema in terms of its performance tradition. Since 1932, when the Hong Kong film industry entered the sound era, Mandarin and Cantonese films have become the two mainstreams of local cinema. Although they were differentiated from each other in terms of the language used, market sectors and production approaches,[1] a common feature could be identified between the two, in that the performances in both cinemas were greatly influenced by the Chinese operatic theatre. As Liu Guojun (2000: 106) identified, performance in the early years of Hong Kong's Mandarin cinema often featured an actor's control of movement, rhythm, exaggerated bodily gestures and facial expressions, which signalled a fixation with a particular moment in acting corresponding to the dramatic and operatic performances on stage. In comparison, Hong Kong's Cantonese cinema, since its very beginning, saw the market potential of screen adaptations of traditional Chinese opera. Often taking as few as seven days for the entire production process (including filming and editing), many Cantonese films produced at the time functioned in effect as a video recording of operatic stars' stage performances (Garcia 2000: 30).

Throughout the period from the 1950s to the early 1970s, both Mandarin and Cantonese cinemas continued to develop and to be influenced by the theatre. In this period, a great number of Mandarin films fell into the category of the two most popular genres, costume dramas (such as *Kingdom and the Beauty* 1959 and *Empress Wu Tse-tien* 1963) and martial arts films (such as *Dragon Gate Inn* 1967, *Golden Swallow* 1968 and *A Touch of Zen* 1971). However, one might note that the costume drama of this period was often shot in the format of *huangmei diao*, a popular folk tune from the Anhui province of mainland China. As in the theatre, singing and dancing formed two important elements of performance in *huangmei diao* films. Similarly, martial arts films often stressed the actors' physical competence and spectacular body movement. Showcasing the actors' skills in singing, dancing and action stunts, performance in Mandarin films, as Li Cheuk-to (cited in Chu 2003: 73) observed, still tended to be 'exaggerated' and 'avoid[ed] a direct outpouring of emotions'.

In contrast to the prosperity of Mandarin cinema, which often had financial support from big film studios, Cantonese cinema gradually lost its appeal to the local public due to low production quality, an oversupply of similar stories, and the popularity of Cantonese programmes on local television since the mid-1960s. The number of Cantonese films in production was declining drastically every year, to the point that only one film was made in 1971 and none was made in 1972 (Cheuk 2008: 40). In 1973, a comedy entitled *The House of 72 Tenants* (1973) was released, and its popularity among local audiences marked the gradual return of Cantonese cinema to the Hong Kong film market in subsequent years. It should be noted, however, that *The House of 72 Tenants*, the only Cantonese film produced in 1973, was in fact a remake of a film produced in mainland China called *The House of 72 Tenants* (1963), which was itself an adaptation of a popular stage comedy of the same title debuted in 1958 by the Shanghai Dagong Comedy Theatre. Comparing the two films to the theatrical comedy, it is not difficult to notice the striking similarities among them in terms of narrative, *mise en scène* and even acting style. Set in the studio, the 1973 film contained many long takes of medium-shot frames. In this case, the film's theatrical *mise en scène*, basic arrangement of camera angles, limited close-up shots and simplified editing continued to blur the line between the film acting and stage-based performances.

During the same period, the post-war generation grew up to become a major group of film consumers. Many film scholars have pointed out that this young generation's educational background, contact with Western media and a growing experience of urban Hong Kong, all meant that a distinct cultural identity attached to these local communities had begun to take shape (Chu 2003: 39; Cheuk 2008: 14). As a result, the rural settings, traditional family-based social ethics and historical narratives found in martial arts cinema, period dramas and comedies could no longer satisfy this audience's expectations. Nevertheless, the conservative film industry failed to identify this shift in the local audience's taste, and was reluctant to hire new talent in the mid-1970s, with the exception of recognising the potential of former TV comedians such as the Hui Brothers. In 1977, Hong Kong's local government relaxed its censorship of nudity and violence in the local media. When Hong Kong's Cantonese cinema entered a period of stagnation in the mid-1970s, many local film studios tried to attract audiences back to the cinema through sensual stimulation rather than seeking to improve script quality and character design (Law 1991: 32).[2]

In this context, it is not difficult to understand why some of Chow's early films during this period were marketed directly as adult-themed dramas. As mentioned in the previous chapter, Chow started working in local film industry in 1976. Within two years, he made eight films for Goldig Films (HK) Ltd (hereafter referred to as Goldig Films). However, the films' promotional materials suggest that the majority of these films used sex and violence to attract public attention. The poster for *The Hunter, The Butterfly and The Crocodile* (1976), for instance, foregrounds nudity through its prominent display of a woman's naked shoulder and legs. The poster also highlights key textual identifiers such as 'erotic storm', 'brutal fight' and 'fierce film' (original poster for *The Hunter, The Butterfly and The Crocodile* 1976). In a similar fashion, the poster for *Bed for Day, Bed for Night* (1977) places pictures of six actors (including Chow) around a cartoon of a naked man and woman sitting in bed, and the promotional leaflet for *Their Private Lives* (1978) displays explicitly erotic pictures, including Chow and a woman having sex in a car, and Chow and a woman lying in bed with only a white sheet covering their bodies (Original promotion leaflets for *Their Private Lives* 1978). These three examples are good illustrations of the production studio's intention to attract the audience's attention via the fetishistic desire for the star's body.

Although Chow did not appear in the erotic scenes in most cases (as with his role in *Bed for Day, Bed for Night*), the films' promotional materials often concealed such information by not even disclosing to the audience which role the star played in the film. Meanwhile, despite the fact that Chow sometimes only appeared in a tiny or supporting role in films like *Miss O* and *Bed for Day, Bed for Night*, his name often appeared at the top of the cast list in promotional materials and opening credits, as if he were the leading man. Such obfuscation demonstrates Goldig Films' intention to capitalise on Chow's (TV) fame and sexual appeal by insinuating that Chow would display his body in the film. In comparison, when Chow did display his body in a film, the studio made it an unmistakeable selling point, as can be seen in one of the promotional leaflets for *Their Private Lives*, which explicitly uses the text 'Chow Yun-fat boldly showing his buttocks' to attract public attention (original promotion leaflets for *Their Private Lives* 1978). In both cases, Chow and his characters became part of the erotic packaging for the film's promotional strategies.

The focus on the star's body and the lack of discourse concerning the star's portrayal of his character indicate that such films had little interest in promoting Chow as a serious actor. As Wojcik (2004c: 170) noted, 'the business of film acting, and especially the star system, relies on recognisability, marketability, and the necessity for known commodities'. In this regard, the discourse of the body in these films simply continued to explore Chow's image as a good-looking and physically charming young man – the *xiaosheng*-type image that had already made Chow a popular TV star. Nevertheless, Goldig Films generally ignored the social sensitivity embodied in Chow's TV *xiaosheng* stardom (such as fighting against the odds to achieve upward social mobility in a rapidly changing, modern Hong Kong). The depiction of sex and violence did not really save the local film market. In fact, many of Chow's early films failed at the box office, suggesting that the one-dimensional focus on the actor's physical charms was not sufficient to attract local audiences (including Chow's TV fans) to the cinema. Disappointed by this situation in the film industry, Chow decided to focus on his career in the local TV industry, and did not make any films for nearly two years as a result.

The situation only started to change towards the end of the 1970s. Confronted with the achievements of young talents, such as Ann Hui and Tsui Hark in the TV industry, film studios started to reconsider their production strategies after the film industry experienced a few years of stagnation. In addition to combining popular genres, film studios became more willing to invest in film genres other than the martial arts, period dramas and comedy. In addition, the breakdown of the studio system not only saw the decline of Mandarin cinema in the Hong Kong film industry, but also contributed to the increase in independent production. Accordingly, a significant number of young TV talents moved their careers to the big screen. Unlike an older generation of filmmakers, such as Li Han-hsiang, King Hu and Chang Cheh, who had come from mainland China or Taiwan, these young filmmakers were either native Hong Kongers or had grown up in Hong Kong from a young age, and many of them had studied film theory and production overseas. Known for their fresh ideas about cinema and their concern for local society, this new generation of filmmakers soon brought the so-called New Wave to Hong Kong's Cantonese cinema. Beginning their careers as marginalised experimentalists, the work of this new generation of filmmakers provided audiences with alternative viewing experiences during the early 1980s. It was in this context that Chow returned to the film industry in 1980 and his big-screen roles became more diverse, in keeping with the preferences of the young generation of filmmakers.

One obvious change introduced by the young generation of filmmakers, according to Sek Kei (1999a: 61), was an emphasis on characters' sentiments and emotions, which is evident in many of Chow's films produced in the early 1980s. For instance, the promotional leaflet for *The Story of Woo Viet* (1981) displayed a number of film stills, including Chow's Woo Viet embracing fellow refugee Shum Ching (Cherie Chung), holding hands with his pen pal Li Lap-quan (Cora Miao) with a wire net partition between them, fighting with gangsters together with his Chinatown friend Sarm (Lo Lieh), and sitting sadly in a small refugee boat with a boy in his arms (original promotional leaflets for *The Story of Woo Viet* 1981). These film stills promoted complexity of character by going beyond discourses surrounding Chow's physical charm, offering audiences a chance to preview different stages of the protagonist's dramatic life experiences. Moreover, the synopsis in the leaflet particularly emphasised Woo's background as a second-generation migrant and his experience as a Vietnamese–Chinese refugee, as well as the character's cultural attachment to, and physical detachment from, his motherland. By repeatedly using terms such as 'loss', 'catastrophe', 'the Exodus', 'drift', 'root' and 'despair', such descriptions worked to direct the reader's attention to the character's struggles when seeking self-identity.

The emphasis on the character's complex emotions and social relationships is clearly echoed in the local critics' film reviews and discussion of social changes in Hong Kong's society. For many critics, the intensified emotions of Chow's characters were an expression of the social mentality during the early 1980s. Li Cheuk-to (1982: 27), Chen Yaocheng (1982: 22–5), Lo Wai Luk (1999: 65–71), Leung Noong-kong (2000: 33–9) and Sek Kei (1999b: 42) respectively claimed that the plot of *The Story of Woo Viet* expressed the anxieties of Hong Kong's local society and increasing concern over Vietnamese refugees, namely boat people, in Hong Kong in particular. According to these film critics, Woo Viet's experience reminded Hong Kongers of their self-identity in a colonial territory, evoking feelings of roots/rootlessness, hope/despair, and home/homelessness. The shifting discourse concerning Chow's presence in his films' promotional materials, as well as the film reviews of local critics, thus suggest that the local film industry and its market began to divert attention from the star's body to his portrayal of the character's emotion. In this sense, the richness of the characters' emotion created a testing ground for Chow's acting skills.

BEING A STAR ACTOR: BETWEEN PERSONIFICATION AND IMPERSONATION

I think that Chow Yun-fat's popularity is largely a result of the audience's predilection for strongly represented emotions. He is also physically appealing and is an extremely skilled actor who has the ability to transform the most banal of scenes into something interesting.

Sek Kei (2000: 108)

The above quotation illustrates that Chow's screen charisma relies not only on his physical charm, but also, and more importantly, on his performances, which conform to local audiences' preferences for watching a well-rounded character whose image is charged with complex emotions. However, one may argue that an actor does not necessarily become a good actor simply because he or she is cast in the role of a sentimental character. For the general public, an actor's ability to deliver a convincing performance is one of the key criteria for judging his or her professionalism. As Michael Kirby (1995: 46–51) noted, good acting does not rest entirely on the side of the performer, and what an actor feels and a spectator believes differ in many cases. In this sense, film reviews offer a window through which we can investigate the local public's perceptions of Chow's performances at the time. In Sek Kei's (1999c: 46) and Huang Zhi's (1985: 27) reviews of *The Story of Woo Viet*, both critics used the words 'touching' and 'convincing' to describe Chow's performance; according to them, Chow delivered the strong emotion of the character perfectly through his subtle performance. Similarly, Qi Fuhui (1984: 22) claimed that Chow and his co-stars in *Hong Kong 1941* 'did a wonderful job' by delivering convincing and impressive performances. These film critics' reviews all suggest that Chow has the ability to deliver a rounded character with multi-layered emotions.

The local film critics' readings of Chow's performance in his post-1980s films agrees well with the message delivered by the films' promotional materials. Rather than an overwhelming emphasis on the star's appearance, physical charm or sexual appeal, as was the case with his TV publicity and early films, Chow's post-1980s films placed more attention on the genuineness of Chow's screen performance even though some of them contained sexually explicit scenes, such as *The Last Affair* (1983) and *Dream Lovers* (1986). For instance, the original promotional booklet for *The Last Affair* (1983: 3) not only placed pictures of Chow (as the star) and Wu Kwong-ping (Chow's character in the film) on the same page, but also asked the direct question: 'Is Chow Yun-fat the Kwong-ping in Paris?' While the booklet reveals that Kwong-ping is a romantic playboy who often feels unsure about his life, it also uses Chow's short marriage[3] to suggest that the star was also a man who became involved in different romantic relationships because of his sense of insecurity. The same situation can be seen in the promotional booklet for *Love in a Fallen City* (1984), in which an article entitled 'Chow Yun-fat's Love Philosophy' repeatedly stressed that Chow and his screen role, Fan Liuyuan, shared similarities in terms of their attitudes towards romantic relationships and their sentimental masculinity, suggesting that rumours about Chow and his co-star Cora Miao's real-life romantic relationship might be true (original promotional booklet for *Love in a Fallen City* 1984: 12).

This star-*is*-character scenario apparently suggested that a 'perfect fit', as detailed by Richard Dyer (1998: 129),[4] existed between Chow and the traits of his on-screen character. However, Dyer's notion of a 'perfect fit' also tends to suggest that the star's construction of the screen character is based on personification. According to Paul McDonald (1998: 185), 'personification foregrounds the continuities of the star's image over and above differences of character'. In other words, there is a strong presence of the star's own constructed personality in the character. Personification, often leading to the perception of stars playing themselves, could thus pose a potential threat to a star's professional reputation as an actor because it invites criticism of a star's inability to play someone else.

In terms of the notion of acting, many film scholars, including Kirby (1995: 44), Phillip B. Zarrilli (1995: 7) and Andrew Higson (2004: 147), have conceptualised it as behaviour involving feigning, pretence, impersonation and simulation. Often invoking the concept of disguise (at both physical and emotional levels), these words all highlight the idea that the sense of 'truth' is an illusion created by the actors' efforts to hide their own personalities. As Barry King (1991: 130) argued, good acting means that the '"real" personality of the actor should disappear into the part', leading to the norm of impersonation. McDonald (1998: 185) had a similar view, claiming that the crucial factor determining whether an actor becomes a respected professional would depend on his or her capacity for impersonation, rather than for personification. What is important in King's and McDonald's arguments is that they underline how differences between the actor and the character showcase the actor's skill in constructing a fictional role during the process of acting. As their arguments highlight, actors' professional reputations are often judged according to their ability to remove these differences by transforming themselves into the character, rather than transforming the character to suit the actors themselves.

It is interesting that while the promotional materials for Chow's films in the early 1980s intended to create the illusion of Chow's authentic performance through the emphasis on similarities between the star and his characters, they simultaneously highlighted differences between the character and the star, which distinguished the New Wave cinema from Chow's early films in terms of their respective star strategies. In the promotional booklet for *The Last Affair* (1983: 4), for example, the character Wu Kwong-ping's wealthy family, overseas higher-educational background and idealistic temperament are highlighted in contrast to Chow's working-class family background, limited schooling and realistic attitude to life. The simultaneous presence of similarities and differences in these promotional materials illustrate that the New Wave cinema had little intention of ignoring or downplaying those aspects of Chow's star image that did not fit in with a film's conception of character. Instead, the presence of these differences promoted Chow as a serious actor who was able to reconcile such contradictions by committing himself to the role.

While Chow's portrayal of these sentimental and emotionally sensitive characters have been recognised by film critics, his acting style has also shaped his reputation as an actor. In the local public media, Chow's acting style is frequently linked to the words 'naturalistic', 'non-artificial', and 'fresh' as demonstrated in Pan Bingchang's (1987: 23) comments on Chow's performance. According to Pan (1987: 23), the characters Chow creates are 'not just images but real people with their own souls'. Similarly, director John Woo (cited in Yang 1995: 28) commented, 'Chow is very spontaneous, very naturalistic . . . His acting is very multiplex [and] vivid . . . He has a remarkable ability to observe.' However, it is worth pointing out that both Pan's and Woo's comments on Chow's professional quality as an actor were made after Chow had reconstructed his extremely successful stardom in the Hong Kong film market following the release of *A Better Tomorrow* in 1986. In fact, Chow's acting was not entirely celebrated before 1986, despite the fact that Chow had already won some acting awards in the early 1980s. For instance, film critic Chen Yaocheng (1984: 30) sharply criticised Chow's performance in *Love in a Fallen City* for being stiff, and the star's delivery of dialogue for being plain and boring.

In terms of different opinions about Chow's screen performances, director Wong Jing (cited in Yang 1995: 25) made a thorough observation of Chow's changing acting style:

> What is the magic in his acting? Let me tell you, it is his eyes and the 'I don't care' attitude on his face. Because of this 'don't care', he acts freely . . . [and] naturally . . . This 'don't care' look and casualness determines Chow's grace. However, his 'don't care' is not inborn. He overacted on the TV until he captured the essence of 'don't care' and naturalness in *The Good, the Bad, and the Ugly* and *The Bund*. The same problem of overacting returned when Chow entered the film industry. Personally, I think his performance in *The Story of Woo Viet* was terrible . . . as was his performance in *Love in a Fallen City* . . . because he cared too much

... Nevertheless, he won the [Best Actor] award for his performance in *Hong Kong 1941* as soon as he gave up over-caring ... and since then he has realised the [significance of] 'don't care'.

From Wong's comments, we can see that although Chow was presented as a fine actor in many promotional materials for his post-1980s films, he was not actually recognised as a good actor in the industry until he overcame the tendency to overact and learned the importance of what Siegfried Kracauer (2004: 20) termed 'breath[ing] a certain casualness'.

As mentioned in the first section of this chapter, before the 1970s, performances in Hong Kong cinema (both Cantonese and Mandarin) were greatly influenced by the theatre. At that time, it was mainly Westerners and the wealthy, well-educated Chinese elite who went to watch foreign films (Lee 1991: 82). Nevertheless, in tandem with educational reform and rapid economic growth, an increasing number of young local citizens had access to Western cinema in Hong Kong. As Cheuk (2008: 21–2) observes, in the 1960s and 1970s a significant number of young local students demonstrated their passion for cinema influenced by American underground films and the French New Wave movement. Since local post-secondary school institutions offered no formal training programmes in film during this period, many young people decided to study film (in either critical or practical aspects) overseas, particularly in America and in Europe. As Liu Guojun (2000: 106) noted, a trend for realism came into force in the 1960s in both American and European cinemas. When this group of young people returned to Hong Kong and finally entered the film industry as part of the group of Hong Kong's New Wave directors, their training and contact with the Western media exerted an unavoidable influence on their understanding of film aesthetics and on their perception of screen performances.

As Chow (cited in Luo et al. 1991: 32 and 34) claimed in an interview, an actor should be able to adapt him- or herself in order to create a character not just according to his or her own creative ideas, but also in conformity with the creative vision of other people involved in the making of the film, such as directors and scriptwriters. Chow confessed that he tried to learn different acting techniques from watching many other actors' films in order to improve his acting skills (cited in Ji 1988: 25). It is clear from Chow's own comments that the star not only consciously applied different tactics to remove (or at least reduce) the lack of congruence between his own personality and that of his character, but also learned from others intentionally, in order to improve his acting skills. In this sense, Chow's mastery of 'don't care' involves his control over his own acting skills, as well as over the cinematic apparatus. As a result of learning and practice, Chow's mastery of 'don't care' and his apparent easiness on screen reveal the actor's efforts to develop his acting professionalism, as recognised by the industry and the market at the time. Chow's adoption of a naturalistic acting style therefore indicates that the star managed to articulate this recent trend in cinematic aesthetics by following the shifting perceptions of screen performance in the local film industry.

What is interesting here is not just how Chow improved his acting skills, but also how local film critics counteracted and modified criticism regarding Chow's responsibility for character failure, to some extent ironically. In fact, Chow's performance (particularly his handling of dialogue) in films such as *Love in a Fallen City* received some negative criticism. However, local film critics paid far more attention to the phenomenon of New Wave cinema and the influence of New Wave directors on the local cinema than they did to a star's performance. One example of this shift in the critical focus is demonstrated by Luo Jianming's (1984: 34) review of *Love in a Fallen City*, in which Luo suggested that it was the director's misunderstanding of the novel that led to the film's flatness. Similarly, local film critics Sek Kei (1999d: 60), Gao Siya (1985: 8), Chen Yaocheng (1984: 30) and De Yu (1984: 3) all argued on various occasions that it was the authors, such as the director Ann Hui and the scriptwriter Peng Cao, who should be responsible for the film's failure to deliver a convincing story and characters. Other examples can be found in the reviews of Chow's other films, including *The Postman Strikes Back* (1982) (Sek 1999e: 170; Feng 1982: 40) and *Women* (1985) (Sek 1999f: 7–8). In all these cases, film critics blamed the film scripts' weak character construction rather than labelling Chow's performance as being lacklustre.

It is important to point out that many of these local film critics were working from the premise that the actor or star simply did not count as one of a film's authors. Similarly, although the emergence of Hong Kong's New Wave cinema has attracted considerable attention from film scholars, little academic and critical attention has been paid to the actors of the time. One explanation for this situation is the general tendency within film studies and criticism to ignore the significance of the actor's role in filmmaking. In particular, the 1970s *auteur* theory had a significant impact on Hong Kong film criticism during the 1970s and 1980s. As Peter Krämer and Alan Lovell (1999: 2) pointed out, *auteur* theory placed the director at the centre of the production, whereas the actor's contribution to the film was 'if acknowledged at all, subordinated to the director's genius'. Although the emphasis on individual creation in *auteur* theory has been comprehensively challenged more recently by the view that films are produced collaboratively, the actor's role was still often concealed behind considerations of film editing, sound recording, *mise en scène*, the director's responsibility, and even audiences' personal interpretations, as shown in many reception studies (Butler 1991: 7; Wojcik 2004b: 2).

By regarding the stars and actors as what Krämer and Lovell (1999: 2) termed 'puppets of the director', the critical discourse on the role of creativity in film production indicates another shift in the cinematic culture of Hong Kong (Cantonese) cinema since the 1970s. Unlike earlier decades, when stars such as Yam Kim-fai and Bak Sheut-sin were deemed to be among the leaders of a film's creative team, especially in the operatic films that dominated Hong Kong's Cantonese cinema during the 1950s and early 1960s, the director started to exert creative leadership in Cantonese cinema in the late 1970s.[5] Accordingly, while stars were an important element in attracting investment and promoting a film, their significance in the team was reduced within the overall filmmaking process. In this sense, the critics' attention to New Wave directors' *auteurship* appropriated a large part of the star's responsibility, and to some degree increased the public's tolerance of a star's unsuccessful performance.

CONCLUSION

During the ten years between 1976 and 1985, Hong Kong cinema reached a new stage in its development. The emergence of New Wave directors started to challenge older practices in local cinema, and gradually transformed the outlook of the industry in terms of camerawork, cinematic technique, approach to subject matter, and perceptions of acting style. With the Hong Kong cinema's increasing focus on narrative and characters' emotions, Chow gained the opportunity to display his acting talent through his performances in non-mainstream New Wave films that highlighted a character's emotional struggles in a changing world. As detailed in the previous chapter, Chow's position at TVB was quickly occupied by new actors shortly after his insistence on acting in *The Story of Woo Viet*. However, the fading of his TV stardom was not entirely a bad thing, as it helped to dissipate Chow's connection with his established screen persona and forced him to try performing different types of roles across different genres. In a sense, this helped Chow to break through the restrictions involved in playing a *xiaosheng*-type character.

Although Chow did not truly establish his significant film stardom during this period, the focus of critics on New Wave directors provided a space for Chow to practise his acting techniques on the big screen during the early 1980s. As Stanley Cavell (2004: 31) suggested, 'the creation of a (screen) performer is also the creation of a character'. In order to convince audiences of the existence of the screen character and to justify the character's emotions, motivations and actions, an actor needs to create a performance through his or her understanding of the character, the genre, the film's narrative, the cinematic apparatus and the audience, as well as through the mastery of acting skills and techniques (such as vocal performance, physical gestures and bodily movements).

When Chow gradually mastered the skills of impersonating his character on the big screen with a sense of naturalness and ease, his performance not only injected sentiment and emotional sensitivity into his screen personae, but also helped Chow to establish his film stardom in later heroic action films such as *A Better Tomorrow* (1986) and *The Killer* (1989), as well as in many other widely circulated dramatic films, including *An Autumn's Tale* (1987) and *All about Ah-Long* (1989). The subsequent public recognition of his portrayal of complex characters was thus a result of the combination of Chow's personal effort, the shifting industrial culture and changing tastes in the local film market at the time. In this specific context, Chow's career move and the shifting of his star image can be seen as illustrative of the new trends in Hong Kong cinema.

NOTES

1. The post-war Hong Kong film market was roughly divided into three tiers in terms of distribution strategy. Imported foreign films occupied the top end of the market, and had the highest admission prices and the most prestigiously located cinemas with the best equipped screens. By contrast, Cantonese films remained at the lowest end. Without financial support from big studios and their own distribution line, locally produced Cantonese films not only cost less in production terms, but were also often released in small cinemas at the cheapest price. Mandarin cinema occupied a position between the two. For a detailed discussion, see Zhong (2004: 138).
2. It is noted that, during the 1960s and 1970s, sexual liberation came into force in many Western countries. Influenced by this trend, Hong Kong cinema became more tolerant of the display of human nudity on the big screen from the 1970s onwards.
3. Chow married actress Yu On-on in 1983, but his first marriage only last nine months. Only a few months before the wedding, Chow was rumoured to have committed suicide over his ex-girlfriend, actress Idy Chan Yuk-lin.
4. Dyer argued that a perfect fit occurs in cases when there is no incompatibility between the star's image and character.
5. The situation was different in Mandarin cinema, in which directors were empowered via creative leadership from a very early stage of its production history.

CHAPTER 3

Star Endorsement and Hong Kong Cinema: The Social Mobility of Chow Yun-fat

Film stars have played an important role in mediating between the cinema and mass consumption in our societies. This chapter examines the dynamic and complex articulation between Chow's star image as a male fashion and lifestyle icon and the local consumer culture during a period in which Hong Kong was experiencing rapid social, economic and cultural changes. In the 1980s, after nearly two decades of industrial restructuring, Hong Kong finally reshaped its image from a regional manufacturing city to a service-based metropolis and global financial centre. Together with this shifting of the city's image came the rise of consumer culture within the local society. Trying to stimulate consumer desire, an increasing number of local businesses and organisations began to seek high-profile endorsements for their products and services.

As glamorous celebrities with public appeal, film stars became the ideal candidates for such endorsement because their prolific (on- and off-screen) images provided a flexible territory in which advertisers could establish symbolic connections between their products (or services) and certain types of lifestyles, images of beauty, or social values. In conjunction with the commercial and critical success of *A Better Tomorrow* in 1986 and the unexpected popularity of the image of its underdog hero Mark Gor, Chow Yun-fat not only became one of the most popular stars in the Hong Kong film industry, but also one of the most sought-after celebrities for local businesses. During the years that followed, a range of companies and charities invited Chow to endorse their products or services, which included menswear and accessories, jewellery, mobile phones, food and drinks, blood donation and even babies' diapers (Li 1992: 22–3).

Paul McDonald (2000: 54) pointed out that stars often represent the ideological values of wealth, freedom and individualism on which a consumer economy is built, and are therefore not only employed to promote movies, but also to sell other commercial products. From Sarah Berry's (2000) observations on the popular fashion discourses informing Joan Crawford's, Greta Garbo's and Marlene Dietrich's stardom, to Gaylyn Studlar's (2000: 159–78) study of the relationship between Givenchy and Audrey Hepburn's star persona, current scholarly attention on the dynamic interaction between cinema and consumer society recognises that female stars often help to define certain types of femininity through the costumes they wear in their films, through which a female audience is encouraged to participate in a fantasy of consumption.

Studying female stars' images as fashion icons in the early 1930s and 1950s respectively, both Berry and Studlar disclosed how fashions and lifestyles function as symbolic gestures crossing class boundaries, and how Hollywood reshaped the female American audience's sense of self during those periods by focusing on the improvement of women's social mobility and their presence in traditionally male-dominated workplaces. Berry's and Studlar's studies of the dynamic interpenetration between stars' personae and the general public's perception of self are certainly valuable in terms of the attention they give to the selective and dynamic components of star image, as well as to the ways in which these components are constantly negotiated through public taste within specific social contexts.

However, we might note that whereas female stars, such as Sharon Stone (see Epstein 2007 for details), continue to attract scholars' attention for their connections with mass consumer culture, male film stars are almost completely absent from these discussions. Nevertheless, I argue that male stars play as important a role as their female counterparts in today's consumer culture. This is not only because many male stars currently appear in commercial or non-commercial advertisements, but also because male audiences are an equally important consumer group for many products, including fashion products. Examples here would include Pierce Brosnan for Ericsson Mobile Phones (1997) and Omega (1995–2005); Brad Pitt for Honda Integra (1996), Rolex (1998) and Heineken (2005); George Clooney for Martini (2000, 2006 and 2007) and Nespresso (2006); Leonardo DiCaprio for TAG Heuer (2010–2015) and Daniel Craig for Heineken (2014).

Moving the attention from Hollywood back to East Asia, we might note that the phenomenon of star endorsement is even more prominent. In Hong Kong, almost every film star (male or female) since the 1980s has endorsed commercial products and services. This is because film acting in Hong Kong has not necessarily earned a high income for stars, especially over the four decades between the 1960s and the 1990s. As a result, appearing in commercial advertisements has become a fast and effective way for stars to increase their income. In addition, stars' associations with certain brands and their salary from the commercial endorsements, as Li Shaomin (cited in Anon. 1999: A12) pointed out, are often regarded as one of the (hidden) criteria for judging their star value.[1] Helping stars to maintain, or even increase, their visibility to the public, commercial endorsement thus functions as proof that the star is popular within the entertainment industry.

In this regard, Chow's case not only helps us to explore the dynamics of a cinematic culture beyond Hollywood, but also offers us an opportunity to investigate male film stars' relationships with mass consumption. In the next two sections, I will demonstrate how the intermediation of Chow's cinematic capacity (as a glamorous star as well as an acclaimed actor) was mobilised by advertisers to generate public desire for consumption. I argue that the interaction between Chow's on-screen image and his presence in consumer commercials creates a public space for Hong Kong's new middle-class citizens to articulate the rise of their political and economic power, and to openly express their emerging sense of being Hong Kongers.

THE RISE OF NEW MIDDLE-CLASS CONSUMERS AND THE TRANS-CLASS MOBILITY IN HONG KONG'S CONSUMPTION CULTURE

Before the industrialisation of Hong Kong's society, many high-ranking government officers (such as governors and chiefs of police) and senior managers were white people who were appointed directly by the British government or by a (foreign) parent company. These *yangren* (foreigners, but the term refers particularly to white people from Western countries), with their political and merchant power, were the real rulers of the city. With the exception of rich Chinese businessmen migrating from mainland China, the majority of Hong Kong's citizens and new immigrants were employed in low-skilled jobs (working, for example, as factory workers, shop assistants, or as low-ranking office clerks). However, as a result of the rapid industrialisation and urbanisation of Hong Kong, there arose a huge demand for junior and middle management personnel and professionals. Together with the series of local educational reforms that took place during the 1960s and 1970s,[2] an increasing number of local citizens entered the middle class and became professionals (such as lawyers, financial consultants and doctors), as well as highly skilled workers and managers over the following decades.

The expanding size of the middle class gave rise to a new market sector that many businesses were eager to explore. As Heather Addison (2000: 8) noted, '[m]ass-circulated images promoted the new standards of behavior [sic], appearance, and lifestyle to which the public began to aspire'. Selected by local advertisers as offering an alluring image to drive public consumption, Chow's star persona in advertisements thus inevitably reflects the social changes of the time.

In his commercial advertisements, Chow frequently appears as an affluent man who enjoys a leisured lifestyle. For instance, between 1987 and 1992, Chow endorsed two men's watches, Guy Laroche and Solvil et Titus. As a brand connected to the French fashion designer, Guy Laroche was sold in Hong Kong exclusively by Dickson Concepts (International) Limited (hereafter referred to as Dickson Concepts), a high-fashion retailer that also deals in such high-status brands as Rolex, Charles Jourdan and Polo Ralph Lauren. In one set of pictures published in *Ming Pao Weekly*,[3] Chow's image as an affluent citizen who enjoys a high standard of material living is highlighted by his smart outfit and large house with its luxurious interior decor (Guy Laroche 1987a). In addition, Chow is shown playing the piano and cello in another set of pictures (Guy Laroche 1987b), projecting an image of a man who has both wealth, because he has the money to afford such expensive musical instruments, and education, because it is implied that he has received training in classical music.

As with Guy Laroche's brand, Solvil et Titus' watch, originally from Switzerland, was also targeted at relatively affluent consumers. In a TV advertisement, Chow and his co-star Jacklyn Wu Chien-lien play a young couple who have to separate because of the war. Before Chow leaves on his mission, he gives Wu a Solvil et Titus watch as a gift, which becomes emblematic of their love (Solvil et Titus 1992). In addition to the classically styled watch, Chow is shown to be the owner of other goods that working-class people could not have afforded during the period of the 1930s and 1940s, such as a camera and a car. At the same time, Chow and Wu are shown going on a date at the cinema. The poster of the Hollywood film *Waterloo Bridge* (1940) (rather than of a Cantonese film, which would arguably have particular appeal to a local working- and lower-class audience) indicates that both characters are urban citizens who probably received a Western education.

Chow's star presence and his connection with the luxury products and leisurely lifestyles depicted in these advertisements strongly demonstrates the intentions of local businesses at the time to promote the desire for a better material life in Hong Kong's consumer culture. As Richard Dyer (1998: 39) noted, America's consumer culture promoted a 'myth of success' that encouraged its consumers to believe that American society was sufficiently flexible for anyone to rise to the top, regardless of class. In this sense, Chow's star presence in these advertisements shares some similarities with the role of Hollywood stars in America's consumer society by encouraging the ordinary public to imagine becoming members of the society's elite.

However, one significant difference between the consumer cultures of Hong Kong and America at this time can be identified. According to Dyer (1998: 39), the circulation of Hollywood stars' presence within America's consumer culture suppresses the depiction of these stars at work. In not being represented as working, these Hollywood stars were therefore deliberately being positioned as symbolising the glamorous and privileged social status of the leisured classes. In other words, the wealthy and leisured lifestyles associated with these Hollywood stars came to represent the notion of success, or more accurately, the result of success.

By contrast, Hong Kong's consumer culture attempted to demystify such images of success by highlighting Chow's profession and work. For instance, Guy Laroche published an advertisement featuring Chow on the same page as a report covering the Hong Kong Film Awards ceremony (Guy Laroche 1987c). Although this picture only features a female model, it is located directly below the photos capturing the moment at which Chow (dressed in the Mark Gor costume[4]) received the award for Best Actor for his performance in *A Better Tomorrow*. A few weeks later, Guy Laroche (1987d) released another set of pictures in which Chow appears in a similar outfit with a long trench coat and a toothpick in his mouth (which has come to be seen as Chow's signature style since the release of *A Better Tomorrow*). It is important to note here that, instead of being released immediately after the film hit the box office, this set of pictures featuring Chow dressed in the Mark Gor style was distributed after Chow had won the award for his performance. Thus, rather than simply being seen as a recreation of the popular character of Mark Gor, Chow's image in this set of pictures should also be understood as the fashion label's strategic capitalisation on Chow's professional achievements as an actor.

Similarly, the Solvil et Titus advertisement clearly communicated the profession of Chow's character as a fighter pilot to audiences by showing the character flying a fighter plane and serving his country during the second Sino-Japanese War. In comparison, Solvil et Titus produced another two TV advertisements during this period, this time starring Anita Mui and Andy Lau, respectively. In the advertisement starring Mui (Solvil et Titus 1988), the star is simply depicted as being associated with luxury and leisure through her sumptuous costume, expensive jewellery, grand car and palatial house, while the advertisement starring Lau (Solvil et Titus 1994) portrays the star as a rebellious youth in the 1960s. In both advertisements, the professions of the two stars and their characters remain unmentioned.

While all three advertisements produced by Solvil et Titus feature nostalgic narrative and filmic references, it is only in the advertisement featuring Chow that the star's profession (as a skilled soldier) is signalled clearly to the audience. The narrative of the star, as well as the character's profession in Chow's advertisements, was clearly different from the typical fashion endorsements made by Hollywood stars at the time, as well as from the commercial advertisements in which many other Hong Kong stars appeared. This leads us to ask how the emphasis on Chow's star image as a professional in these advertisements – both through the narrative of Chow's profession as an actor and through the professions of the characters that he portrays – helped local businesses to target their specific markets at the same time as a leisured lifestyle was being idealised in the consumer society.

As McDonald (2000: 9) noted, although stars often occupy one of the highest positions within a hierarchical workforce structure in the film industry, they are also '[i]n the labour pool of actors'. It should be noted that, in the 1980s and early 1990s, many of Hong Kong's film actors (including Chow) worked very hard under taxing conditions and for extremely long hours even after they achieved top stardom. For example, Chow starred in ten films in 1986, eleven in 1987, eight in 1988 and six in 1989. Chow's case was not uncommon at the time. In other words, the capacity for working hard was an essential element that became incorporated as part of the elite status of Hong Kong's film stars. In this sense, Chow's commercial endorsements in the late 1980s provide a different model from those promotional images of stars used in the Hollywood system by suggesting that professional development is an indispensable element in attaining a materially better or leisured lifestyle. In delivering a message that is absent from the discourse on female stars' relationships with high fashion, this emphasis on professionalism in Chow's star endorsements transforms the meaning of luxury and leisure from an upper-class lifestyle to a symbol of career achievement.

Taking the market position of these consumer brands into consideration, Chow's advertisements were clearly targeted at a group of consumers whose income allowed them to consume expensive goods. As noted earlier, an increasing number of local citizens have entered Hong Kong's middle class since the 1970s. Positioned between the upper class who control the majority of social power in Hong Kong, and the lower or working classes who make their living through physical labour and spend a great portion of their income on basic needs such as housing, food and medical treatment, the middle class has quickly become a powerful consumer group in Hong Kong's mass market.

Since many middle-class citizens were originally from working- or lower-class families, they would have climbed the social structure through a similar career path to that of Chow himself. Accordingly, they could identify easily with Chow as being similar to them, and the narratives conveying his profession in Chow's endorsements thus allowed this group of consumers to regard owning luxury products and enjoying leisure activities as a standard part of their own lifestyles. As Addison (2000: 3–4) argued, advertisements are an effective marketing tool that product or service providers adopt to convince consumers of the satisfaction that consumption brings, such as happiness, success, youth and beauty. In this sense, Chow's star image in these advertisements not only symbolised the trans-class mobility of Hong Kong at the time, but also turned expensive consumer goods into the anticipated reward of the middle-class citizens for their hard work and diligence. The combination of leisure and work as the essential components of Chow's star image in these commercial advertisements therefore allowed local middle-class consumers to celebrate their own social status through consumption.

BEYOND THE CINEMA: SCREEN CHARACTERS AS FASHION AND LIFESTYLE ICONS

In her study of Hollywood's consumption culture, Addison (2000: 9) argued that motion pictures and consumer culture are 'perfect complements for one another', as '[m]ovies inspired wants that advertisers could exploit, and advertisements incited wants that movies could vicariously satisfy, establishing a cycle in which these phenomena tended to reinforce each other in a symbiotic fashion'. Addison's observations regarding the inter-relationship between Hollywood cinema and American consumer culture could certainly also be applied to the situation in Hong Kong. One of the direct examples is that, parallel to the circulation of Chow's middle-class male image in local advertisements, an increasing number of local films cast Chow as a middle-class or upper-class man, such as musician Song Yu in *Dream Lovers* (1986), bank broker Chow Chen-fat in *The Diary of a Big Man* (1988) and millionaire Lam Bo-sun in *The Fun, the Luck & the Tycoon* (1990).

Unlike in Hollywood, where many production companies and their parent companies (such as MGM, Viacom's Paramount Pictures and the News Corporation's 20th Century Fox) focus their business on the entertainment-related and media industries, many Hong Kong film production companies, especially the independent studios, received investment from businesses outside of these two industries, and thus often have a significant obligation to promote consumer values on the big screen in ways that reflect the interests of investors. For example, during the mid-1980s and early 1990s, Chow starred in a few films produced by D&B Films Co. Ltd (hereafter referred to as D&B). Co-founded by Sammo Hung and Dickson Poon Dik-sang – the executive chairman of Dickson Concepts – D&B is a studio closely related to the retailer Guy Laroche. Therefore, D&B often credits Dickson Concepts and its products for their sponsorship at the end of its films. Accordingly, Chow and his 'middle-class man' image in the film often function as an indirect endorsement of products sold by Dickson Concepts.

Nevertheless, not every D&B film casts Chow as a middle-class man; in *An Autumn's Tale* (1987), Chow plays Boat-head, an illegal immigrant who lives in the Chinese ghetto in New York. How do Chow's different images work together to promote the brands sold by Dickson Concepts in such a context? As Lim Chiu-wing (cited in Sek et al. 2000: 104) claimed, while the film portrays Chow as a poorly educated illegal immigrant, it also tells a love story across social classes. The film's ending, with its depiction of Boat-head's reunion with Jennifer (Cherie Chung) whom he has a crush on, and his material success as a restaurant owner, suggests that Boat-head finally manages to achieve his 'American dream', a notion defined by Stacilee Ford (2008: 22) as the 'faith that [an] individual can attain success and virtue through strenuous effort'. Although the film fails to give any clues as to how Chow's character achieved his American dream, the ending offers Hong Kong audiences a fantasy of crossing divisions of social class, as Shu Kei noted (cited in Sek et al. 2000: 109). In this sense, Chow has transformed the character's American dream into a middle-class dream for the local public.

These cross-class dynamics suggest, on one hand, that Chow's middle-class image does not (and could not) disconnect him entirely from his working-class background; on the other hand, it reveals that an appreciation of Chow's working-class image is often related to his cross-class success. It should not come as a surprise that such cross-class mobility contributed to Chow's popularity when we place his star persona within the social context of Hong Kong. As mentioned earlier, the majority of the local middle class was from lower-class family backgrounds. Unable to obtain social or cultural capital from their families, members of this post-war generation had to depend on themselves to improve their professional knowledge and living conditions. Supported by local educational reforms and the rapid economic growth of the city, people in this demographic group gradually approached the peaks of their careers in the late 1970s and 1980s (Zhang 1987: 10–11). Although many of them became well established, with careers in management, professional or government bodies, their career successes could not be separated from their personal experiences of working hard during difficult times. While Chow's own working-class background would make this middle-class dream more feasible for working-class consumers, it would also resonate with middle-class consumers, given their relatively recent experiences of striving for social mobility.

However, it should also be noted that Chow's screen image does not always signify the crossing of boundaries of social class. In D&B's 1986 production *The Lunatics*, Chow plays Chung – a vulnerable, mentally ill patient who is unable to look after himself and his family. Unlike his role in *An Autumn's Tale*, Chow does not cross class boundaries and remains at the lowest end of the social scale throughout the film. Interestingly, a picture of a Guy Laroche watch appears immediately after the film's narrative stops on the screen. Appearing even before the cast list, this picture announces the close relationship between Guy Laroche and the film's production. To some extent, this endorsement has similarities to the brand's appropriation of Chow's image as Mark Gor, an underdog action figure in *A Better Tomorrow*. Although *A Better Tomorrow* was not produced by D&B, Guy Laroche, as described in the

Figure 3.1: Chung (Chow Yun-fat) in *The Lunatics*, film, dir. Yee Tung-shing, Hong Kong: D&B, 1986.

previous section, still decided to use Mark Gor's image to market its product. Here, we may note that these screen characters do not fit the brand's image and market position, which challenges Addison's aforementioned observation about the mutual relationship between the prerogatives of cinema and those of consumer culture to some extent.

The question then is how Chow's underdog screen image helps Guy Laroche to market its product to local middle-class consumers. As Sek Kei (1999g: 175–6; 1999h: 177–8) stated, *The Lunatics* is a film calling for greater awareness of, and less social phobia regarding, mentally ill people. Casting many film stars, including Chow, Tony Leung Chiu-wai, Paul Chun, as the mentally ill patients, the film tried to raise public awareness of this vulnerable group's social welfare. In this sense, although Chow's on-screen character stays at the bottom of the social structure, Chow and other filmmakers and stars involved in the production also represent the participation of professionals (and by extension of the local middle class) in caring for the socially marginalised. In other words, the delivery of Chow's middle-class image through commercial advertising, as well as his professional identity as a film star, complicates his screen image in the film.

Zhang Bingliang (1987: 11) argued that the experience of working their way up not only determined the new middle-class Hong Kong citizens' sense of self-reliance, but also made them sensitive to social problems and to the poor social care for the vulnerable. Since Hong Kong was where the new middle-class citizens grew up, established their careers and had families, they not only had a much stronger sense of local identity than did people of their parents' generation, but also constituted a group of people who cared (and worried) deeply about Hong Kong's current affairs and future (Zhang 1987: 11). Understood in this social context, we can see how Chow's participation in *The Lunatics* helped Guy Laroche to target local, newly middle-class consumers by fulfilling their desires to assume responsibility and take leadership in the management of local affairs.

This also helps to explain why Chow's Mark Gor became a fashion icon in Hong Kong's consumer culture.[5] Some scholars and film critics have argued that Chow's Mark Gor became a film icon as well as a fashion icon because he provided local people with an opportunity to vent their anxieties during the transitional period of Hong Kong's return to China prior to 1997. Tony Williams (1997: 69), for instance, claimed that John Woo's post-1986 films (many of which starred Chow) expressed the local citizens' despair, uncertainty and insecurity. Analysing a series of critical opinion pieces published in such Western media outlets as *Economics* and *Variety*, Williams (1997: 70–1) concluded that most Hong Kong residents regarded 1997 as 'an apocalyptic "end of world"', and as a threat to Hong Kong's 'quintessential hybrid and heterogeneous nature'. Similarly, Jillian Sandell (2001: n.p.) argues that in *A Better Tomorrow*, as well as in *The Killer* (1989) and *Hard Boiled* (1992), Chow represents the fantasy of fighting against the imminent social deterioration threatened by China's governance of Hong Kong, which reflects the fears of local citizens concerning Hong Kong's sovereign return to China – a 'differently organized and "less developed" kind of economy and a mode of social relations that has strong ties to its feudal past'.

By contrast, other scholars have regarded local action films as revealing the dark side of Hong Kong society by disclosing the colonial government's hypocrisy and incapacity in the face of corrupt forces. Poshek Fu (2000: 73–4) argued that there was no representative democracy or guaranteed political rights for local citizens, and many local people, except for a small group of 'anglicized Chinese elites', were in fact second-class subjects, not citizens. Although Fu's argument is not specifically related to the cinema of the 1980s, his point of view is certainly shared by Wang Haizhou, a film scholar from mainland China. Wang (2000: 185) argued that Chow's action films represent society under the colonial administration as corrupt and irrational, a social and legal system in which local individuals were victims of exploitation. According to Wang (2000: 191), Chow's action heroes not only forcefully expressed local citizens' anger regarding their oppressed social status under the colonial government, but also represented a new force challenging the malfunctioning of the social system during the reign of the colonial government. Accordingly, Wang suggested that the change of sovereignty and administration allowed Hong Kong's citizens to reconsider their social status, and opened a window for them to criticise the colonial government's political system and social policies.

In comparison to these two opposing arguments (from Western and mainland Chinese scholars), many local film critics held a somewhat ambivalent view of such social anxieties. Shu (cited in Sek et al. 2000: 109) stressed that Mark Gor offered local audiences the fantasy of seeing an oppressed man's ultimate triumph against the odds. Unlike other scholarly arguments, which clearly locate Chow's popularity in terms of the frustrations of local citizens with regard to returning to China, or their dissatisfaction with the colonial administration, Shu does not specify the exact meanings of 'oppressed' and 'ultimate triumph' in his review of the film.

As Zhang (1987: 14) argued, many upper-class and traditional middle-class Chinese citizens migrating from mainland China did not have a strong sense of being Hong Kongers, because they only regarded Hong Kong as a place where they could accumulate capital. According to Zhang, this group of people had already prepared to abandon the city and migrate to a different place once more should their living conditions deteriorate with the approach of 1997. Meanwhile, many members of the working and lower classes, as Ma Junxiong (1988: 94) revealed, were unconcerned about political change or were unable to spare the time to participate in local affairs because of the pressure of making a living.[6] In this sense, the post-war, locally born new middle class became the group most likely to be affected by this social change because of their growing experiences of and emotional attachment to the territory of Hong Kong (Zhang 1987: 14).

Having developed the strongest sense of being Hong Kongers and being the most anxious about the city's future and their positions in a changing society, new middle-class citizens were thus the keenest group of local citizens to hold a strong desire for social autonomy. As Zhang (1987: 12) described, the colonial government had gradually begun to open its doors and improve its communications with local people since the 1960s. As such, some well-educated middle-class citizens of Hong Kong managed to enter the colonial government because of localisation projects that had been sponsored by the government since the 1970s. The Chinese government's promise of *gangren zhi gang* (Hong Kongers governing Hong Kong) created hope that local people might assume leadership in governing Hong Kong after the handover. However, because of mainland China's poverty and the social turbulence caused by the closed-door policy in the 1960s and the subsequent Cultural Revolution, Hong Kongers were rather sceptical about China's administration, and were uncertain whether the Chinese government would keep its promise of letting Hong Kongers govern Hong Kong, or whether it would continue the British colonial government's past policy of favouring the upper-class elite as a result of an over-reliance on their control of capital.

Given this context, Hong Kong's local film critics' interpretations of the popularity of Chow's Mark Gor image in and beyond cinemas indicates that local citizens' perceptions of social anxiety brought about by the political change were much more ambiguous and complex. As Lai Kit (cited in Chua Lam et al. 2000: 93) suggested, the handover should be understood as providing a social context for interrogating the social values of local citizens, and their commitment to the identity of Hong Kong and to their compatriots. Unlike his friend Ho (Ti Lung), who espouses tolerance and self-sacrifice and chooses to leave Hong Kong silently in the face of Kit's (Leslie Cheung) anger and Shing's (Waise Lee) provocation, Mark Gor clearly tells the audience that he wants to fight for the chance to be master of his own fate. Meanwhile, Mark Gor, through his sensational speech at the top of Victoria Peak about Hong Kong's striking landscape, and in his final return for the last fight of the film, voices the emotional attachment of new middle class to the city of Hong Kong. Mark Gor is, of course, an underworld gangster. Nonetheless, his actions for honour, his compassion for the Hong Kong people and the land, and his strong sense of autonomy and control over his own fate, would have had clear and appealing resonances with the new middle class' concern during Hong Kong's transitional period.

In this sense, Chow's Mark Gor enacts the aspiration of the new middle class to seize a historical opportunity to fight for an improved social position. Since 1997 entailed both excitement and anxiety for the new middle class, it is understandable why the interpretation of social anxiety inscribed in Chow's characterisation of Mark Gor by local film critics, as represented by Shu and Lai, is somewhat ambiguous. It is worth pointing out here that while the critical discourse of film is invariably influenced by multiple determinants, including political and social issues, we should not overlook the fact that many of these local film critics were also members of the new middle class. In this sense, these local critics' ambiguous readings of Mark Gor's image and his social anxieties mirror the dilemma of the new middle class in the changing political climate of Hong Kong. Returning to the widespread dissemination of Chow's Mark Gor look in the luxury Guy Laroche advertisements, we can therefore observe that Chow's Mark Gor blurred the line between underdog hero and middle-class icon in a way that proved socially attractive.

CONCLUSION

The classification of social class differs widely owing to the multiplicity of the different criteria employed (such as wealth, social power, profession, education and so on) across different cultural spaces and historical periods. Precisely because it singles out a characteristically transitional demographic group, 'middle class' is an ambiguous and plural concept. Located at an intermediate position within the social structure, the middle class, with its upper end often mixing with the upper class and its lower end gradually merging with the working class, is not a predetermined or fixed category (Zhang 1987: 11). Since the 1960s, local educational reform, industrial restructuring, localisation projects sponsored by the colonial government and involvement with global financial and business systems have created an increasing number of opportunities for Hong Kong's young people to improve their social status. During the late 1970s and the 1980s, these young people became an important workforce in society, and many of them developed careers in management or professional bodies.

In this context, Chow's middle-class image in the advertisements can be identified as offering recognition and a declaration that the new middle class had become an important market sector within the mass consumer culture of Hong Kong in the 1980s. Meanwhile, Chow's middle-class image was reinforced by a series of local films in which he was cast either directly as a middle-class man, or as a man who successfully crosses class boundaries or shares a similar social attitude and mind-set with the new middle-class citizens. This does not mean, however, that Chow's working-class background was completely expunged from his star image. Instead, Chow's working-class background became fully incorporated into his successful, upwardly mobile star image, serving as the starting point for a middle-class dream that attracted both working-class and middle-class audiences. The interaction of the multiple dimensions of Chow's star image thus captured the complex factors determining social mobility in Hong Kong, forming a key reason for his popularity with the local public at the time.

NOTES

1. Li Shaomin is the marketing director of Marketing Decision Research (Pacific) Ltd (MRD), which since its foundation in 1993 has conducted research and published reports on actors' and singers' fees for endorsing commercial products and services for local businesses. For details, see Anon. (1999: A12).
2. The educational reforms at the time included the provision of more primary and secondary schools and the implementation of six years of compulsory education in 1971 and then nine years of compulsory education in 1978, as well as the establishment of a second university, the Chinese University of Hong Kong in 1963, and other new vocational colleges.
3. First issued in 1968, *Ming Pao Weekly* is one of the leading entertainment, celebrity and lifestyle magazines in Hong Kong.
4. Chow was filming *A Better Tomorrow II* (1987) when the Hong Kong Film Awards was taking place in 1987. He went to the ceremony venue directly from the film set. Having no time to change clothes, Chow received his award in the same costume he wore in the the film.
5. In addition to the Guy Laroche advertisement, which copied Mark Gor's look directly, there is a popular saying that many local young men bought themselves a 'Mark Coat', despite the humid climate, after watching *A Better Tomorrow*. Meanwhile, there is also a persistent rumour that Alan Delon wrote Chow Yun-fat a personal note of thanks for boosting the sales of his signature sunglasses, which further acknowledges Chow's appeal in the fashion market. Although neither story has been empirically verified, the widespread nature of these rumours in itself serves to demonstrate the influence of Chow's Mark Gor image in Hong Kong's men's fashion culture of the mid-1980s. These two stories are also recorded in Yi (2006: 52) and in Stokes and Hoover (1999: 56).

6. Ma's article lists interview responses from a number of working- and lower-class interviewees, including factory workers, vendors and residents of public and temporary houses made of wood frames and zinc plates. These interviewees expressed their indifference to the 1997 issue since they believed the transition would make little practical difference to them.

CHAPTER 4

'Come Laugh with Me': The Construction of Cosmopolitan Residentship in Chow Yun-fat's Comedies

For many Hong Kong audiences, Chow Yun-fat is not only an action or melodrama star, but is also a good comedy actor. Many of his comedies yielded a good investment return for the film studios during the late 1980s and early 1990s. For example, Chow's *The Eighth Happiness* (1988) and *God of Gamblers* (1989) reached box-office totals of HK$37,090,776 and HK$37,058,686 respectively, and both topped the local box office in the year of their distribution (Hong Kong Film Archive n.d.a, n.d.b). In fact, Chow's comedies not only featured consistently in Hong Kong's local box-office top ten between 1986 and 1995, but also often outperformed Chow's own acclaimed action films at the box office. His *Now You See Love, Now You Don't* (1992), for instance, earned HK$ 36,475,536, nearly double the box office take generated by his well-known action film *Hard Boiled* (HK$19,711,048), and more than double that of *Full Contact* (1992) (HK$16,793,011) (Hong Kong Film Archive n.d.c, n.d.d, n.d.e).

Jenny Kwok Wah Lau (1998: 24) pointed out that 'the recognition of humor depends heavily upon the understanding of the complex dynamics involved in the interaction of the symbolics, such as gestures, icons, linguistics, and so on, which are defined by their own social and cultural traditions'. Although Hong Kong comedies, as noted by many film scholars and critics, could sometimes be regarded as a less sophisticated stream of mass culture because of their depiction of jokes about people's appearances, accents, sexual orientations and even disabilities (Sek, as cited in Chan et al. 2000: 125; Lau 1998: 24), they are valuable for investigating specific local experiences at the time. What, then, was the kind of specific, local social mentality expressed in Chow's comedic images in the late 1980s and early 1990s.

In order to understand the popularity of Chow's comedic image, this chapter pays particular attention to Chow's music albums *12 Fun 10 Fun Chuen* (1988), in addition to the original film posters for Chow's comedies.[1] *12*

Fun 10 Fun Chuen is one of only two music albums that Chow ever released. It consists of only two songs in total, one of which bears the same title as the album, while the other is the theme soundtrack to Chow's 1988 comedy *The Diary of a Big Man* – 'Very Nice'. While it was popular practice in Hong Kong for stars to perform across media, the album's comic style extended Chow's comedic image beyond the cinema. Through a detailed analysis of these two types of prefigurative materials, this chapter argues that the popularity of Chow's comedic image in Hong Kong's film market was closely engaged with Hong Kong's urban history, in particular with the city's further transformations into a cosmopolitan metropolis with its own significant status in the world at the time.

FROM URBAN CITIZEN TO COSMOPOLITAN RESIDENT

In the studies of local comedy, Hong Kong's urban history often plays one of the most important factors in film narrative, as does its role in shaping the stardom of many Hong Kong comedians. Film scholar Lau (1998) and critic Sek Kei (1985), respectively, argued that one of the reasons that the Hui Brothers' comedies became so popular in the 1970s is that their films began to see Hong Kong as a modern metropolis and captured a sense of urban-based culture as a way to differentiate the city from agricultural China. Although Hui Brothers' comedies, such as *Games Gamblers Play* (1974) and *Security Unlimited* (1981), still strongly featured traditional Chinese moral norms, they no longer regarded the city as an evil place where people lost their innocence to urban material life, a narrative in contrast to the popular theme portrayed Hong Kong comedies of the 1950s and 1960s (Lau 1998: 26). As Lau (1998: 29) demonstrated, many of the early Hong Kong comedies were generally 'China-centered [sic]', while Hong Kong was quite often positioned in terms of its otherness and 'capitalistic faults' because many of the audiences and filmmakers were refugees from mainland China. However, Hui Brothers discovered a new sense of identity in the 1970s through their comic evaluation of Hong Kong's modernisation and economic achievements. In Hui Brothers' films, many of the on-screen characters represent new migrants to the city (very often from mainland China), and are often portrayed as exuding an otherness indicative of people who were not only unfamiliar with the city's lifestyle but also often presented themselves as ludicrous characters in their encounters with modern, metropolitan Hong Kongers. As such, the local comedies of the late 1970s and 1980s inverted these symbolic roles, repositioning Hong Kong as the 'self' and mainland China as the 'other'.

The Hui Brothers' portrayal of an ordinary man in the fast-paced modern society of Hong Kong was inspiring and, in the 1980s, many filmmakers and stars, such as Karl Maka and Jackie Chan, urbanised the settings of their comedies. Placing his analysis within the historical context of Hong Kong in 1997, Cheng Yu (1985: 42) suggested that these urban comedies satisfied the local Hong Kong audiences' escapist urges during the period of governmental transition. Similarly, Sek Kei (1988: 18–19), working according to the assumption that the audiences for these local comedies were primarily from working- or lower-class backgrounds, argued that the 'vulgar, boorish qualities of the common people' in local comedies – such as their penchant for petty quarrels, their greed and obsessive urges to gamble, their dishonesty, iniquities, lewdness and childish play-acting – allowed ordinary audiences to release their anxieties and frustrations caused by being deprived of full citizenship status through laughter.

At first glance, the popularity of Chow's comedies seems to be just another case of combining the story of ordinary Hong Kong people with the local public's anxiety about the 1997 handover. In a similar vein to Cheng's and Sek's readings of Hong Kong comedies, Gordon Chan (cited in Chan et al. 2000: 125) claimed that Chow's comedies, such as *God of Gamblers*, allowed audiences to enter another world by allowing them to 'vent their anger and frustrations and throw themselves wholeheartedly into the story'. However, we may notice that although Chan tried to uncover the reasons behind the popularity of Chow's comedies, he did not tell us exactly what attracted local people to the cinema to see these films. If his observations about the escapist character of Hong Kong's local mentality at the time are right, then the reason that local audiences went to see Chow's comedy films was to seek entertainment that specifically did *not* deal directly with Hong Kong's political transitions, or remind them of their own social and political uncertainties. Instead, we might assert that, in some sense, Hong Kong audiences were self-consciously avoiding watching or thinking about such social and political anxieties and were looking for something else to make them laugh.

Although the issue of the 1997 handover was often used to justify the vibrant and dynamic elements manifest in Hong Kong cinema of the 1980s and 1990s, and has been seen as a critical historical moment awakening the local citizens' sense of self, generalisations concerning the effects of 1997 on Hong Kong tend 'to erase the concrete details of cultural experiences and [cover] up the complex social and psychological realities of life in Hong Kong' (Lau 1998: 22). While Chow's comedies seem to extend the style of the Hui Brothers' urban comedies by telling the story of an everyday man's life in modern Hong Kong, we might ask exactly what has been updated in Chow's urban comedies, and what differentiates his comedic image from that of the Hui Brothers or those of other comedy actors during the late 1980s and early 1990s.

Here, I would first like to invite readers to consider a quotation from the lyrics of Chow's medley *12 Fun 10 Fun Chuen*:

My good friend, what do you like to eat? *Hanbao bao* [hamburger], *yuliu bao* [fish burger], *jiwei bao* [baked coconut bun], *naiyou bao* [steamed custard cream bun], *boluo bao* [baked pineapple bun]. Foreigners like *hanbao bao*, Chinese from other provinces like Shanghai-style *bao*. Exactly what kind of *bao* do Hong Kongers like – *hanbao bao*, *jiwei bao*, Shanghai-style *bao* . . . (Chow Yun-fat 1988)[2]

Deliberately using a flat voice, Chow gives an unconventional vocal performance by naming a list of different types of *bao*, a word used to refer both to Chinese-style steamed buns and to Western-style hamburgers and breads. Whilst Chow clearly claims that migrants from mainland China like the Shanghai-style buns and foreigners prefer hamburgers, he does not specify a definite answer concerning Hong Kong people's preferences for any particular type of *bao*. Instead, he repeats all the different choices. Since food has its own cultural meanings, the list of assorted *bao* that Hong Kong people might like indicates both that the city is a place that embraces different cultures, and that its citizens are flexible and adept when it comes to accessing these cultures.

This message is reinforced in the song by the various languages in which Chow sings. Switching frequently between Cantonese, Mandarin, Hakka, Hokkien, English and Japanese, Chow's vocal performance not only connects Hong Kong with mainland China, Taiwan, and South East Asian countries with large Chinese migrant populations, but also connects Hong Kong with Japan – the biggest economy in Asia in the 1980s – and many Anglosphere countries that have loosened migration control for Chinese-born migrants, especially those with Hong Kong citizenship, since the 1970s. In the late 1980s, as has already been mentioned, Hong Kong developed into a dynamic and mature metropolis and established its global status as an important centre for international finance and trade. Together with the city's entrance into a new stage of urban history by becoming a cosmopolitan metropolis, migration and travel into and beyond the city's territory became once again an important part of local citizens' lives. In this sense, Chow's *12 Fun 10 Fun Chuen* deftly captures Hong Kong's urban dynamics and the cultural hybridity of the time.

Similarly, in many of Chow's comedy films, the star plays the part of a man who often changes his citizenship (or nationality), or demonstrates his mobility through a relationship with something or somebody related to a place outside of Hong Kong. Chow's image as a cosmopolitan citizen is particularly highlighted in the posters promoting these films. For instance, half of the poster for *The Diary of a Big Man* (1988) is designed as a calendar, in which each date is filled with images such as a US dollar, the Statue of Liberty, the Eiffel Tower and the English words 'Love' and 'Very Nice!'. While Chow's smiling face almost dominates the other half of the poster, the calendar seems

Figure 4.1: Three protagonists: Red Bean (Cherie Chung), James (Leslie Cheung) and Red Bean Pudding (Chow Yun-fat) [from left to right] in *Once a Thief*, film, dir. John Woo, Hong Kong: Gold Princess Film Production, 1991.

to indicate that his character is happy with a lifestyle that involves frequent international travel and contact.

Similar motifs can also be found in the three posters promoting *Once a Thief* (1991). While the translation of the film's Chinese title means crossing the world freely, the three leading stars are captured in a state of mobility in the first two posters, one showing Chow and his co-stars Leslie Cheung and Cherie Chung sitting in a car and the other showing them walking along a road. Of the three stars, Chow is the figure whose image specifically incorporates the idea of mobility. This is demonstrated by the third poster (which was published for the film's opening day), in which the three characters are given nicknames in addition to the ones they have in the film. While both Cheung's *bianfu dadao* (Bat Larcenist) and Chung's *miaoshou huakui* (Deft-handed Beauty) disclose their characters' thief identities, Chow's nickname *tianya langzi* (Sky-edge Vagabond) emphasises his image as a global traveller.

Why, then, is Chow singled out to represent the growing social mentality of cross-border mobility among Hong Kong citizens at that time? As I discussed in previous chapters, throughout his acting career Chow has built up a strong star image associated with his credentials as a local citizen of Hong Kong. Whereas the cross-border mobility of his comedic image expresses the desire of local citizens to explore new opportunities in different places, Chow's star image as a Hong Konger also conveys local audiences' perceptions of the city as the site of their cultural roots. Despite their flexibility to move around the world, Hong Kong always stands in the background of Chow's characters' personal stories, such as being the place where he finds love, as is evident in *The Greatest Lover* (1988) and *The Fun, the Luck & the Tycoon* (1990). Even in *Now You See Love, Now You Don't* (1992), in which Chow's Ng Shan-shui breaks up with his girlfriend Firefly (Carol Cheng) at the very beginning of the film, the two characters' romantic relationship is revived after they move to an urban area in Hong Kong.

In addition to finding his true love in the city, the depiction of the family in Chow's comedies is also distinctive, suggesting his character's emotional attachment and sense of belonging. Unlike many of his action or dramatic characters who are alone, Chow's comedic characters often have a family, such as brothers in *The Eighth Happiness*, and grandmothers in *The Fun, the Luck & the Tycoon*. Even in *God of Gamblers*, Chow's character Ko Chun develops a family-type relationship with Knife (Andy Lau), Jane (Joey Wong) and Knife's grandmother (Chan Lap-ban), who look after Ko when he injures his head. In these comedies, Chow is no longer a lonely hero whose action is glorified. Instead, he is a man enjoying support and care from his family and friends.

As with the theme of international mobility, Chow's characters' emotional attachment to the city is also highlighted in the film posters. For instance, both *The Eighth Happiness* and *Now You See Love, Now You Don't* use Hong Kong night scenes as their backgrounds. In the poster promoting *The Eighth Happiness*, eight small pictures showing eight stars making phone calls are inserted into a larger picture of the city's nightscape. Although it is difficult to tell exactly where these stars are located geographically and who they are talking to in the small pictures, the large background picture of Hong Kong's skyline suggests their association with the city. Similarly, in the poster for *Now You See Love, Now You Don't*, Chow and his co-star Carol Cheng are shown dancing together on a Hong Kong street. Their smiling faces and bodily gestures suggest their attachment to the city and their happiness at being Hong Kongers.

In terms of the concept of roots, Sheldon H. Lu (2005a: 298) argued that many Hong Kong films produced during the 1980s and 1990s often resulted in an identification with an ultimate 'homeland' – mainland China – during the process of searching for its own identity. However, Lu's argument does not apply to Chow's comedies, as these films rarely trace their origins back to China's history and cultural heritage, or even to a period before Hong Kong's metropolitan history. In many of Chow's comedies, mainland China is either completely absent from the narrative (as in *The Diary of a Big Man* and *The Fun, the Luck & the Tycoon*) or is simply portrayed as one of the character's many travel destinations (as in *God of Gamblers II*). Even in *The Greatest Lover*, in which Chow plays a character from the mainland, China soon vanishes from the narrative and Hong Kong becomes the place where Chow's character Locomotive expands his vision of modern society and obtains more freedom by accessing foreign cultures, such as learning English, tasting French wine and appreciating Western ballroom dancing in order to behave more like a Hong Konger.

Unlike in the films of Hui Brothers or of other comedic actors, in which a comic element is often located at the moment when a character confronts new technologies or modern ways of approaching problems (such as new manage-ment), speaking a different language or enjoying wine and entertainment in Chow's films may not in themselves necessarily relate to the characteristics of modern urban life. However, these actions are cultural signifiers that represent access to the world. All these factors, together with the huge hamburger Chow is holding in the film's poster, extend Locomotive's Hong Kong life from a simple urban experience to a cosmopolitan experience.

From the above analysis, we can see that Chow's comedic characters and their cosmopolitan experiences help to define Hong Kong as a vibrant, multi-cultural city with local citizens who are geographically and culturally flexible. As a small island on the world map, Hong Kong therefore represents not only a site that its citizens experience as a notion of home (where they are from and whither they can return), but also a symbolic location that increasingly gener-ates cultural hybridity through its global interactions. In other words, Chow's comedies distinguish Hong Kong's inhabitants from mainland Chinese citi-zens more generally through the depiction of Hong Kong citizens' privilege of global mobility.

Here I would like to note that, as a man who has not quite yet mastered the cosmopolitan lifestyle, Chow's character as bumpkin mainlander Locomotive in *The Greatest Lover* serves to challenge many of the star's own screen images as a diligent Hong Kong citizen, such as Ching Wai in *The Good, the Bad, and the Ugly* (1979), as detailed in Chapter 1. However, the comedian often pre-sents a spectacle of otherness by locating 'an eccentric individual who (know-ingly or unknowingly) disrupts conventional modes of behaviour, thought and identity' (Krutnik 2003: 3). Presenting Locomotive as a laughable character because of his provincial behaviour and lack of knowledge about the cosmo-politan lifestyle, Chow uses his performance to confirm Hong Kong citizens' self-perception as that which Steve Fore (2004: 94) termed 'denizens of the transnational cultures'. In this sense, Chow's comedic image as the mainlander Locomotive serves the same function as his other serious roles depicting Hong Kong citizens, in suggesting the cultural superiority of Hong Kong's citizens to their mainland Chinese neighbours.

Not only do Chow's characters allow Hong Kong citizens to feel good about themselves in front of mainland Chinese, they also reveal the pleasure that Hong Kong citizens feel as a result of their intelligence, capabilities and even their slyness when they encounter people from other parts of the world. Chow's Ko Chun in *God of Gamblers*, for example, is a Hong Kong gambler who easily beats his rivals from Japan, Singapore and Taiwan. Similarly, Chow's Red Bean Pudding in *Once a Thief* escapes under the eyes of a group of French gangsters who are chasing him with the intention of killing him. As Sek Kei (1999i: 36) commented in his review of *Once a Thief*, the film was extremely popular because it told a story about Hong Kong people travelling around the world, making money and defending themselves through their wisdom. In this regard, the characters Chow played in local comedies signified the local citizens' unique and honorific sense of the significance of being Hong Kongers, not just in East Asia, but in the world.

Considering the emphasis on the presence of Hong Kong in these films is thus particularly important in understanding the popularity of Chow's comic image in local cinema. As Sek Kei (cited in Chan et al. 2000: 126) stated in his review of *God of Gamblers*, 'Hong Kong people like to travel abroad but this doesn't mean they want to stay all their lives in a foreign country'. Chow expressed a similar point of view when discussing his own experiences of global travel in an interview in 1990. In this interview, Chow admitted that he liked travelling, but did not like to leave Hong Kong for a long period; what he preferred was a situation in which he could 'come back to Hong Kong for a while and then go out again' (Chow, as cited in Weng 1990: 33). Chow's views on global travel, his star persona as a Hong Konger and the cultural flexibility inscribed in his comedic image thus underline the perceptions of local citizens of themselves as cosmopolitan citizens, constructing both their cultural roots and their transcultural mobility through the global city of Hong Kong.

ADOPTING FLEXIBLE IDENTITIES: OPPORTUNITIES AND DILEMMAS

Many studies of the Chinese diaspora have argued that the meaning of international migration has undergone a remarkable conceptual shift in recent years. Laurence J. C. Ma (2003: 1) noted that, historically, the term has implied 'permanent, unidirectional, and onetime movement of people from one country to another often under economic, religious, or political duress at the places of origin'. However, more recent definitions of the term identify the process as involving complex 'geographic expressions of human interaction across global space', created as a result of varied forms of transmigration and transnational economic activity (Ma 2003: 6–7). As Ma (2003: 6) pointed out, in this process of definitional shift, 'the negative memory of oppression and the gnawing desire for return have been suppressed', and positive connotations, such as 'supermobility', 'flexible identities' and 'multiculturalism' have been brought to the foreground instead. In a similar vein, Lu (2005a: 301) argued that today's diaspora is not necessarily a 'condition of homelessness, exile, and dislocation', as migrants could become empowered through their migration. While contact with foreign cultures and the concept of roots continue to function as two important elements in both old and new notions of diaspora, the overall conceptual shift indicates that the new Chinese diaspora has adopted more dynamic, multiple and flexible identities.

Chow's comedic image conforms precisely to these new features that are being critically interrogated within the diasporic experience and its relationship with Hong Kong's new cosmopolitan status. As in the four images that feature Chow on the front cover and in the lyric booklet of his music album, there is no explicit connection between each image: In one, he is a white-collar yuppie wearing a suit and tie; in a second, he is dressed as a street vendor in a blue apron, three-quarter pants and a pair of clogs, holding a big bamboo steamer of steamed *bao*; in a third, he is dressed as a Chinese folk musician holding an *erhu* (Chinese two-stringed fiddle), while in the fourth he appears as a rock 'n' roll singer holding an electric guitar. However, by encompassing a wide range of dress codes signifying Chineseness and Westernness, modernity and tradition, and middle class and working class, these costumes and props emphasise Chow's star image as a man with multiple identities.

Chow's image, as presented in this album, can be seen as a direct extension of his image in the film *The Diary of a Big Man*. In this film, Chow sings the theme song 'Very Nice!', at a point where the star also frequently changes his image. In addition to appearing as the character, Chow also dresses up in traditional Mexican costume and a sombrero, as well as in the typical dress of a cook working at a street stall. As with the images found in the album booklet discussed above, Chow also plays different musical instruments in the film, including the saxophone, guitar, and maracas (also known as rumba shakers or shac-shacs). In addition to surprising the audience, these seemingly irrelevant narrative images serve to remind them of the flexible cultural identifications embodied by both Chow and the characters he plays.

The multiple and flexible identities inscribed on Hong Kong's emerging cosmopolitan mentality is one of the common themes in Chow's comedies. In *God of Gamblers*, the behaviour of Chow's character Ko Chun turns into that of an eight-year-old boy after a head injury. In *God of Gamblers II*, Chow, as a real gambling master, pretends that he is not such a man. Other examples include characters such as the villager in *The Greatest Lover*, who pretends to be an urban upper-class man, and the multi-millionaire in *The Fun, the Luck & the Tycoon* who disguises himself as a working-class waiter in a small restaurant. Whether as the result of an accident or as a volitional act of free will, these disguised identities reveal the ways in which being able to adopt a new identity often provides Chow's characters with solutions to their problems or ways of achieving their goals, such as getting revenge in *God of Gamblers*, or finding true love in *The Greatest Lover* and *The Fun, the Luck & the Tycoon*.

Given the social context at the time, the popularity of Chow's multiple and flexible images in his comedies is understandable. As detailed in the Introduction, the fast-growing local economy, shifting immigration rules in Western countries and an integrated global network all enriched the diaspora in the imagination of Hong Kong citizens. According to Ronald Skeldon (1994: 41), the ability to move around the world has not only helped to fulfil the Hong Kong people's dreams of exploring various opportunities in different places, but has also served to reduce the risk of Hong Kong's citizens becoming restricted to any single geographical location. In a sense, mobility has become an effective means for Hong Kong citizens to realise their goals in real life, such as exploring new business opportunities in East Germany (Zhang 1990: 41), seeking a British passport for the convenience of travelling and for better social welfare and education (Gu 1990a: 88), or taking advantage of lower costs and enjoying life in a place where people speak the same language by migrating to mainland China (Gu 1990b: 86–7). While Hong Kong gradually transformed itself from a colonial city to a metropolis playing an important role in the global financial markets and trading, its citizens also started to seek an identity, or more accurately identities, that could match Hong Kong's global metropolitan status.

Unlike serious diasporic dramas produced during the same period, such as *Farewell China* (1990), *Song of the Exile* (1990) or Chow's *An Autumn's Tale* (1987), which were direct portrayals of the stories of Chinese migrants struggling to live abroad and the hardship involved in their necessary identity shifts, Chow's comedies offered local audiences optimism and hope regarding changing identities. For example, Chow's character resolves his dilemma of having two wives by converting to Islam in *The Diary of a Big Man*, and his Lam's disguise helps him to avoid an arranged marriage and find his true love, Hung Leung-yuk (Sylvia Chang), in *The Fun, the Luck & the Tycoon*. In a relaxed and entertaining format, the happy endings afforded to Chow's comedic characters thus appear to reward Hong Kong's citizens for their flexibility and pragmatism.

However it is equally important to note that many emigrants from Hong Kong in the 1980s were well educated, highly skilled or possessed considerable wealth, as Skeldon (1994: 33) pointed out. Skeldon's research suggests that Hong Kong's citizens did not have equal opportunities for global travel due to many countries exerting their requirements by demanding evidence of personal skills and property during the application procedures for migration and travel. In terms of the migration threshold, money plays an important role in a person ability to become globally mobile. Exploring opportunities within films therefore presented an associated phenomenon in the popularisation of gambling and odds. In *The Fun, the Luck & the Tycoon* the minor taxi driver character Mr Stink (also played by Chow) becomes a multi-millionaire because he looks similar to the real millionaire in the film, Lam Bo-sun, not to mention Chow's iconic image as god of gamblers Ko Chun. As Cheng Yu (1998: 32) and Cheung Chi-wai (2012:150) pointed out, Hong Kong comedies of the 1980s no longer viewed gambling or trickery as the origin of sin and greed – a popular message delivered in comedies of the 1950s and 1960s. Instead, citizens started to regard gambling as a fast, legitimate way of getting rich.

This explains why, in Chow's musical medley *12 Fun 10 Fun Chuen*, an entire section of the lyrics is dedicated to the jargon used in different (gambling) games. In comparison to his own *xiaosheng* image, which encourages achieving success through hard work (as detailed in Chapter 1), the associated themes of gambling and odds in Chow's comedies and in his musical medley would have resonated with the opportunistic mentality of local audiences at the time, providing audience members from lower- or working-class backgrounds with a fantasy of becoming rich quickly, as a way of helping them to remove one of the major obstacles to global migration and travel.

Of course, the popularity of Chow's comedic image cannot be exclusively explained in terms of the fantasy he represented to his local audiences in the 1980s and 1990s. In addition to the cinematic fantasy of success or travel, Chow's comedic images also presented the dilemmas and social problems experienced by the local citizens in Hong Kong's cosmopolitan environment. In the theme song from the film *The Diary of a Big Man*,[3] Chow sings:

> The Big Man is me, Oh very nice; I love the right and I love the left;
> You very nice;
> Two lovers, same love, I am dealing with both;
> I am with two, the right and the left;
> Shuttle between the two, Oh, very nice . . .

In this song, Chow portrays a male chauvinist, the 'Big Man', who has a marital relationship with two women, which mirrors his character's situation in the film. When these two women finally discover their husband's secret in the film, Chow's character's marriages reach a crisis point. The family problem is nevertheless resolved when both of his wives start to accept the fact that they love him and are willing to share a husband. This 'Big Man' theme is also featured in Chow's *The Eighth Happiness* (1988), in which Chow also plays a playboy-type character – 'Handsome' Long, who in addition to having a steady girlfriend Do-do (Carol Cheng), also regularly dates different girls in each of Hong Kong's nineteen districts, particularly Beautiful (Cherie Chung).

The narratives of these two films, as well as Chow's song medley, pose an important question concerning why Chow's comedic image as a 'Big Man' became so popular in the late 1980s. According to the *Hong Kong Economic*

Times (Anon. 2000: C01), since polygamy has been illegal in Hong Kong since 1971, Chow's image in *The Diary of a Big Man* offered local men a sexual fantasy of continuing to have two or even more wives. However, as Cheng (1985: 44) pointed out, although Hong Kong remained a society in which male chauvinism prevailed in the 1950s and 1960s, many Cantonese comedies created intelligent and independent female characters. Similarly, as Chapter 1 on Chow's TV stardom discusses, one of the reasons that Chow became so popular in the local TV industry was that his *xiaosheng* image showed his respect for the new woman. Why, then, did audiences accept Chow's comedic image as a 'Big Man' who, as Cheng (1985: 44) stressed, 'shamelessly exploit[s] the female sex'?

The answer suggested by the *Hong Kong Economic Times* (Anon. 2000: C01) and Laikwan Pang (2005: 8) is that local comedies were produced mainly for male audiences, and such gender-oriented cinema provided a space to accommodate patriarchal ideology. Similarly, Cheng (1985: 44) and Sek Kei (1999j: 105–6) argued that the revival of patriarchal ideology in Hong Kong fostered the success of Chow's 'Big Man' comedies. However, if these critics and scholars are right, then how are we to understand the resurgence of male chauvinism in the modern Hong Kong of the late 1980s? Moreover, the experience of female audiences who are faced with this kind of comedies should be considered, even if women account for only a small share of the audience.

One may notice that in both films, Chow is engaged in a relationship with air hostesses, Sally (Sally Yeh) and Do-do, and his character is able to be with other women because he seizes the opportunities brought about by the frequent absences of his wife or girlfriend in their capacity as air hostesses, flying between Hong Kong and overseas destinations. Such narratives can be identified as mirroring local citizens' dilemmas as they faced the problems arising from global migration and travel. As Ma (2003: 34) noted, a unique set of social problems was created by global migration and travel, as some emigrants became *kongzhong feiren* (frequent fliers), who travelled frequently to different locations. Problems such as long-distance relationships, extra-marital affairs and emotional stress among those diasporic and transnational families became conspicuous (Ma 2003: 34). Since these social problems were closely related to the daily lives of local people at the time, they became one of the key concerns of cosmopolitan Hong Kongers in the late 1980s and early 1990s (whether they stayed in their host countries, flew frequently between different countries, remained in their home city, or experienced these difficulties via migrating family members or friends). In this regard, the 'Big Man' theme may have provided some men with the fantasy of solving their dilemmas or problems by getting involved in extra-marital affairs without damaging their family relationships.

However, instead of endorsing such behaviour, Chow's comedic performances often mocked local men who perpetuated patriarchal gender relations by taking advantage of global mobility. While Chow's 'Big Man' characters often experience a happy ending in the films, he also portrays these characters as risible figures who receive due punishment for cheating on their wives or girlfriends. In this sense, Chow's 'Big Man' image captured the social and psychological dilemmas experienced by local citizens concerning this increasingly severe social problem. In this regard, they gave other members of the audience the pleasure of seeing these 'Big Men' receive their due punishment for their cheating behaviour and the abnegation of their commitment and responsibility to their families in the social context of rapid cross-border migration and travel.

CONCLUSION

As Geoff King (2002: 4) argued, '[n]othing is *just* comic: things are comic in particular ways and for particular reasons'. To understand the popularity of Chow's comedic image, we therefore have to look closely at its specific context. While the comic elements and characters in Hong Kong comedies of the 1970s have been urbanised and modernised, Chow's comedic image of the late 1980s and early 1990s reflects a city undergoing further transformations into a cosmopolitan metropolis with its own significant status in the world. While local citizens distinguished themselves from other Chinese residents through their cultural flexibility and the privilege of global mobility, they also traced their confidence and self-esteem back to the cosmopolitan city.

It is not just these characters' cosmopolitan experiences that made Chow a popular comedic actor at the time, but also the fact that his comedic image addressed specific social issues at a time when Hong Kong was experiencing a new stage in the history of its urbanisation. With the city being increasingly involved in global business and gradually becoming a global financial centre, local citizens noticed the opportunities created by new social and geographical mobility. In this new pattern of transnational experience, Hong Kong migrants began to adopt multiple and flexible identities in order to explore opportunities in different global locations, and to reduce the risk of residing in a single place. Chow's comedic characters thus provided hope and vehicles for the fantasies of local people, as they became successful and achieved increasingly ambitious personal goals by exploring their multiple and flexible identities within different global contexts. However, frequent travelling between different locations also brought about social problems, such as the stress placed on the interpersonal relationships of family members. By projecting these social concerns onto the big screen and outside of the cinema in a comic way,

Chow turned those opportunists into objects of ridicule. In this sense, Chow's comedic image also addressed the social dilemmas inaugurated by increasing global migration and the cosmopolitan lifestyle that became prevalent in Hong Kong's society in the 1980s and 1990s.

NOTES

1. This music album was released in LP format by Cinepoly Record Co. Ltd in 1988. Cinepoly Record Co. Ltd was a music company co-founded by Cinema City & Films Co. and PolyGram in 1985, with the former holding larger shares at the time it was founded.
2. Translation of the various *bao* quoted in the lyric is added by the author.
3. This song, entitled 'Very Nice!', is also included in the music album *12 Fun 10 Fun Chuen*.

PART II

From an Expatriate Hong Kong Star to a Returning HKSAR Star: A Chinese Icon in Transnational Cinema from 1995 Onwards

CHAPTER 5

The Birth of a Hollywood Star: An Asian Hero in America

As the centre of global commercial cinema, Hollywood has a long-term appeal for many Chinese actors. However, historically, very few (with the exceptions of Anna May Wong and Bruce Lee) have managed to achieve stardom in America.[1] This situation seemed to change in the 1990s when Hollywood saw an influx of Hong Kong film stars, including but not limited to Chow Yun-fat, Jackie Chan, Jet Li and Michelle Yeoh. A number of factors have contributed to this change. First, the prosperity of Hong Kong cinema and the rise of other East Asian film industries during the 1980s captured global attention. Through video circulation, film festivals and art-house releases, East Asian films found a strategy for entering the American film market. Although the distribution of those films was limited, it cultivated a group of cult fans in America. Through those films, Hong Kong film stars demonstrated their cross-racial and cross-cultural appeal.

Secondly, a shift in consumer power was taking place in the American and global film markets.[2] Whilst the rapid growth of the Asian economy over the past three decades has enhanced the status of the East Asian film market in Hollywood's global distribution strategy, the demographic structure of Hollywood's domestic market has also changed. The population of Chinese migrants and their descendants, for example, was increasing at a rate between four and five times faster than the growth rate of the total population of the United States (Skeldon 2004). In comparison to the older generation of Chinese migrants, an increasing number of new Chinese migrants started to work in high-status jobs as lawyers, businessmen and scientists as a result of America's new rules on immigration, particularly the Immigration Act (1990).[3] Such a shift meant that the Chinese community started to possess new and increasingly significant powers of consumption in the American domestic market.

However, the employment of Chow, and of other Hong Kong stars, has proved to be a challenge to the status quo in Hollywood, not only because the

Asian presence has long been marginalised in Hollywood, but also because stars like Chow already enjoy huge popularity in the Asian film market. As Chow (cited in Smith 1995: 10) commented:

> A good role is important. But more than that is the script. Because for me, an Asian, I have a lot of fans, people that support me. If I choose the wrong role in a movie, they will feel ashamed. For me and for them . . . If I say that going into Hollywood is one of my dreams, well, maybe the dream comes true and helps my career. On the other hand, maybe it spoils my career, too, if I'm not careful.

Understandably conscious of his established stardom and fandom in Asia, Chow clearly understood that his performance in Hollywood films would be likely to impact on his popularity in both the new and the established markets. In this sense, Chow provides a compelling case for interrogating the transition of a Hong Kong star's career from the Asian to the American film market, as well as for examining Hollywood's shifting star strategies in relation to its racial narrative.

THE CREATION OF AN ASIAN HERO IN HOLLYWOOD

Hollywood is notorious for its stereotypical portrayal of Asian men as either 'primitive, infantile, carnal, effeminate, backward, and in need of the paternalistic benevolence', or as a 'threat' to American society (Marchetti 2001: 37 and 47). In both cases, Hollywood is criticised for favouring white supremacy through its discriminative depiction of the subordinate Oriental as the yellow peril. Hollywood's conception of the yellow peril provides a popular explanation for the low numbers of Asian actors being cast as leading men in Hollywood cinema. As Jachinson Chan (2001: 57) pointed out, Hollywood's fear of Oriental 'otherness' led to the widespread practice of whitewashing Asian characters on its silver screens from the 1920s to a period long after blackface casting became taboo in America's film industry. Referring to this situation, Chan (2001: 57) argue that yellowface casting effectively excluded Asian actors from the workforce, which resumed the historical elimination of Chinese migrants from labour competition in America.

Although yellowface casting has become less common in recent years, many film scholars, such as Gina Marchetti (2001: 37 and 52) and Lo Kwai-cheung (2004: 69), believed that Hollywood's idea of oriental otherness has not changed much despite the arrival of Chinese stars in America in the 1990s. For them, Chow's Hollywood films, such as *The Replacement Killers* (1998), *The Corruptor* (1999) and *Anna and the King* (1999), are just further examples confirming Hollywood's Orientalist depiction of Asian men (Marchetti 2001: 37, 52; Lo 2004: 69).

While Marchetti's and Lo's studies are important for revealing the restrictions that many Asian actors have encountered in America, considering three additional factors helps us to investigate the construction of the Asian image in Hollywood cinema in depth. First, as I mentioned at the beginning of the chapter, the career moves of the Hong Kong stars in the 1990s did not imply that they were about to abandon the Asian market and start afresh as new personalities in Hollywood. With something unique to offer, including their various cinematic skills, filmmaking knowledge and appeal to Asian markets, these stars exerted a degree of power when it came to negotiating their roles in Hollywood films. In this sense, the consideration of star power in film production needs to be examined.

Secondly, star presence beyond Hollywood's silver screen requires interrogation. As director Antoine Fuqua (cited in *Director's Commentary on The Replacement Killers* 2002) claimed, Chow's Hollywood debut in *The Replacement Killers* (1998) would make audiences feel that the film was America's version of Chow's acclaimed Hong Kong film, *The Killer* (1989). Deliberately recreating the Hong Kong action style (such as slow-motion gun shots and stylised body movements) in its production, Columbia Pictures thus showed it was making an effort to incorporate Hong Kong's cinematic language in its own action cinema. By so doing, the studio not only intended to attract fans of Hong Kong's action cinema, but also to promote Chow as a star who would bring new viewing experiences to audiences that were only familiar with Hollywood action films.

Thirdly, the shifting demographic structure of the film industry and the film market should be taken into account. As Marchetti (1991: 278) argued, Asian characters have to sacrifice their subjectivity and any desire to maintain their self-identities in order to be accepted by the white-dominated society represented in Hollywood cinema. Although Marchetti employed a historical approach in her study, her argument still assumed that Hollywood and the American mainstream market were dominated by white middle-class men to a degree. However, being overly reliant on the structural binary of a colonial relationship between the Occident and the Orient, Marchetti's study of Hollywood's depictions of the Asian image in an interracial relationship becomes increasingly questionable in contemporary social and cultural contexts in which increasing global mobility and cross-cultural communication have become the norm. The increasing pace of international migration and travel (both for leisure and for business), interracial marriage, and the shifting demographic structure of the American domestic market have transformed the American public's general perception of Asian migrants fundamentally, rendering such social and racial perceptions as multiple and in flux. Thus, while Marchetti's reading of the cultural assimilation implicit in cinematic representations of the Orient suggests that the Asian man's racial and cultural independence and subjectivity have historically been refused by Hollywood cinema, we should also consider how shifting social contexts have shaped the industry's depiction of the cultural identities enacted by Asian stars.

Despite the Orientalist narrative conveyed in Chow's Hollywood films (I will come back to this point later), one key difference could be identified in these films' marketing strategies. In contrast to the processes of cultural assimilation and the objectification of Asian characters as represented in early Hollywood cinema, all of Chow's Hollywood films have highlighted the ways in which the Asian man asserts his influence over his white partners, demonstrating Hollywood's attempt to incorporate Asian subjectivity. This is particularly evident in Chow's first Hollywood film *The Replacement Killers* (1998), in which Chow's character John Lee partners with a dealer of forged documents called Meg Coburn (Mira Sorvino) and defeats the powerful gang lord Terence Wei (Kenneth Tsang). Lee's moral standard and his action also gain him the respect of detective Stan 'Zeedo' Zedkov (Michael Rooker). Despite the film's discourse of partnership, its original theatrical trailer (1998) placed Lee's white partner Coburn and the detective Zedkov in the background, while simultaneously presenting the Chinese hero as the outright central figure who carries most of the narrative and action, clearly marketing the film as a star vehicle for Chow.

In comparison, the original theatrical trailer for *The Corruptor* (1999) narrates two parallel stories about Chow's Nick Chen and Mark Wahlberg's Danny Wallace. Although the trailer seems less prominent in terms of the narrative of Chen's authority, the negotiation of Asian subject matter certainly underlines the production of its content. As senior vice-president of New Line Cinema's Creative Marketing Department Lori Drazen (cited in 'From the (under)ground up' 1999) disclosed, the studio produced three trailers before the film was released in cinemas. The first two focused on Wallace's dual identity as a new cop in Chinatown and as an inspector from internal affairs, but both trailers failed the market tests.

As a result, the studio adjusted the key features involved in the two main characters' relationship in its third trailer. Telling the story from both Chen's and Wallace's viewpoints, the third trailer not only removes Wallace's role as an inspector from internal affairs completely, but also places emphasis on Chen's role as Wallace's 'mentor', who has something from which the new cop is going to learn. Although Drazen did not reveal who attended the marketing tests for the first two trailers, the shifting emphasis of Chow's position in the evolution of the trailers indicates that utilising images of Oriental objectivity, notwithstanding their still being persistent and prevalent in Hollywood, was no longer an easy option for studios when promoting the film.

The publicity for Chow's third Hollywood film, *Anna and the King* (1999), also confirmed that this negotiation of Asian subjectivity and Oriental objectivity was taking place in America. At first glance, the marketing of *Anna and the King* seems to follow Hollywood's traditional narrative of the Oriental objectification of Asian characters by placing Chow in the background behind his co-star Jodie Foster in the film's poster. Exalting Anna's position in the story and highlighting Foster's image as the top-billed star, the film poster appears to support Marchetti's (2001: 46–7) argument that the Orientalist idea of Asian people as an inferior race that needs to experience salvation continues to dominate the racial narratives delivered by Hollywood's silver screen.

Nevertheless, if we look at the promotional materials and publicity surrounding the film more closely, we can discern another narrative. The film's original theatrical trailer (1999), for instance, explicitly states that the film is about 'two people from different worlds who share an extraordinary moment'. In line with the message delivered by the film trailer, Emanuel Levy (1999) wrote an article in *Variety* before the release of the film, acknowledging the equality of King Mongkut and Anna – significantly, neither is superior to the other – despite their different social and cultural backgrounds.

It might be noted that in this different-but-equal relationship, both Anna and King Mongkut stand out from their countrymen in the film's trailer and in other publicity. While Anna openly criticises the West's colonisation of Asia, distinguishing herself from other one-dimensional British characters who symbolise colonialism, Chow's King Mongkut differentiates himself from other Siamese aristocrats via his vision of the modern world, as well as through his determination to defend the country's independence. Signifying mutual understanding, the romantic spark between the two characters therefore serves as a foil to their countrymen's ignorance, conservatism and self-centred arrogance. As such, Chow's *Anna and the King*, like his first two Hollywood action films, also highlights an interracial partnership that involves a transformation from tension at the beginning of the film to the development of mutual understanding at the narrative's culmination. The bi-directional path of the main characters learning from each other, as depicted in these three films' trailers and publicity, not only retains the distinct subjectivity of the main Asian characters within the interracial partnerships, but is also interwoven with an understanding of the need to develop a new West–East relationship (from both sides) within the rapidly changing global context.

Examining the publicity for these three films, we should not deny Hollywood studios' efforts to promote Chow as a new Asian icon who challenges the conventional Hollywood representation of inferior Oriental men in America. Nevertheless, I have no intention of ignoring Lo's (2004: 67–8) reading of Chow's casting as Hollywood's superficial demonstration that the American film industry has become more globalised and multicultural. Although Chow's characters were endowed with Asian subjectivity at times, Hollywood's portrayal of these screen images is by no means unproblematic. One may note that Chow's on-screen action in his Hollywood films is largely restricted to Oriental spaces, such as Chinatown or a Siamese palace, the production design creating ambiguity about the place of Asian stars in Hollywood. Norman K. Denzin (2002: 15) noticed that contemporary Hollywood frequently complicates its cinematic portrayals of racial subjects by its tendency to place good and bad dark-skinned characters together. In fact, in all three of the films mentioned above, Asian villains are included as part of Hollywood's creation of an Asian hero. Confined to a restricted domain of action, Chow thus negotiates his on-screen Asian subjectivity in Hollywood cinema in opposition to the Oriental objectivity incorporated in other Asian characters.

The subjectivity of Chow's heroes in Hollywood films became more ambiguous when the studios tried to bring the character's personal story into the narrative. Unlike those mysterious Asian villains whose personal background is almost completely occluded in Hollywood cinema, Chow's Hollywood films produced at the end of the 1990s all attempted to inform American audiences about where the character was from, and how he developed into the character they were seeing in the film. For example, it is revealed in the extra features on the DVD of *The Replacement Killers* that Lee's father was a general who was imprisoned during the Cultural Revolution because of his disagreement with Chairman Mao.[4] Although this scene was deleted from the film's big-screen version because the studio was considering releasing the film in then Chinese-administrated Hong Kong – one of the major film markets in which the studio intended to capitalise on Chow's fandom[5] – it is restored as an extra feature in the film's DVD, which was released in North America in order to inform audiences about the reason behind the enhanced partnership between Lee and Coburn, as Fuqua revealed (cited in *Director's Commentary on The Replacement Killers* 2002).

Nevertheless, this kind of supplementary stories delivered a somewhat ambiguous result. On one hand, it demystified the character and helped American audiences to understand the Chinese hero's motivation for his actions. On the other hand, by telling American audiences that this scene was removed because the studio was worried about censorship by the Chinese government, this extra feature reinforced Hollywood's characterisation of China as an alien, communist country that has a low tolerance of free speech and diverse opinions. Diverting the audience's attention from racial tension to political tension between two social systems, such a message thereby conforms to an idea of the diversity of the Asian subject-object in association with the post-Cold War ideologies that is crucially shared by many societies, communities and individuals around the world.

In addition, the on-screen depiction of sexual intimacy during the construction of an interracial romance continued to cause problems for the construction of an Asian man's subjectivity in Hollywood. Steve Seidman (1991: 2) pointed out that Hollywood's ubiquitous depictions of romance between two white characters are often sexualised via visible physical intimacy. The absence of such intimacy between Chow's character and a white woman, such as Coburn in *The Replacement Killers* and Anna in *Anna and the King*, seems to offer further evidence of the industry's stereotypical portrayal of the Oriental man as an asexual, impotent and unromantic figure. However, if we examine Chow's performance in Hong Kong films, we will see that Chow, since achieving top stardom in 1986, has rarely relied on explicit sexual scenes for the cinematic construction of a romantic relationship or for the suggestion of a man's sexual potency. It might be true that depicting on-screen physical intimacy is a popular method of conveying the cinematic representation of sexual relationships in Hollywood cinema, but such means are not the only expression of romance. The overemphasis on physical intimacy in Hollywood films would not only reduce the diversity of cinematic expressions of sexuality, but also risks overlooking the subtle dynamism that can be portrayed through different romantic gestures. Thus, it is overly simplistic to criticise Chow's screen hero for losing subjectivity simply based on the lack of physical contact.

In addition, Evelyn Iritani and Marla Matzer (1998: 1) reported in the *Los Angeles Times* that, out of consideration for historical accuracy, a Thai historian urged the studio to remove any depiction of physical contact, even eye contact, between the two protagonists in *Anna and the King*. Andy Tennant (cited in *Director's Commentary on Anna and the King* 2000) also revealed that the studio had to rewrite the script for the scene on the beach in which the King shows Anna the letter from American president Abraham Lincoln. Out of respect for Malaysian law that forbids showing a woman's naked body on the beach, the scene has been changed to show Anna dressed in her gown instead of being naked after skinny dipping in the sea, as written in the original script. Informing audiences that the studio had tried to respond to the demands of the Thai and Malaysian governments concerning such representational changes over the course of five months, and that the script had been rewritten and turned down four times, the *Los Angeles Times*' report and Tennant's comment indicate that 20th Century Fox had tried to retain Hollywood's conventional representation of heterosexual intimacy in the film.

Nevertheless, like the ambiguous result created by Hollywood's decision to add a Chinese hero's personal background to the film's narrative, Iritani and Matzer's report, and Tennant's comments about Hollywood's struggle to include interracial intimacy in *Anna and the King*, have a threefold implication. First, the account of consulting on scripts with Thai historians and respecting Malaysian custom and law instils Asian subjectivity into the process of Hollywood filmmaking. Secondly, it highlights particular scenes (either those

Figure 5.1: Anna Leonowens (Jodie Foster) and King Mongkut (Chow Yun-fat) in *Anna and the King*, film, dir. Andy Tennant, United States: Fox 2000 Pictures, 1999.

that made the final cut or those that were eventually deleted) in order to establish a connection between the film's non-erotic scenes and its depiction of a sexual relationship. Thirdly, the comments made by journalists and the film's director suggest that the desexualisation of the film's interracial romance was a response to Asian sensitivities which, to some extent, defended Hollywood's historical avoidance of sexualising the interracial romance between an Asian man and a white woman. As a result, Hollywood's construction of the image of the Asian man, and his gender and racial identity, has remained fluid and conflicting.

Chow's star presence in Hollywood films and publicity for those films demonstrate the awkward position that Asian stars faced in Hollywood at the turn of the twenty-first century. On one hand, Chow was presented as the Asian hope of challenging Hollywood's Oriental stereotypes. On the other hand, Hollywood studios were struggling to produce convincing scripts without being haunted by their historical, stock depictions of Orientalist imagery, despite filmmakers' attempts to recreate the cinematic style of Hong Kong cinema.

In order to recreate Chow's acclaimed image as a sentimental action hero, both *The Replacement Killers* and *The Corruptor* tried to embed emotional struggle, typically seen in melodramas. In comparison, the promotion of and publicity for the romantic epic *Anna and the King*, as Bob Graham (1999: C-1) pointed out, appeared to wish to trade on Chow's action star vehicle. However, unable to fully embrace Asian subjectivity, Chow's first three Hollywood films suffer from a somewhat uneven tone in terms of genre conventions, which was one of the reasons that these films did not perform well at America's domestic and international box offices.[6]

Despite Hollywood's feeble attempt to transplant Chow's Hong Kong stardom and genre creativity, to some degree (albeit ironically) this does suggest the industry's acknowledgement of Asian influence. The ambivalent message conveyed by promotional materials in this regard is a significant revelation of how Hollywood's global marketing concerns have begun to shape narrative development, and of how the involvement of different historical and political forces has started to complicate Hollywood's construction of its image of the Asian man.

THE INTRODUCTION OF A HONG KONG STAR IN AMERICA

Introducing Chow to the American public in the 1990s was not an easy task. Although he was a huge star in the Asian-American community and had already achieved cult stardom in America, his name was still relatively unknown to many American audiences at the time. In order to capitalise on Chow's stardom in America, Hollywood needed to negotiate different expectations from audiences who may or may not have been familiar with Chow and his Hong Kong films. One strategy that Hollywood adopted was to associate Chow with established stars with whom the American public was already familiar.

One year before Chow's Hollywood debut in *The Replacement Killers* reached audiences, the *Los Angeles Times* published an article by Cheo Hodari Coker (1997: 8), describing Chow as a man 'more elegant than Pierce Brosnan, more agile than Jean-Claude Van Damme, more honor-bound than Steven Seagal and wrapped up in Denzel Washington's smoldering sex appeal'. It is widely known that Brosnan is an Irish actor, Van Damme is originally from Belgium, Seagal is a white American actor known for his competence in Asian martial arts, and Washington is an African-American actor. While these stars are clearly associated with different ethnic/racial identities or non-anglophone cultures, their presence is also evoked by Hollywood to shape the industry's image as a global film centre embracing racial and cultural diversity. By comparing Chow with these stars and stressing his extraordinary screen charisma, Hollywood indicated that his screen persona could easily transcend racial and cultural differences, and that his Asianness should also be embraced as part of Hollywood's global strategy.

What is also important in American media's publicity regarding Chow's career move is that it highlights the hybridity of Chow's star qualities, such as stylishness, elegance, sexiness, agility and honour. In an interview about the cast of *Anna and the King*, Tennant (cited in Short 1999: n.p.) stated:

Speaking from a purely heterosexual point of view, he is a really cool, sexy, strong, charming, funny guy. The other thing about Yun-fat was that when I learned King Mongkut had spent many years as a monk, there's a certain stillness and gentleness in Yun-fat that really captures the essence of that.

Listing a number of personal attributes and mannerisms that seem incongruous with each other, such as coolness and funniness, stillness and sexiness, gentleness and strength, Tennant's comments not only indicate that the star's personal charisma suits well with his on-screen role, but also vividly echoes the American media's comments about the multidimensional nature of Chow's star quality.

Through such discussions of Chow's star charisma, the media publicity repeatedly communicated to American audiences that the arrival of the star in Hollywood would introduce an alternative Asian image to America – one that could dispel the prevalent and stereotypical Orientalist image of Asian men as weak and inferior. To cater for Asian-American audiences' sense of self, Hollywood went even further and became critical of its own past ignorance of Asian sensibility, predicting that Chow's star charisma and screen presence might help the industry, and American society in general, to change its racist reputation. James Foley (as a white director), for example, argued that although American audiences in the 1990s were not yet used to seeing Asian people as leads in American films, Chow's Chinese persona and Hollywood's decision to make him an American star would improve the familiarity of the American general public with Asian ethnic groups (Foley, as cited in *Chow Yun-fat Goes Hollywood* 2002).

In similar terms to those of Foley, such ethnic filmmakers as African-American director Fuqua (*Director's Commentary on The Replacement Killers* 2002) and Chinese-American producer Terence Chang (cited in *Chow Yun-fat Goes Hollywood* 2002) asserted that Chow's presence not only helped to broaden Hollywood's view of minority actors and migrants from East Asia, but also gave them a glimpse of a promising future in which Asian actors might receive more opportunities to be cast in Hollywood films as well as in global cinema. The filmmakers' comments all indicated that Hollywood would try to retain Chow's Asian persona during his career move and to present Chow as an influential public icon whose Asian subjectivity would help the industry and its American audiences to expand their vision and understanding of Asia, Asian culture and Asian people.

The filmmakers' comments about Chow's stardom were well received in American film critics' reviews of Chow's screen performances, especially those referring to *Anna and the King*. Chow's King Mongkut, for instance, is described as a powerful, strong, sophisticated and mighty leader (Arnold 1999; Lamb 2000: A2). This is in contrast to the discourse about Yul Brynner's performance of the same character in *The King and I* (1956), which often focused on the character's exotic looks, savage beauty and amusing behaviour (Iritani and Matzer 1998: 1; Levy 1999; Churchill 1999; Holden 1999; Bernard 1999). In addition to the professional film critics, Chow's star image was also well received by the general public in the American film market. Just two of the many examples include Zarminae Ansari (2000: n.p.), who argued in a student-run journal that 'Besides the charisma, Yun-Fat [sic] is a great actor; an Oscar nomination is definitely deserved here'. From Ansari's point of view, Chow's performance exceeded that of his co-star Jodie Foster, twice an Oscar winner, and convinced American audiences that this Asian man was not only a star but was also a fine actor. Similarly, Beth Armitage's (n.d.: n.p.) review described Chow as 'tremendous, and utterly compelling', and that she would like to see the star being cast as James Bond, an iconic fictional and screen figure. Taken together, these film reviews, published on various media platforms, including a mainstream newspaper, a semi-professional journal and personal website, illustrate that Chow confronted American audiences with a powerful new image of a kind of Asian man rarely seen in the previous decades of Hollywood's cinematic history, and enhanced the American film market's understanding of an Asian star's screen value with regard to global cinema.

Like his role in his on-screen partnerships, Chow was also presented as the more senior and experienced member in Hollywood's depiction of his off-screen interracial partnerships. For instance, Fuqua's status as a first-time feature film director is reiterated several times in the DVD's extra features by the director himself and by other crew members and the cast, as well as by critics and journalists in the film's media publicity. According to Fuqua (cited in Coker 1997: 8), Chow not only understood the film frame and responded very well to camera movement, but also was a star with some very special qualities that many Hollywood actors do not usually possess (such as designing his own action sequences). Although Chow was not responsible for making key decisions regarding camerawork, his suggestions and his creativity were deemed by Fuqua to be inspiring. Through Fuqua, Hollywood conveyed a message that the experience and knowledge that Chow had gained from working in the Hong Kong film industry was highly valuable.

Similarly, the audience is informed of the director's concern about casting Mira Sorvino (despite the fact that she was already an Oscar-winning actress) and Mark Wahlberg because of their inexperience in action cinema (Fuqua, as cited in *Chow Yun-fat Goes Hollywood* 2002; Foley, as cited in 'From the (under)ground up' 1999). Recognising Chow's acting skills and star power on and beyond the big screen, the introduction of his stardom in America, rather than converting Chow to Hollywood filmmaking culture, actually implied the opposite – Hollywood was learning from Chow, a narrative contesting with Steve Fore's (1997: 248) assumption that Asian stars tended to lose their Asian hallmarks when they moved to Hollywood.[7]

However, as with Hollywood's ambiguity when introducing Chow's on-screen Asian hero to an American public, Hollywood's discourse on Chow's star quality was also characterised by friction and internal conflict. This can be seen in Hollywood's depiction of Chow's new star persona as its (unofficial) consultant regarding Asian culture, a role that was used to confirm as well as to challenge the stereotypical image of the Orient in Hollywood. As a way of emphasising the value of Chow's skills, knowledge and experience, Hollywood studios communicated to their audiences the ways in which the star's sensibility concerning Asian culture influenced the film's production. For instance, there is a bathhouse scene in *The Corruptor* in which Chow's character Chen tries to persuade Henry Lee (Ric Young) to give up the idea of corrupting his new working partner, Wallace. As Foley revealed, in the film's original script, Chen's prostitute girlfriend May (Marie Matiko) was engaging in oral sex with Lee when Chen walked into the bathhouse. According to the director, this scene was changed to May feeding Lee grapes because Chow pointed out that Chen could never be with May again if he – as a Chinese man – saw her having sex with another man (*Director's Commentary on The Corruptor* 1999). This message is reinforced by the director's commentary on another scene in which Chow uses a Chinese breathing technique as a method of releasing stress. Regarding Chow's suggestion to make the scene more 'authentically Chinese', Foley decided to change the original script, in which Chow's Chen was supposed to punch a mirror and damage a paper towel dispenser. Through these two stories, it is implied that Chow's opinion and his Chineseness have been respected by the studio as a way of improving the portrayal of Asian elements.

Nevertheless, Chow's image as an Asian cultural expert is dubious. For example, in the two action films, Chinatown appears on screen as an exotic and mysterious place where street violence, drug transactions, prostitution and forced sexual slavery, smuggling, gambling, and corruption are everyday occurrences. Although both Fuqua and Foley admitted that they were unable to film in the real Chinatown because the place did not match their idea of what Chinatown should look like, both directors insisted that their recreation of Chinatown, as a place with 'nasty alley ways and buildings' (Fuqua, as cited in the *Director's Commentary on The Replacement Killers* 2002) and a 'piggy city' (Foley, as cited in *Director's Commentary on The Corruptor* 1999), captured the essence of the place. Hollywood's portrayal of these mysterious and violent characteristics associated with Chinatown concurs with Marchetti's (2001: 52) and Lo's (2004: 68) observations that Hollywood continues to draw disproportionate inspiration from illegal Chinese migrants and to label Asian-Americans in terms of their cultural otherness.

While the filmic Chinatown represents the perceptions of Hollywood's filmmakers or, more accurately, their imagined Oriental space, it also reveals that Chow was unable to change a Hollywood narrative that might be seen as racially clichéd and even offensive. Given Chow's image as an expert on Asian culture (as promoted by the film's distribution materials) and the star's own comments that he would not accept an unsuitable script due to his fidelity to his loyal fan base in the Asian market (as mentioned at the beginning of the chapter), Chow's appearance in the films and his silence on the directors' recreation of Chinatown condone to some degree the authenticity of the gang-ridden image of Chinatown depicted in the films. As a result, Chow's star image becomes conflicted at this point, alternating between his expertise as a highly skilled migrant with Asian sensibility and his endorsement of Hollywood's Orientalist construction of a lawless Chinese community.

The ambiguity of Chow's star quality is also conveyed by the publicity surrounding Chow's English-language skills. Promoting Chow as a new Hollywood leading man, Hollywood reportedly tailored the film script to cater for him. Yvonne Tasker (2006: 441) argued that action heroes often use their bodies as a sort of armour, so that being silent becomes a symbolic method of avoiding the penetration of any softness into his persona. Claiming that Chow's lack of dialogue in *The Replacement Killers* would remind audiences of 'a sort of silent strength' that traditionally appeared in spaghetti Westerns, Fuqua's (*Director's Commentary on The Replacement Killers* 2002) comment confirms Tasker's argument to some degree. In this sense, Chow's silence in the film seems to conform to Hollywood's traditional configuration of an action hero, as well as corresponding to Chow's personification of a silent hero in his Hong Kong action films, such as Ah Jong in *The Killer* (1989).

Nevertheless, Mathew Baer (cited in *Chow Yun-fat Goes Hollywood* 2002) revealed that cutting down long monologues and dialogues was not only a decision to rewrite Chow's character as a strong and silent persona, but was also the result of catering to Chow's level of English. Once again, Chow's star quality becomes conflicting at this point. The story of the tailored script suggests on one hand that Chow is recognised as an important star, who is welcomed by the Hollywood industry regardless of his command of the English language. On the other hand, the tailored script also highlights Chow's lack of ability in English. As a key skill for a migrant worker to gain employment in the United States, English is particularly important for actors, as they need to speak the language in front of a camera.

Unlike other English-speaking stars, such as Clint Eastwood or Sylvester Stallone, whose on-screen silences do not diminish their (English) speaking abilities, Chow's silence in the film, and the accompanying story about the film's tailored script, indicate that the language barrier restricted the types of roles available to him in Hollywood. In critically placing Chow's facility for modifying the script and performing as a typical silent hero, alongside his inability to master the English language, we can identify that Hollywood simultaneously accommodated and limited Chow's star presence within the industry.

In fact, Hollywood's promotion of Asian stars reveals that the industry has been compelled to improve the diversity of its cinematic representations of Asian characters within a rapidly changing global context. Nonetheless, the persistently insufficient casting of Asian stars as leads, especially as romantic leads, reveals Hollywood's inability to produce scripts featuring the kinds of sophisticated interracial narratives that could cater for the diversified social perceptions of an Asian image in today's global film market. Such a situation has not only frustrated many Chinese actors, but has also, at least partially, contributed to the shifting production and distribution strategies of Hollywood studios over the past few years. Instead of importing Asian stars directly and casting them as leading men or women in Hollywood-produced films, Hollywood is increasingly involved in co-productions with the Asian film industry, including financial investment and the global distribution of films produced in Asia.[8] In conjunction with the rise of Asian cinema, it is not difficult to understand why many Hong Kong stars, including Chow, decided to move their careers back to the Chinese film industry a few years later.

CONCLUSION

Prior to the end of the twentieth century, the cinematic images of Asian men in Hollywood films were predominantly associated with Orientalist depictions of the yellow peril. The fear of cultural and political threats from the Orient resulted in many Asian men being portrayed as asexual, emasculated and feminised characters in Hollywood films. Racial tensions in American society were further underscored by the phenomenon of yellowface, which was used to portray Asian characters on the screen. As a result, Hollywood only provided very limited and proscribed opportunities for Asian actors. To demonstrate its awareness of cultural diversity, Hollywood became particularly eager to make cultural differences visible in its productions in the 1990s. As with other American businesses that tried to enhance their positions in the global market, Hollywood studios began to recruit Asian stars to improve their market share in Asia, as well as to provide alternative cinematic images for multi-ethnic domestic audiences.

It is safe to conclude from the analysis in this chapter that Chow has introduced a more positive and complex image of Asian men to American audiences. Unlike the conventional portrayal of a good Asian who loses his or her ethnic characteristics and self-identity in order to become assimilated into American (white) society, Chow's cultural background and his professional skills gained from Hong Kong filmmaking were actually highlighted by the industry as valuable assets, demonstrating Hollywood's accommodation of cultural diversity and Chinese subjectivity. By so doing, Hollywood tried to attract Chow's extensive Asian fan base and his American cult fans, as well as a mass audience unfamiliar with Chow's earlier (Hong Kong) stardom. However, Hollywood's depiction of Chow's Asian subjectivity is somewhat unstable. Restricting the domain of action afforded to Chow's on-screen heroes, and parallelling his autonomous Asian subjectivity with residual depictions of Orientalised objectivity, Chow's Hollywood characters are imbued with Hollywood's clichéd perceptions concerning Chinese otherness. In addition, as the North American promotional materials for these films reveal, Hollywood also made Chow's star persona problematic through its ambivalent attitudes towards his professional skills (such as his command of the English language) and demonstrated a persistent obsession with the imagined, 'authentic' and Oriental overtones associated with Chinese immigrants. As a result, a distinct representational ambiguity became inserted into Chow's Hollywood stardom, and the Asian star's position in Hollywood remained simultaneously accommodated and marginalised.

NOTES

1. Despite her acting ability and linguistic talents, America-born Anna May Wong was cast in stereotypical Asian roles, and was frequently denied the chance to play the lead in Hollywood films. She was even rejected as the lead in a film in which the main character was supposed to be Chinese. With regard to *The Good Earth* (1937), for instance, the director refused to consider her for the leading role of O-Lan, but chose instead to cast white actress Luise Rainer in the role.
2. In 1980, there were 366,500 Chinese immigrants in America, accounting for merely 2.6 per cent of all foreign-born nationals. By 2000, the number increased to 1,192,437, and the amount of Chinese immigrants jumped from tenth position in 1980 to the third largest group in America. For more details, see McCabe (2012).
3. The Immigration Act (1990) increased the number of legal immigrants allowed to enter the United States from 700,000 to 1,375,000 each year from 1995 onwards. Among the 675,000 new visas, 140,000 are employment-based. Aiming to attract highly skilled global labour, the new system set up a preference system, with priority given to those professionals with in-depth knowledge of and/or profound experience in certain areas, such as science, art, athletics, scholarship and other fields. For more details, see the US Citizenship and Immigration Services (n.d.: 3).
4. The DVD versions analysed in this chapter, especially those of *The Replacement Killers* (1998) and *The Corruptor* (1999) were released in the US and Canada only. The Region 1 code effectively restricts the DVD's circulation in areas outside of North America. In other words, the extra features contained in these two DVDs are specifically targeted at a North American audience and thus help us relate the analysis of Chow's star image to the American social context at the turn of the twenty-first century.
5. *The Replacement Killers* finished filming before Hong Hong's handover, but it was not scheduled for theatrical release in Hong Kong until January 1998.
6. Marketed as B-movies, *The Replacement Killers* ranked ninetieth in 1998 in America's domestic gross, and *The Corruptor* ranked ninety-first in 1999. As a blockbuster with a $92

million budget, *Anna and the King* generated only $39,263,420 domestically, standing at fifty-eighth place in America's domestic gross in 1999. For more details, see Box Office Moji (2015).

7. In his study of the distribution of Jackie Chan's *Rumble in the Bronx* (1995) in the American market, Steve Fore argued that Chan's foreignness was removed in the Hollywood distribution exhibition as a way to reduce the expectation of difference.

8. Examples include Chow's *Crouching Tiger, Hidden Dragon* (2000), a co-production mainly invested in by Asia Union Film & Entertainment Ltd, China Film Co-Production Corporation, Columbia Pictures Film Production Asia and Sony Pictures Classics. Warner Bros partnered with the China Film Group and the Hengdian Group to create Warner China Film HG Corporation in 2004. The company invested in Jet Li's *The Warlords* (2007). The Weinstein Company established a fund for the production of Asian films in 2007, and the company worked as the distributor for *The Forbidden Kingdom* (2008) and Chow's *Shanghai* (2010).

CHAPTER 6

Middle-aged Men in the Transnational Martial Arts Cinema: Ageing Stars and the Myth of Midlife Angst

In 2000, forty-five-year-old Chow Yun-fat played a middle-aged martial artist, Li Mubai, in *Crouching Tiger, Hidden Dragon*. Released in Chinese language, this film not only achieved critical and commercial success, but also enhanced Chow's stardom in the global film market. Three years later, Chow starred in *Bulletproof Monk* (2003), which was deemed by many film critics to be an example of Hollywood's attempts to reproduce the success of *Crouching Tiger, Hidden Dragon* in the global film market (Koehler 2003; Ebert 2003). Despite their different market performances, both films were somewhat unusual at the time for allowing an older-generation martial artist to play central characters given the genre in which the two films are situated, namely martial arts.

One may note that, in the majority of Hong Kong's martial arts films produced from the 1960s to the 1990s, older generation-martial artists are either presented as a supporting character or are simply absent from the narrative (such as in *Once Upon a Time in China* I–III 1991–1993, *New Dragon Gate Inn* 1992 and *Heroes among Heroes* 1993). A significant reason behind this situation is the genre's convention of emphasising the actor's physical potency, adaptability and flexible movement, all of which are often associated with the notion of youth or young bodies.

In order to perform within the parameters of the genre's demanding physical culture, many film stars in martial arts cinema are trained extensively. Examples include Bruce Lee, who developed his own style of martial arts in *Jeet Kune Do*; Jackie Chan and Sammo Hung, who both received martial arts training at a Peking Opera school and worked as stunt performers before becoming stars; and Jet Li, who started learning martial arts at the age of eight and won multiple gold medals in Chinese national martial arts championships prior to acting. Although cinematic techniques (such as special effects, stunts and computer technology) are widely known to be used to make the stars' bodies and physical performances more powerful, they are often downplayed in a film's publicity. Instead, the martial arts training background of these stars was often highlighted to demonstrate the authenticity of the action sequences in their films.

By contrast, Chow did not receive any formal training in martial arts, and nor did he appear in any martial arts films before the release of *Crouching Tiger, Hidden Dragon*. In this sense, Chow's screen image as a middle-aged martial artist approaching retirement doubly challenges the traditions previously upheld by the genre. Through the comparative analysis of the mass media publicity in China and America that accompanied the releases of *Crouching Tiger, Hidden Dragon* and *Bulletproof Monk*, this chapter explores how specific market conditions impact upon the screen image and acting career of ageing stars.

THE MYTH OF MIDLIFE ANGST IN ACTION-ORIENTED CINEMA AND THE PUBLIC PHOBIA OF LOSING SOCIAL POWER

As Chris Holmlund (2002: 9) noted, being young is important for both women and men in the film industry because of the public's apparent 'distaste for ageing'. The workforce structure in the film industry supports Holmlund's observation. According to figures from the United States Bureau of Statistics (2014), nearly 74 per cent of the industry's employees are aged forty-four or younger. As shown in Table 6.1, whereas the percentage of employees in all industries drops sharply in the age group of sixty-five and over, which reflects the average retirement ages in most industries, people leave the film industry at a much younger age than the average age of retirement.

Since many administrative, management and logistics staff working in the film industry retire at similar ages to their counterparts in other industries,

Table 6.1: US employment by industry and age group, 2013 (US Bureau of Labor Statistics 2014).

Age group	Motion picture and video industries (median age 34.4)	All industries (median age 42.4)
16–19	41,000 (10.1%)	4,458,000 (2.9%)
20–24	59,000 (14.6%)	13,599,000 (8.8%)
25–34	112,000 (27.7%)	31,242,000 (20.3%)
35–44	86,000 (21.3%)	30,650,000 (19.9%)
45–54	52,000 (12.9%)	42,523,000 (27.6%)
55–64	41,000 (10.1%)	23,776,000 (15.4%)
65 and older	13,000 (3.2%)	7,681,000 (5.0%)

their retirement age keeps the average figures higher in the industry than it would otherwise be, which means that the ages of actors and other creative workers leaving the industry is even lower than the table illustrates.

America's labour structure undeniably indicates that, for many middle-aged stars, ageing probably means either volunteered or forced retirement from the industry due to reduced contracts or salary offered to older actors. Arnold Schwarzenegger provides a good example, as the star moved his career into an area generally more tolerant to ageing (or old age) and became a full-time politician in 2003 at the age fifty-seven.[1] This phenomenon is particularly evident for martial arts or action stars, who often face public questions concerning how long they can continue to fight convincingly on the big screen after they reach their mid-forties. For instance, in 1998 Rone Tempest (1998: 5) wrote that Jackie Chan, who was forty-four at the time, had to deal with the challenge posed by younger rivals, along with increasing concerns that his film career would shortly be eclipsed as a result of his age. Similarly, Tom Brook (2001) stated that many highly bankable leading action men in Hollywood from the 1980s and 1990s, including Sylvester Stallone, Bruce Willis and Kevin Costner, started to find their chances of leading a Hollywood film being reduced, and their box-office clout (in the action cinema) became much lower after they entered their late forties.

The championing of youthful bodies in the film industry is certainly not unique. As Mike Hepworth (1999: 33), Georges Minois (1999: 328) and Sara Arber and Jay Ginn (1991: 169) have pointed out, many of our societies tend to associate youth with physical strength and sexual virility, whereas old age is associated with physical and mental frailty. As such, many of our societies frequently represent the image of getting old in extremely stereotypical terms, constructing what Mike Featherstone and Andrew Wernick (1995: 8–9) termed a return to 'the disruptive role' of being children again. In other words, getting old is often related to the perception of losing or exiting mature adulthood.

The fear of growing old probably explains why many of our modern societies believe that middle-aged men are widely haunted by a sense of having a midlife crisis, even though this group of men is simultaneously considered to be the most powerful age group (Featherstone and Wernick 1995: 8). Standing in a position that bridges youth and old age, middle-aged men not only signify the social power that young people long to possess, but also hold the mature manhood of which old people are deprived. In this sense, the midlife crisis does not convey people's concerns about middle age per se, but rather reveals the fear of approaching a certain age that signifies exiting the most powerful age group in society in the future.

Arber and Ginn (1991: 50) argued that these popular concerns about ageing are largely a product of the industrialisation of society. According to them, the mandatory retirement and pension system of modern industrialised societies not only forces people to leave their jobs at a certain age (regardless of their competence), but also forms a subclass of frequently impoverished retired people as a result of pension costs. With an increasing number of modern societies having growing ageing populations, this crisis of middle age has also become more visible in the media since the 1990s. Sceptical attitudes towards the competence of middle-aged martial arts and action stars in the film industry, the increasing production of such films addressing middle-age crises as *The Bridges of Madison County* (1995) and *American Beauty* (1999), and the intensification of media attention to measures against ageing such as plastic surgery, body shaping and physical fitness (Squires 1999: Z20; Sky News 2007; Parker-Pope 2008; Carrell 2011) are only a few examples of the widespread attention focused on midlife crises in the global media.

However, some stars, such as Robert De Niro, Dustin Hoffman and Meryl Streep, have successfully managed to maintain their stardom on the big screen despite their high-profile ageing. Why, then, are some ageing stars able to maintain their popularity, stardom and employability, while others fail to do so? Holmlund (2002: 145–6) argued that ageing stars often deny their age by clinging to a youthful look through methods such as make-up and even plastic surgery. Similarly, Leon Hunt (2003: 159), in his study of Mel Gibson's and Danny Glover's performances in *Lethal Weapon 4* (1998), claimed that the two 'ageing heroes' must ultimately prove to themselves that 'they are not "too old"' to take on the impossibly agile and martial arts master'. Both Holmlund's and Hunt's arguments suggest that presenting a youthful body is key for ageing stars to convince audiences that their agility remains at the same level as (or even at a higher level than) it was in their earlier films in order to defend themselves against public interrogation about their age. Through downplaying their reliance on special effects and stunt doubles, ageing stars like Jackie Chan and Jet Li may continue to play roles younger than their real age.

Nevertheless, Chow, together with the aforementioned stars who are ageing successfully on the big screen, illustrates the case that the articulation between a star's age and screen career is far more complicated than these studies might acknowledge. As mentioned above, an increasing number of films are depicting middle age and senior life. This is a crucial point, as the production of such films allows some middle-aged stars to portray the dilemmas associated with their ageing and their transition across the generations on screen. Rather than denying their age or pretending to be young, these ageing stars are, through their accomplished performances and their own star images, diversifying the cinematic images of middle-aged people getting older. Moreover, the audience's understanding of film genres, as well as social attitudes to ageing, also determines how the age issue impacts on a star's screen career. Chow and his screen image as an ageing martial artist thus provides a compelling case study for revealing the complex interactions between genre traditions, the film industry's practices of star employment, and the wider social understanding of ageing.

THE BODY CULTURE OF MARTIAL ARTS CINEMA

As a middle-aged star who had not been trained in martial arts playing an ageing martial artist who is seeking retirement, Chow delivered the ambivalence associated with the prowess and incompetence of an ageing man's body as mediated through the transnational martial arts cinema. In comparison to other ageing stars, such as Jackie Chan and Jet Li, who chose to continue to perform challenging sequences of martial arts in their films produced in the 2000s, Chow appeared in only three fighting scenes of about six minutes in total in *Crouching Tiger, Hidden Dragon*. Instead of demonstrating the character's physical competence through action, Chow's Li is often shown at moments when he is teaching Jen (Zhang Ziyi) in such martial arts as *jiandao* (sword ethics) and *jiande* (sword morality). By transferring the popular cinematic understanding of martial arts from a physical spectacle to a philosophical contemplation, Chow's Li not only demonstrates his knowledge of the *jianghu* (the martial arts world) and his authority in the discipline of using a sword, but also minimises the audience's attention on his bodily movement.

Even in the fighting scenes, Chow's body is still positioned between being able and unable in martial arts. For instance, in his first fighting scene, Chow's Li defeats Jen easily using only one hand. Demonstrating greater skill than the younger martial artist, Li successfully displays his physical prowess

Figure 6.1: Li Mubai (Chow Yun-fat) in *Crouching Tiger, Hidden Dragon*, film, dir. Ang Lee, Taiwan, Hong Kong, USA and PRC, Asia Union Film & Entertainment Ltd, China Film Co-Production Corporation, Columbia Pictures Film Production Asia, and Edko Films, 2000.

despite his age. However, equally important is that the choreography of the character's extremely simple movement has effectively hidden Chow's lack of proficiency in performing complicated martial arts movements. In fact, except for this scene, the audience struggles to see Chow captured in the same frame as his opponents when a dual or group fight is taking place. More often, Chow appears on the screen alone, even in scenes such as Li's last battle, in which Li wields a sword to block poisoned needles from Jade Fox (Cheng Pei-pei), who is actually out of the frame. The isolation of Chow's body reduces the demand on the actor to control his movements accurately and precisely in terms of the rhythm, speed, strength and bodily stance required for an action sequence.

The absence of Chow's physical performance of martial arts is clearly illustrated in the American media. In November 2000, the *Los Angeles Times* published an article reporting on the production of one 'key action scene' that had been scheduled for Chow. In addition to the introduction to the film's action choreographer Yuen Woo-ping and his previous work on *The Matrix* (1999), Cheng Scarlet, writing for the *Los Angeles Times* (Cheng 2000: 1), described in detailed the preparations of the stunt team that doubled for the 'flying' action and Chow's delivery of a 'valiant pose' in front of the camera, as well as the computer special effects that were going to be used in post-production to remove the wire. Clearly telling readers that Chow has never made a martial arts film before, this report highlights Chow's star image as an actor rather than as a martial artist. Similarly, *Variety* (McCarthy 2000) and *The New York Times* (2000) emphasised the film's unconventional hybridisation of the martial arts genre with melodramatic narrative by stressing the actors' portrayals of complex emotions and feelings. All told, the authenticity of the star's mastery of martial arts is de-emphasised, and the public's attention is diverted from Chow's action skills to his acting skills, from the physical spectacle to the visual spectacle of Yuen's choreography and special effects.

In comparison, the attitude of the Chinese media to Chow's casting is more complex. On one hand, as in the reports that appeared in the American media, some Chinese-language media reports also placed their attention on the character's subtle emotional range (*Hong Kong Economic Times* 1999: C02; Di 2000: n.p.). Emphasising that Chow was playing a type of character that he had never previously portrayed on the big screen, these reports evoked a public anticipation of Chow facing a new acting challenge. On the other hand, some newspapers and magazines questioned the suitability of casting Chow as the great martial artist Li. *Ta Kung Pao* (1999: D08) and *Ming Pao* (Ah 1999: C01), for example, expressed doubts as to whether Chow's ageing body was able to cope with the intensity of physical combat before the release of the film, and they argued that casting Chow in the role would sacrifice the physical authenticity of the martial arts genre.

The aforementioned media reports reveal the different understandings of body culture in martial arts cinema in the two different film markets. As mentioned earlier, the authenticity of the martial arts cinema conventionally comes from its stars' martial arts training backgrounds and their images as real martial artists. In the Chinese media, the combination of the expectation of the physical tradition in the martial arts genre, as well as social perceptions of the lack of potency of ageing bodies, generated scepticism about Chow's competence to deliver an intensive physical performance.

However, Chow's reputation as an accomplished actor not only helped the star to confront the difficult issue of his age and to allow him to be represented as growing old on the big screen, but also turned Chow's age into a new aspect of his acting to some degree. Consequently, the Chinese media could still highlight different dimensions of his performance in order to divert the audience's attention away from Chow's limited physical martial arts performance. In this sense, Chow managed to challenge the physical conventions in the martial arts genre by demonstrating that an ageing star who has an acclaimed reputation for acting does not necessarily experience diminished employability in the action-oriented cinema or in the industry overall. This last point may be one of the reasons that so many action stars wish to be considered seriously as dramatic actors and not just as martial artists.

By comparison, as a foreign genre, martial arts cinema (especially the sub-genre of the swordplay film) is relatively new to American audiences. The correlation between the genre's physical authenticity and a star's physical performance had not really been established at the time of the film's release. The emphasis in the American media on the film's special effects and choreography suggested that the American audience did not necessarily see the genre's visual spectacle as relying on the star's agile body. The different understandings of the martial arts cinema in the Chinese and American film markets therefore generated different attitudes to the issue of physical performance and visual spectacle in a martial arts film, which confirms Sheldon H. Lu's (2005b: 226–7) argument that the reception of transnational films varies from region to region as a result of audiences' different understandings of film genres, artistic conventions and film history.

Nevertheless, performing in this genre was not a straightforward task for an ageing star. In the Hollywood-produced martial arts film *Bulletproof Monk*, Chow played a nameless monk who is immune from ageing because of a powerful scroll. In contrast to the presentation of his body in *Crouching Tiger, Hidden Dragon*, Chow was required to demonstrate the physical prowess of a genuine martial artist throughout the film.

Reaction to the film in the Chinese and American media, however, was strikingly similar. Despite acknowledging Chow's acting talent, both overwhelmingly considered that the star's ageing body failed to deliver the action sequences that are supposed to be congruent with what the character's ageless body is supposed to be able to do (Koehler 2003; LaSalle 2003: D-1; Er 2003; *NetEast* 2003). In contrast to Holmlund's and Hunt's observations that portraying younger characters or disguising their age helps ageing stars to overcome the career crisis associated with their fears of losing their physical prowess, the denial of Chow's age in *Bulletproof Monk* had the opposite effect of inviting more critical scrutiny of the impact that ageing has on a star's employability in action-intensive films.

It is worth noting that both Chinese and American media discussions of Chow's performance in both films constantly separated the physical performance of martial arts from dramatic acting when portraying complex emotions, despite the performance of martial arts being a crucial part of portraying a martial artist in the genre. Whilst *Bulletproof Monk*'s strategy of denying Chow's age (by depicting him as ageless, and with infinite physical prowess) ironically served to make of the signs of Chow's ageing even more visible on screen, it was Chow's ageing body, rather than his acting skills, that was blamed as one of the reasons for the film's failure.

Chow's screen image also reveals the divergent perception of an ageing man's sexuality across the two film markets. As the *Los Angeles Times*' Scarlet Cheng (2000: 1) claimed, *Crouching Tiger, Hidden Dragon* is set against the backdrop of two love stories: 'an older, repressed romance between Shu Lien and Mu Bai' and 'the younger, wilder romance between Jen and Lo'. In a similar vein, *Rolling Stone* (Travers 2009), *New York Times* (2000) and *Variety* (McCarthy 2000) all promoted a similarly stereotypical understanding of the generationally bound nature of heterosexual relationships that the film explores. This predominant ageist perception of an asexual ageing man in the American media might not be surprising, given the film's narrative of these two generationally different romantic relationships.

In contrast to the young male bandit Luo Xiaohu (Chang Chen), who stridently declares his love to Jen, Chow's Li barely acknowledges his love for Shu Lien until the last minute of his life. While Luo travels thousands of miles from the Gobi desert to Beijing in order to stop Jen's arranged marriage, Li avoids developing any relationship with Shu Lien beyond friendship. Moreover, while the young couple experience a passionate sexual intimacy only a few days after they first meet each other, the older couple consistently suppress their feelings for each other over the course of several decades, despite receiving encouragement from the people around them, such as Li's treasured friend Sir Te (Lung Sihung).

It is interesting to note that Li became desexualised and was in a sense castrated, as this great martial artist was understood as not able to cope with a heterosexual, romantic relationship. Suggesting the sexual impotency of the ageing man, American media's focus on Li's reluctance to make any romantic commitment reinforced the myth that ageing men lose interest in sexual activity, despite still expressing heterosexual affection. Such an interpretation is somewhat in agreement with the so-called 'normal' and 'appropriate' age-bound sexuality determined by 'social norms' (Gott and Hinchliff 2003: 63). In this regard, the desexualisation of Li in the American media not only underlined conventional perceptions differentiating between the sexuality of younger and older men, but also suggested that Chow's star image as a public icon with great heterosexual charisma was under threat because of his age.

In comparison, several Chinese newspapers offered a different interpretation of Li's sexuality by sexualising the relationships between Li and Shu Lien, as well as the master–apprentice relationship between the ageing Li and the young Jen (Sek et al. 2000: C06; Wen Wei Po 2000). *Ta Kung Pao*'s Ximen Yi (2000: D08), for example, argued that Li's care for Jen is ambiguously positioned between benign, platonic affection and the desire for physical relations. As Larry A. Morris (1997: 59) pointed out, the majority of older people, both men and women, are sexually active and regularly engage in sexual intercourse. In identifying Chow's Li as attracting both of the film's main female characters (Shu Lien and Jen), *Ximen* and many other Chinese newspapers thus viewed the middle-aged Li as offering a stronger image of male sexuality than his younger on-screen rival Luo. In this sense, Chow's Li challenges stereotypical perceptions concerning the age determinations of on-screen male sexuality.

I would like to ask, then, why are media perceptions of the sexual appeal and potency of Chow's middle-aged character different in the American and the Chinese markets? We should consider Morris's (1997: 57), argument that an ability to attract sexual partner(s) is one of the key elements that contributes to social perceptions of manhood (and, as such, men's sexual liaisons with women) carries the symbolic meaning that an ageing man can retain his mature adulthood. With this in mind, we can assert that, in equating the exhibition of sexual contact with the broader notion of sexual competence per se, the America media denies the mature manhood of Chow's Li in *Crouching Tiger, Hidden Dragon* because of his lack of physical involvement in sexual activity with any of the film's female characters.

However, as I argued in the last chapter, the cinematic expression of love and sexual relationships should be viewed as multi-faceted and heterogonous, varying across different cinematic cultures. As some Chinese film scholars, such as Ma Sheng-mei (2005: 112) and Jia Leilei (2003: 240–1) have pointed out, the representation of male sexual prowess in martial arts cinema is often delivered via the discourse of the action skills and mastery of weapons demonstrated by the films' martial artists. As both Ma (2005: 112) and Jia (2003: 240) argued, the sword of Green Destiny (*Qingming*) in *Crouching Tiger, Hidden Dragon* is a phallic symbol for the film's male martial artists. Going into more detail, Jia (2003: 240) argued that, from the perspective of the female characters, what Jen steals from Li is not just a sword, but his heart and body; similarly, what Shu Lien defends is not just Green Destiny, but the sexual relationship between herself and Li. In these Chinese scholars' readings, the powerful Green Destiny sword not only represents the superior martial arts skills that its master Li possesses, but also symbolises Li's mature sexual prowess and charisma. Therefore, we need to take the Chinese market's understanding of the semiotic index constructed within the martial arts genre into account if we are to understand what it is that allows local Chinese – and not American – newspapers to identify with the film's sexual undercurrents. In demonstrating a different approach to the cinematic depiction of men's sexual vigour, martial arts cinema may therefore prevent those audiences who are not familiar with the genre from seeing any sexual implications in what appears to be a sex-free narrative.

It is worth paying some attention to Chow's image in *Bulletproof Monk* at this point. In comparison with Li's involvement in the complicated hetero-sexual relationships that are played out in *Crouching Tiger, Hidden Dragon*, Chow's nameless monk in *Bulletproof Monk* is denied almost any participation in narratives of romance and heterosexual relationships, reflecting the rule of celibacy in Buddhism. The film's desexualised narrative of Chow's monk is reflected well in both the American and the Chinese media. Whilst Chow's monk is absent from discussions in the American media regarding the film's sexual relationships and the characters' sexuality, the Chinese media clearly observes the differences between this asexual role and Chow's earlier sexu-ally charged screen characters in the star's Hong Kong films. For instance, Zi Teng (2003: 35) criticised Hollywood's prevalently Orientalist and ageist attitude as the reason for the industry's reluctance to offer Chow a romantic role in the film. As such Zi expressed the view that Chow should be allowed to restore his sexual charisma on the big screen and receive more contracts that appreciated his romantic image regardless of his age. In inviting complaints from the media about the Hollywood studio's stereotypical portrayal of ageing and Asian men as asexual, Chow's monk has therefore encouraged a critical reconsideration of the complex relationship between film genres, industrial conventions and on-screen representations of ageing men in Hollywood cinema.

AN AGEING STAR IN AN INTERGENERATIONAL RELATIONSHIP

Ageing means different things to different people. As Jeff Hearn (1995: 100), Minois (1999: 329) and Stela Bruzzi (2005: 157 and 188) argued, for a young man, ageing often means entering into fatherhood, a symbol of maturing into adulthood and a notion that traditionally offers men a sense of superiority and authority over younger descendants and dependants. However, ageing, as detailed in the first section of this chapter, also tends to be associated with the stereotypical perceptions of a middle-aged man exiting adulthood; this includes the reduction and even complete loss of control over his (adult) children. Holmlund (2002: 149) argued that ageing men have to demonstrate that they are still physically mobile and mentally alert in order to be allowed to continue playing the socially prescribed role of the father. In other words, holding on to their status as fathers (or often being reimaged as masters in martial arts cinema), and continuing to play an active role in educating younger people helps ageing men to remain in society's power group.

In both *Crouching Tiger, Hidden Dragon* and *Bulletproof Monk*, the fatherliness of Chow's characters is clearly referred to in the film's publicity in the American media. For instance, Richard Corliss (2000: n.p.) notes the intergenerational relationship in *Crouching Tiger, Hidden Dragon* in *Time*:

> In this war of the generations, the adults are as eager to instruct the young as the kids are to rebel against authority. In life as in martial arts, knowledge is power. And only the most powerful, like Chow's Mubai, can share it. He hopes to share it with Jen. Teaching this bright, wilful girl is as close as he will come to fatherhood – even if the job carries fatal risks.

Similar comments concerning the master–apprentice relationship can be found in the reviews of *Bulletproof Monk* by Robert Koehler (2003), Roger Ebert (2003), and Mick LaSalle (2003: D-1). In these reviews, Chow's Li in *Crouching Tiger, Hidden Dragon* and the monk in *Bulletproof Monk* are identified as representing two middle-aged men who possess greater professional knowledge and social authority than do the younger characters, and are understood as wanting to educate the younger martial artists in order to pass on their understanding of adult social responsibility to the younger generation.

However, Corliss' and other critics' statements also suggest the instability of Chow's on-screen representation of fatherhood. First, the younger generation is not only deemed to be bright and wilful, but also represents a rebellious force that could potentially undermine the paternal authority of Chow's characters. This reading echoes Jay Ginn and Sara Arber's (1999: 62 and 66) argument that, while the advantages of ageing are that younger people are able to enter the workforce to replace older employees, ageing also means that middle-aged and older employees subsequently become devalued and are increasingly likely to leave the labour market because of redundancy, or the mandatory retirement system in modern industrialised society. The hegemonic mode of age-determined employment and redundancy within the capitalist labour market can therefore be identified as contributing to social conflict between different age groups.

In addition, these critics' writings suggest that it is Chow's character, the middle-aged man, who is eager to fulfil his role of fatherhood. This can be supported by the observation that, in every scene in which Chow encounters his young pupils in these two films, the ageing martial artist physically chases them, defeats them with his skills and knowledge, and tries to transform them mentally with his superior experience and knowledge of martial arts and of the *jianghu*, or society. Unlike the narrative framework in many Hong Kong martial arts films whereby younger characters have to prove their intelligence and competence in order to be accepted into the power institutions of martial arts, Chow's Li and the monk strive to convince the younger martial artists of their capacity for fatherhood. In this sense, fatherhood is not an identity that appears to come naturally to Chow's characterisation of middle-aged martial artists. In being deprived of the social and authoritative status accorded to their mature manhood and physical prime, Chow's characters have to fight hard to retain their roles as father figures. Their struggles to participate in the process of gaining fatherhood therefore represent a middle-aged man's sense of crisis; both within the family as well as in the public domain of the labour market (the professional domain).

However, we should observe that different societies and cultures have different understandings of, and attitudes towards, ageing. As Shuichi Wada (1995: 48) pointed out, East Asian societies, profoundly influenced by the idea of *kõ* (filial piety, *xiao* in Chinese) in the Confucian doctrine, traditionally show more respect for elderly people than that afforded to older citizens in many industrialised Western societies, despite industrial and political modernisation having changed people's attitudes towards elderly citizens to varying degrees. Originating in China, Confucianism and its associated concept of *xiao* are reflected well in traditional martial arts cinema. For instance, in many Hong Kong martial arts films (especially those set in pre-modern China), older-generation stars, though often only appearing in supporting roles or as minor characters, are frequently portrayed as key figures in the process of transforming the young martial artists from childish juveniles into adults who assume authority and social responsibility, such as Jackie Chan's master Yuen Siu-tien in the films *Drunken Master* (1978) and *Snake in the Eagle's Shadow* (1978) and Jet Li's master Yu Hai in the film *The Shaolin Temple* (1982), who also appeared as Jet Li's father in *Kids from Shaolin* (1984).

Whereas the American media focused on intergenerational conflict and the marginalisation of older characters by younger characters (subverting the master–apprentice relationships common in martial arts films) in *Crouching Tiger, Hidden Dragon* and *Bulletproof Monk*, the interpretation by the Chinese media of intergenerational relationships in these two films demonstrates the

impact of Confucianism on Chinese considerations of Chow's stardom as an
ageing star. For instance, although he is not a trained martial artist, many
Chinese newspapers and magazines argued that only Chow could deliver Li's
transcendent power in *Crouching Tiger, Hidden Dragon* because of the authority that has become associated within his star persona (Wen Wei Po 2000;
Lin 2000: C08; Yu 2000: 12). Similarly, Ang Lee (cited in the *Sing Tao Daily*
2000: A35) openly stated in an interview that Chow was an ideal candidate
for the role, because the star shares some similarities with the character of
Li in terms of leadership, manners and status (in the film industry and in the
jianghu). In these comments, Chow is clearly identified as an eminent figure
– an actor who had risen over a period of nearly thirty years to become a top
Chinese star and had won many awards by the time he was cast in *Crouching
Tiger, Hidden Dragon* – and whose charisma and status in the industry matched
the outstanding martial arts skills of the on-screen masters of *jianghu* he was
playing.

In addition to his image as a respected master on the big screen, Chow was
also deemed to be a respected mentor for the films' new stars. *Wen Wei Po*
(2000) and *Ming Pao* (2000: C07) reported how Chow and his co-star Michelle
Yeoh taught the young starlet Zhang how to concentrate and to overcome her
nerves in a scene. In a similar vein, believing that the global recognition of
Chow's stardom helped the film to improve its success at global box offices,
many Chinese media publications argued that Chow's stardom helped to
introduce the films' young stars to a wider range of audiences in the global film
market (Xiao 2000: i; Yu 2000: C14). In these media reports, Chow is represented as a high-profile star who has considerable experience in the film industry, and who has become an important mentor figure by sharing his knowledge
and professional networks with his younger co-stars.

Believed by Chinese media to be helping young stars to launch or improve
their careers in the industry, Chow mirrors the role of the master in martial
arts films, guiding his pupils and sharing his wisdom with them. In contrast to the discussions of Chow's ageing star image in the American media,
the Chinese media's coverage of Chow's mentoring role suggested that the
social power associated with fatherhood or master status had already become
incorporated into Chow's stardom. In this sense, from the perspective of the
Chinese media, both Chow and the middle-aged martial artists he was portraying on the screen enjoyed the age-related power and respect bestowed by
traditional *xiao* concepts of Confucianism on attitudes towards age and ageing
within Chinese society.

Nevertheless, the industrialisation and modernisation of Chinese society
has had some impact on such traditional ways of thinking. This change in
attitude is reflected in the potential career threat posed by younger-generation
stars, particularly in cases where younger actors have strong personalities and

the potential to mature quickly within the industry (for example by building up their own networks, gaining experience of dealing with the public media, and making appearances at various public occasions). For instance, Zhang is deemed by some Chinese newspapers and magazines to be a talented and lucky young actress who steals the show from the film's two ageing stars as a result of the strong and complex personality of her role in the film (Yu 2000: 12; *Ming Pao* 2000: C07). Such comments about the emergence of young actors perceived to be stepping into their own period of stardom indicate that this younger generation of stars is starting to take over those roles that used to be played by established (but now ageing) stars when they were younger. This also suggests the unrelenting competition in an industry in which the growth of young stars is likely to force older-generation stars to retire if the ageing stars are not able to adjust their star personae or find their niches in the industry. In this sense, the public discourse about Chow as a middle-aged star and his on- and off-screen image as an ageing master reflects shifting social attitudes towards ageing, both in the Western media and in the industrialised and modernised society of present-day China.

CONCLUSION

As Hearn (1995: 99) noted, ageing is an essential element in the representation of men and of masculinity whether this be in images, texts, social practices or social structures. My analysis of Chow's image as an ageing star, and of his career in the martial arts cinema, demonstrates that an understanding of an ageing star's body depends on the specific conditions in different markets, including the familiarity of audiences with the star, their knowledge of the particular film genre, and wider social attitudes towards ageing, although the publicity for the films in both the American and in the Chinese media reinforced, to varying degrees, the social perceptions that associate ageing with an actor's decline in physical ability and performance.

Aging is a process that everyone experiences in their lives. Nevertheless, people's perceptions and attitudes to ageing not only vary across different societies and cultures, but also shift over time. These different market conditions explain one of the reasons that many of China's ageing martial artists, such as Jackie Chan and Jet Li, have adopted different strategies to maintain their stardom in different markets. Whilst the use of technology and special effects has impacted increasingly on their Hollywood-produced martial arts films, such as Chan's *The Tuxedo* (2002), and Li's *The One* (2001) and *The Mummy: Tomb of the Dragon Emperor* (2008), their Chinese-produced films, such as Chan's *New Police Story* (2004) and *Shinjuku Incident* (2009), and Li's *Fearless* (2006) and *The Warlords* (2007), are emphasise increasingly their character's emotions and the stars' acting abilities. All of these factors suggest that ageing male stars are understood and consumed differently by different film markets. In examining the different conditions between different film industries and markets, I therefore argued that Chow's physicality and sexual potency are simultaneously emphasised and de-emphasised within the transnational martial arts cinema in order to mediate different perceptions of ageing, and of how the career of an ageing star in the highly competitive film industry should be managed.

NOTE

1. Since the 2010s, a new trend has emerged in the film industry whereby a number of ageing action stars, including Arnold Schwarzenegger, have returned to the silver screen and have attempted to recapitalise on their stardom in action cinema. However, there is a shifting focus on their physical performance, such as the comic effect created by self-parody and self-satire in films like *The Expendables I–III* (2010, 2012, 2014). Due to the scope of the book, this issue will not be fully addressed here.

CHAPTER 7

Glocalising Chinese Stardom: Internet Publicity and the Negotiation of Transnational Stardom

Within the half year between the 2006 Christmas season and the 2007 summer season, Chow appeared in two blockbusters, the Chinese-language film *Curse of the Golden Flower* (2006) and the English-language film *Pirates of the Caribbean III: At World's End* (2007, hereafter referred to as *At World's End*). With 360 million RMB investments,[1] *Curse of the Golden Flower* was, from the very beginning of its production, marketed as the most expensive Chinese-language film ever made to date (Li 2006). In a similar manner, *At World's End* was also rumoured to be the most expensive film in Hollywood history at the time.[2] Clearly targeted at a global film market from their inception, both films were promoted as 'event films' with large casts.

Chow's star presence in both films illustrated the shifting global marketing strategies of the Hollywood and Chinese film industries. In order to expand its overseas markets and consolidate its dominant position within the global commercial film market, Hollywood has a tradition of recruiting foreign stars, such as Spanish stars Antonio Banderas and Penélope Cruz, Australian stars Nicole Kidman and Hugh Jackman, and French stars Juliette Binoche, Audrey Tautou and Jean Reno, to name just a few. Together with the ascendency of Asian film markets in Hollywood's global strategy, an increasing number of Chinese stars have joined this list since the 1990s (as discussed in Chapter 5). Meanwhile, Chinese cinema has shown growing ambition to enter the global commercial film markets, many of which were and still are dominated by Hollywood films. Both industries' new global strategies have facilitated the creation of so-called 'global', 'international' or 'transnational' Chinese stars, whose names are assumed to attract audiences beyond the domestic film market.

To understand Chow's stardom in the global film market, this chapter once again adopts a comparative approach. In addition to industry-produced promotional materials for *Pirates of the Caribbean* and *Curse of the Golden Flower*, this chapter focuses in particular on the Internet publicity for these two films in both Chinese- and English-speaking markets. As many film scholars have already pointed out, the Internet has had a considerable impact on the star system (Redmond and Holmes 2007b: 309, 311; McDonald 2000: 105–6). Paul McDonald (2000: 105–6) argued that the Internet has made the stars' names 'a link that traverses sites', and the emergence of official film websites, online star profiles and various fan forums has dramatically extended the presence of star appeal. In this sense, the Internet not only enhances public consumption, but also improves the interaction of the production, distribution and reception of star images. However, unlike printed publicity, the content of online publications may be altered without notice, and the public may not always be able to identify such changes. Therefore, the date of access becomes particularly important. Accordingly, this chapter has restricted its scope of online research: all the information analysed in this chapter was accessed before the release of *Curse of the Golden Flower* and *At World's End*.

I would like to stress here that language plays an important role with regard to the websites that people have the linguistic competence to access, despite the Internet having broken down the geographical boundaries of information distribution to a great extent. In this sense, language (Chinese and English in this case), with its capacity to impact on people's consumption of information, can be identified as one tool with which to differentiate the two key markets in which Chow started, and has developed, his film career and stardom. By examining Chow's presence in two virtual cultural markets, this chapter argues that Chow's stardom is simultaneously globalised and localised in transnational cinema.

IDENTIFYING INTERNATIONAL, GLOBAL AND TRANSNATIONAL STARDOM

As businesses, commercial studios need to make a profit from their products, namely films. Therefore, maximising profits at the box office in both domestic and global film markets is crucial to film industries around the world. As a result of sales of a film on overseas markets, as well as co-productions between different film industries across national borders, many stars achieve fame beyond their domestic markets. Variously referred to as 'global', 'international' and 'transnational' stars, these stars often have a stronger box-office value in today's film industry than their domestic peers. However, film scholars have not yet differentiated film stars' market status within the global context. For example, in her study on Leslie Cheung's posthumous fandom, Wang Yiman (2007: 333 and 336) refers to the star as 'global' as well as 'transnational'. Jackie Chan is referred to as a 'global superstar' by Chris Berry and Mary Farquhar (2006: 1), an 'international' star by David Desser (2006: 152), and as a 'transnational film star' by Zhang Yingjin (2003: 37). Without further elaboration, these terms seemingly become interchangeable, and they are simply used as what Will Higbee and Song Hwee Lim (2010: 10) called 'shorthand' for a cross-border mode of film production and consumption. Generalising the global status of stardom, however, not only conceals the hybridity of industrial demands and market tastes, but also obscures the complex articulation of a star's image(s). Thus, it is important to clarify the meaning and scope of these terms and to consider how they apply to the extension of stardom around the world according to the understanding that the globalisation of the film market increases a star's labour flow across national borders.

In his study of Hong Kong stars' presences in Hollywood, Lo Kwai-cheung (2004: 66) argued that stars like Jackie Chan, Jet Li and Chow are 'no longer exported to the global film enterprise as "products made in Hong Kong"', but instead they become more like 'expatriates or migrant workers' in their new host country. Similarly, Desser's (2006) understanding of Jackie Chan's 'international' stardom is based on his perception of Chan's success in breaking the national boundaries of Hong Kong filmmaking. Both Lo's and Desser's observations focused on the star's career moves and involvement in foreign film industries. For them, the stardom of Chow and other Hong Kong stars became internationalised when they entered a film market or industry beyond their domestic base, regardless of whether their stardom established in their domestic market has changed or not.

Whereas the perception of 'international stardom' focuses scholarly attention on a star's employment in different film industries, or his or her public presence beyond the domestic market, the understanding of 'global stardom' is seemingly more focused on the interconnection of a star's presence across different film markets around the world. In terms of what it means for a film to be 'global', Steve Fore (1997: 258) argued that a 'relatively universal marketability is the signature'. Similarly, Fredric Jameson (2010: 315) claimed that '[t]he totality today is surely what we call globalization'. In light of this logic, many film scholars see a global star as a figure that public discourses tend to conceptualise as an omnipresent image, fusing different tastes across different film markets. For instance, Berry and Farquhar (2006: 196) claimed that Bruce Lee's global stardom developed from the worldwide consumption of his star image that was initially exported by Hong Kong cinema. In a similar vein, Fore (1997: 245) argued that Jackie Chan entered the global film market as a result of his performance in the Hong Kong cinema even before he had started to work in Hollywood. The emphasis on Lee's and Chan's Chinese roots and the stars' already established personae in Hong Kong cinema suggest that these stars' global reputations are determined not only by the consumption of their images in the global film market, but also by the penetration of their core images into different markets.

Nevertheless, conceptualising globalisation as a process leading to homogenisation often reduces its significance to a hegemonic operation enacted by one dominant culture. Kai Hafez (2007: 87) argued that the de-differentiation of world cultures and the accompanying de-cultured commercialisation is the key to Hollywood's global strategy. According to Hafez, Hollywood blockbusters mix various cultural elements into a standardised 'global' formula, intending to consolidate rather than to respond to local tastes across global film markets. Many other film scholars, such as Desser (2005: 218) and Anne T. Ciecko (1997: 222), share Hafez's view and have argued that globalisation in the film industry runs the risk of becoming a process of Americanisation. Seeing Hollywood as a dominant force in today's global commercial cinema, these scholars' arguments tend to construct the notion of being 'global' as equivalent to accepting Hollywood's cultural hegemony. We may then question whether a blockbuster film that aimed at making profit in the global film market is really able to standardise the tastes in various local film markets. Furthermore, how do stars communicate their image to audiences and fans in different film markets with their own cultural particularities?

As a contrast to the aforementioned scholars who regarded globalisation as a process leading to standardisation and homogeneity, an increasing number of film scholars have argued that the cultural heterogeneity during the process of cross-border filmmaking, marketing and viewing should be recognised. Michael Curtin (2007: 14 and 19) argued that selling a film to various foreign markets demands a consciousness of market considerations because of 'sociocultural variation'. Similarly, Rob Wilson (2005: 260) noted that behind its 'image of wholeness and completion and fusion-culture', globalisation is an action full of motion, combination and interconnections to various spaces. Although neither Curtin nor Wilson specifically focused on a star's global presence, their studies demonstrate that understanding how to respond to local variations plays a vital role in the circulation of cultural products globally.

Other scholars have gone further and have tried to capture the nuances of different experiences of 'globalisation' by using alternative terminology. Mette Hjort (2010: 15) pointed out that the valuable forms of cinematic 'transnationalism' rely on their resistance to globalisation as cultural homogenisation, as well as on 'a commitment to ensuring that certain economic realities associated with filmmaking do not eclipse the pursuit of aesthetic, artistic, social, and political values'. Hjort's argument echoes Berry and Farquhar's (2006: 4) claim that the term 'transnational' incorporates the notion of 'exceeding [the] national' with specific experiences of 'the particular places and times in which they operate, the particular people they affect, and the particular ways they are constituted and maintained'. Arguing that 'transnational' should not simply be seen as a higher order, both Hjort's and Berry and Farquhar's studies remind us of the multiple and different experiences involved in the processes of cross-border communication, as well as underscoring the notion that interrogating a star's presence in the global film market does not necessarily mean distilling the distinctions between different cinematic cultures and market specificities into a larger cultural unity.

In a similar vein, I would like to suggest that transnational stars are those whose images are constantly adjusted to cater for different market specifications. As Aihwa Ong (1999: 4) pointed out, the prefix 'trans' in the word 'transnational' not only means moving through space or across lines, but also means 'changing the nature of something'. As a contrast to the discourses on global stardom that attempt to consolidate distinct market tastes by imposing a universal core image, the circulation of transnational stardom does not intend to exhibit the universality of the star's public image. Instead, it deliberately displays the multiplicity of a star's image in different film markets. In this sense, transnational stardom is the outcome of glocalising a star's image – a process of establishing a star's global presence while at the same time adapting his or her image to respond to the local sensitivity of different markets. I would like to stress here that the division of these three concepts of 'international' 'global' and 'transnational' stardoms is by no means rigid, because neither stardom nor global status is a predetermined social status. However, such distinctions help us to understand the pluralisation of the global star system and the mobility of star value across national and cultural borders.

A CHINESE STAR IN THE ONLINE MARKETING CAMPAIGN OF A HOLLYWOOD BLOCKBUSTER

The success of *Pirates of the Caribbean: The Curse of the Black Pearl* (2003) saw the production of its sequels, *Pirates of the Caribbean II: Dead Man's Chest* (2006) (hereafter referred to as *Dead Man's Chest*) and *Pirates of the Caribbean III: At World's End* (2007), both of which aimed to capitalise on China's film market. As Chu Yiu-wai (2005: 319) noted, 'the "local" has been successfully (re-)appropriated by transnational capital to become part of the globalizing process'. Similarly, I argue that rather than standardising market taste, Chow's presence in Hollywood blockbusters plays a territorially defined role in the worldwide distribution of a Hollywood blockbuster, signifying the localisation of the studio's global marketing strategies.

When *Dead Man's Chest* was still at the announcement stage, the news that Chow had accepted a role in the film appeared on many Chinese news websites. As early as 16 December 2004, Song Fangcan (2004) reported on Chinanews. com that 'Chow will play a Chinese pirate in the film', and two days later, Liang Ning (2004) confirmed on CRI Online, a government news website affiliated to China Radio International, that Chow had signed a contract for the sequels to *Pirates of the Caribbean*. According to these reports, the director of *Pirates of the Caribbean*, Gore Verbinski, made a special trip to Hong Kong in order to invite Chow to act in both *Dead Man's Chest* and *At World's End*.

About two months before *Dead Man's Chest* started filming, more Chinese websites reported that Chow had joined the cast. To invite public interest in the film, the online news in particular tried to prove to readers that Chow was going to challenge himself in his new screen role as a pirate. Some websites, such as Sina.com[3] (Ye 2005) and *People's Daily* (Da 2005), even published a photo of Chow's off-screen image, which showed the star with a newly grown beard. Since Chow had rarely appeared in public with a beard either on- or off-screen before, this image was introduced as part of the new experience that would be offered to Chinese audiences by watching Chow in the sequels to *Pirates of the Caribbean*.

The Chinese online publicity clearly placed great emphasis on the star's significance in the cast. On 23 May 2006, a month before the film's release in the United States, QQ.com[4] posted a video clip from the Guangdong TV station (2006), which reinforced the message that Chow's role in *Dead Man's Chest* was second only to the character of Captain Jack Sparrow played by Johnny Depp. More interestingly, when reports about Chow's casting and his new image came to dominate discussion about the film, details of Chow's new character, such as the character's name, relationship with other characters, and his costumed image in the film, were 'successfully' kept secret. The seemingly well-protected screen image duly stimulated Chinese audiences' curiosity about the film and the mysterious image of the pirate role played by Chow.

Ironically, in June and July 2006, the release of the film in the United States and Europe revealed that Chow was not in *Dead Man's Chest* at all. However, since the film was still trying to gain permission for release in mainland China in August,[5] Chow's name was still ambiguously connected with the film in online Chinese-language publicity during the summer of 2006. Although in many cases the words 'Dead Man's Chest' had been removed from the film's full title, the word 'sequel' was still widely used. Furthermore, some online reports about the film became somewhat ambiguous during this period. For example, a report from China.com (2006) about the opening event of *Dead Man's Chest* in California used the title 'Grand opening event of *Pirates of the Caribbean II*; Chow Yun-fat plays a pirate captain as a guest star'. Although the report did not openly say that Chow played a role in *Dead Man's Chest*, the connection between the two parts in the report's title preserved the illusion that Chow would appear in the film. These online reports and the general public's discussion surrounding Chow's image thus created a deceptive impression of market demand for watching the film during the period when *Dead Man's Chest* was still striving to obtain a release quota under China's revenue-share scheme.

The online discourse surrounding Chow's casting in *Dead Man's Chest* on Chinese-language websites becomes particularly interesting when we compare it to the online discourse about the film on English-language websites. Concentrating on the 'return' of the major players, including director Gore Verbinski, screenwriters Ted Elliott and Terry Rossio, and stars Johnny Depp, Orlando Bloom and Keira Knightley, English-language websites made much less of such kinds of 'factual mistakes'. In fact, *Variety* was the only source to publish an article in which Chow was briefly mentioned as appearing in *Pirates of the Caribbean II* (cited in Fleming 2005). No other online publicity on English-language websites has yet been found containing the same mistake. Most English-language websites clearly used the term 'Pirates of the Caribbean 3', 'Pirates 3', 'At World's End' or 'the third instalment of "Pirates of the Caribbean"' to refer to the film in which Chow appears (D'Alessandro 2006; Chang 2005; Cohen 2005).

The differences in the two markets' publicity of Chow's presence in the film thus raises the question of why few English websites made such a 'mistake', and why Chinese-language websites continued spreading false information about Chow's casting in *Dead Man's Chest* even after the film was released in Western cinemas. The answer might be Walt Disney's intention to manipulate the public's expectations through its localised marketing strategy. By emphasising Chow's importance in the film, *Pirates of the Caribbean* clearly intended to capitalise on Chow's popularity and box-office appeal in the Chinese film market. Although *Dead Man's Chest* finally failed to obtain a release quota from the Chinese government, the marketing campaign had successfully generated a high level of expectation about the film and public curiosity about Chow's new image. Such expectations and curiosity subsequently became part of the marketing campaign when preparing for the release of *At World's End*, in which Chow was confirmed as playing Captain Sao Feng, a Chinese pirate.

Disney's localised star strategy in promoting *At World's End* is further demonstrated by the different presentations of Chow's star status on English- and Chinese-language websites. Empirical research on the Internet suggests that Chow's star value differed widely not only in quantity but also in content in the two virtual markets. Carried out on 18 November 2006 – about half a year before the global release of *At World's End* – this online research examined six websites, *Variety*, *Entertainment Weekly*, *The New York Times*, *Los Angeles Times*, Sina and Sohu,[6] and two search engines, Google.com and Yahoo.com. The results are presented in Table 7.1.

From the perspective of quantity, the results found on Sina and Sohu suggest that roughly 8 to 13 per cent of texts mentioning *Pirates of the Caribbean III* included Chow's name. By contrast, the figure is much lower for English websites. The results found for the *Los Angeles Times*, *Entertainment Weekly*, *The New York Times* and *Variety* indicate that few of the online

Table 7.1: Online search result for *Pirates of the Caribbean* on English and Chinese websites and search engines.

Search term	'Pirates of the Caribbean 3'	'Pirates of the Caribbean 3' + 'Chow Yun-fat'	'加勒比海盗 3'	'加勒比海盗 3' + '周润发'	Percentage of times Chow's name mentioned with film
Websites					
Variety (English)	766	4			0.52
Entertainment Weekly (English)	52	0			0
The New York Times (English)	173	0			0
Los Angeles Times (English)	6	0			0
Sina (Chinese)			1,220	102	8.36
Sohu (Chinese)			309	42	13.59
Google (English and Chinese)	231,000	899	36,000	12,300	0.39 (English) 34.17 (Chinese)
Yahoo (English and Chinese)	147,000	1,280	22,600	1,690	0.87 (English) 7.48 (Chinese)

reports from the English websites deemed Chow's presence to be an essential element in promoting *At World's End* at that point. Meanwhile, the results from the two biggest Internet search engines, Google.com and Yahoo.com, confirmed these market differences. Although the figures see a variation for different websites and search engines, the search results clearly illustrate that Chow's star presence played a far more important role in promoting the film in the Chinese-language market than it did in the English-language market.

Whilst the figures contained in these results indicate that Chow's star value in Hollywood's blockbuster was defined by a specific market, the content of these search results also demonstrates the local responsiveness to Chow's transnational stardom. For instance, among the four results found on *Variety*'s website, two were actually identical, and it was the only publication that placed Chow's name in its titles and introduced information about Chow's character Captain Sao Feng (Cohen 2005; *Variety* 2005). In the other two articles, Chow's name only appeared in the cast list, and nothing else about his star image or character was mentioned (Chang 2005; D'Alessandro 2006).

However, the results found on the Chinese websites show a completely different picture. For example, on 15 July 2006, Sina.com (2006a) published an article in which not only was the character Sao Feng's relationship with Captain Jack Sparrow highlighted, but Chow's costume and make-up (such as his scarred face, grey beard and uneven teeth) were also described in detail. Other examples highlighting the significance of Chow's role in the film include but are not limited to the online publication of information detailing how Chow's character saves Captain Jack Sparrow's life, and how Chow's star quality as a comedic actor and his appeal to the Asian market would help the film to continue its box-office success (Xiao 2006; Sina.com 2006b). Although Chow only appeared in the film for about twenty minutes, he certainly became one of the top stars and central characters in its marketing campaign on the Chinese-language websites.

Hollywood has long been interested in China's rapidly expanding film market. However, the quota of imported foreign films determined by the Chinese government suggests that only a limited number of Hollywood-produced films will be allowed to be released in mainland China. As a means of protecting China's domestic film industry, the implementation of this quota system suggests that Hollywood studios need to compete with each other to receive a release permit. However, the restriction on the number of foreign films also suggests that once a film has obtained permission for release in China's mainstream market, it will encounter relatively low competition due to the limited number of films available on the market. Adding a Chinese element, including star presence, is one of the key strategies that Hollywood studios have adopted to improve their chances of obtaining the quota from the Chinese government, and maximising future box-office sales in mainland

China. In these pre-screen promotional activities, the presence of Chinese stars provides a familiar element for local audiences, playing an important role in promoting a Hollywood film in China's film market.

HYBRID STARDOM IN THE TRANSNATIONAL CHINESE-LANGUAGE BLOCKBUSTER

While Hollywood continues to be the major player in the world's commercial film market, many other countries have joined in the competition. China is one of them, and unstintingly endeavours to obtain recognition from overseas markets. Competing against Hollywood in both China's domestic and overseas markets, an increasing number of Chinese-language blockbusters have been produced since the mid-2000s. Unlike Hollywood's transnational star strategies – which valued Chow's star presence mainly for his ability to promote its films to the Asian market – the transnational Chinese-language blockbusters recognised Chow's star appeal in both China's domestic and global markets. As do the Hollywood studios, the transnational Chinese-language cinema tailors its online marketing campaigns and star presentation in order to attract audiences around the world. Whereas Chow's global image is highlighted in the Chinese market as a way of justifying the film's production quality and standard, his Asianness and Chineseness are emphasised in the English-language market as a way to promote the Chinese blockbuster's 'authentic' Chinese features and its spectacle of Oriental exoticism.

As Chris Berry (2003: 218) observed, Hollywood blockbusters virtually dominate market attention throughout the global film market via the industry's 'exceptional bigness – big budgets, big stars, big effects, big publicity campaigns'. In order to promote their films' production quality and visual spectacle when competing against the Hollywood blockbusters appearing in China's domestic market, Chinese studios have also adopted various strategies to emphasise the 'bigness' of their blockbusters, and casting a 'global' star has emerged as one of the most successful elements in promoting these Chinese-language blockbusters in China. Although many of these films are based in mainland China and the majority of stars and crews are ethnically Chinese, promotion in China's domestic market constantly attempts to connect these films with global productions. Through the discourse about their crew and cast members' nationalities, funding resources, international awards attained by its crews and stars, and even overseas locations for a film's pre- and post-production (such as the location of special effect creation and sound mixing), these Chinese-language blockbusters present themselves as quality pictures on a par with the grand spectacle offered by Hollywood cinema.

Directed by one of the most prestigious Chinese directors, Zhang Yimou, the historical epic *Curse of the Golden Flower* was an adaptation of a well-known play, *Thunderstorm* – a dramatic tragedy written in the early 1930s by one of the most famous Chinese playwrights, Cao Yu, who had the reputation of being a 'Chinese Shakespeare' (Bulag 2002: 90; Li 2010). Moving the story's background from its original setting in the early 1930s to the Tang dynasty one thousand years earlier – which is arguably one of the highest points in Chinese civilisation – this film presents a picture of royal luxury and opulent grandeur. As part of the entire package that tried to secure the 'best' and 'biggest' of everything, Chow and Gong Li, two Chinese top stars, were selected to play the leading characters, the Emperor Ping and Empress Phoenix.

The film's pre-release campaign on Chinese-language websites tried hard to convince audiences that this film was going to provide the public with a high standard of visual spectacle and intense dramatic narrative, no less accomplished than those delivered by Hollywood blockbusters. In this context, Chow was repeatedly presented as a 'Hollywood' or a 'global' star from the very early stages of the film's production. For instance, two reports posted on Sina.com, which also sponsored the film's official Chinese website, revealed that Chow's salary was calculated in US dollars in accordance with Hollywood employment practices, in which travelling time and even hours spent in traffic jams were included in Chow's working hours (*Sichuan Daily* 2006; Shan 2006). From the contract details of Chow's salary and working hours to the star's practice of Mandarin (*Beijing News* 2006), from his status in the crew to his appearance in Hollywood-produced films (Sina.com 2006c; 2006d), the online publicity about the star on Chinese websites all highlighted his star appeal in the global film industries and markets. As such, these Chinese online reports not only indicated the film's commercial potential in overseas markets, but also presented the Chinese audience with a picture of the rise of Chinese-language cinema on the global stage.

As Sheldon H. Lu (2005a: 300) argued, identity is no longer defined in terms of original nation-states in today's transnational culture, but implies local participation and global imagination. The emphasis on Chow's Hollywood-ness and global appeal helped the studio to encourage film consumption by fulfilling the desire of local audiences for Chinese-language films to be recognised globally. As in Hong Kong in the 1980s, when rapid economic growth accelerated the cosmopolitan confidence of local citizens, many people in mainland China are also no longer satisfied with the nation's image as a mere world factory after nearly two decades of rapid economic growth. Along with China's increasing participation in global affairs and business since the turn of the century, the nation also seeks more recognition and respect in the global arena.

As a result, a new nationalism has gradually emerged, a point I will discuss in more detail in the next chapter. Unlike the nationalism promoted by the government in previous decades, especially before the country started its economic reform, which featured a protective sense of defending the country's security and territorial integrity from the threats posed by foreign superpowers, this new nationalism is armed with an active display of the nation's economic and political power and an intention to impose a strong influence on various international relations. Accordingly, many people believe that the country could, and should, be a major player in world affairs in the twenty-first century. Indicating that a Chinese-language blockbuster is going to be a competitive force in domestic as well as global commercial film markets, the emphasis placed by the film's domestic marketing campaign on Chow's Hollywood-ness and global achievements therefore fulfils some local audiences' imagination of participating in global business and restoring national glory to China across the world.

Nevertheless, this film's global dimension disappeared on its English-language websites. As a way of differentiating the film from Hollywood blockbusters in the global film markets, the distribution of *Curse of the Golden Flower* particularly stressed the film's Asianness, which confirms Julian Stringer's (2003a: 9) and Julie F. Codell's (2007: 206) arguments that constructing cultural distinction is crucial for non-Hollywood cinemas competing in different global film markets. As part of the film's global strategy of sinicising the film, Chow's image as a 'global' star also shifted to that of a Hong Kong or Chinese star. For instance, in an article published on *Variety*'s website (Associated Press 2005), Chow is described as a 'Hong Kong Hollywood star', and 'The *Crouching Tiger, Hidden Dragon* star'.

The report's emphasis on Chow's Hong Kong identity and his star image in Asian cinemas matches the message developed in the film's English-version trailers. In the film's first trailer launched in North America on 1 September 2006, both the stars' and the director's names are followed by mention of their previous films. Rather than mentioning Chow's Hollywood-produced films, the trailer listed two of Chow's films with strong Asian connotations: *Crouching Tiger, Hidden Dragon* – the winner of the best foreign film in the 2000 Academy Awards, and *The Killer* (1989) – Chow's Hong Kong-produced action film, which achieved cult status in Western film markets in the early 1990s. As Darrell William Davis and Emilie Yeh Yueh-yu (2008: 113) noted, Hollywood film buyers tend to posit an alignment of nation and genre, 'assigning individual Asian countries to recognizable types, thus promoting the entry of domestic Asian hits'. In contrast with the film's online publicity on Chinese-language websites, which highlighted Chow's global cinematic achievements, the English trailer's reference to Chow's performances in *Crouching Tiger, Hidden Dragon* and *The Killer* not only firmly repositioned Chow's star image in Asian cinema, but also helped the Hollywood distributor to create a link between *Curse of the Golden Flower* and what Davis and Yeh (2008: 117–18) called 'signature' genres, such as martial arts films from Chinese cinema and action films from Hong Kong cinema.

In addition to the trailer, the presentation of Chow and his screen character Emperor Ping in the film's '"Making of" featurettes' further reinforced the film's self-Orientalism. Released on the film's English official website, the '"Making of" featurettes' repeatedly emphasised the complex relationships in the Chinese imperial family and the secrecy surrounding battles for power in Chinese history. According to the programme, Chow's role represents the time during China's feudal history when men dominated both society and the family. Emphasising Emperor Ping's cruelty, slyness and loneliness, the programme invited English-speaking audiences to find out how the power battle in the private chamber affected the Emperor as an individual. The stress on Emperor Ping's power, desire and Machiavellian machinations also catered to the Western audiences' imagination of the dark side of imperial Oriental life. Unlike the content of the film's online Chinese publicity, neither Chow's Hollywood working experience nor his cross-market appeal was mentioned to promote the expectation of quality.

Davis and Yeh (2008: 5) argued that 'Asian pictures might be delocalized in terms of higher quality, especially in marketing, while concurrently re-localized in subject matter, stars and genres'. The emphasis of English-language websites on Chow's roles in Chinese-language cinema and his Asian origins illustrated the promotional strategies of the studio by distinguishing *Curse of the Golden Flower* from other Hollywood blockbusters through what Chu Yiu-wai (2005: 324) has called 'exporting Chineseness'. In this sense, the attention given to Chow's Asian stardom and the Oriental myth surrounding his screen image on these English-language websites represents a symbolic gesture towards the globalisation of the Asian cinema, as well as signifying a spectacle of Oriental otherness.

CONCLUSION

The online publicity for Hollywood and Chinese blockbusters demonstrates that the perception of a star's global status shifts across different markets. As Chu Yiu-wai (2004b: 126) suggested, 'one must refuse to believe that identity is a kind of determinate "being"'; the formation of star identities should be understood as a process of becoming. Restrictions on time and space thus not only decide how identities are circulated, but also which specific components of identity are promoted under different market conditions. Although many stars are involved in a film's multinational or multiregional production and distribution, the online distribution of their films constantly repositions star identities in order to cater for local markets. As a result, a star's global status varies considerably across markets.

The wide gap in the empirical online results that I outlined when researching Chow's presence in *Pirates of the Caribbean* – in which Chinese-language sites considerably outnumbered English-language sites in their references to Chow's star personality and to the significance of his involvement in the production – indicates that Chow's global stardom is a concept facilitated mainly by local support from Chinese markets. Although Chow only appeared in a supporting role in *At World's End*, his presence played a vital role in promoting the film in China and helped Hollywood studios to encourage local consumption. Meanwhile, as the publicity surrounding Chow's star image in *Curse of the Golden Flower* illustrates, this local responsiveness does not apply only to Hollywood studios in the Chinese film market, but also to the Chinese film industry in the anglophone film markets. The different presentation of Chow's star image on English- and Chinese-language websites thus indicates the Chinese star's hybrid identities within transnational cinema, as well as suggesting that stars often function to help a transnational blockbuster respond to local markets by repackaging their image.

NOTES

1. This was roughly equivalent to US$45 million at the time.
2. The production cost of *At World's End* is estimated at around $300 million. For details, see Imdb (n.d.).
3. Sina and Sohu are two leading online media sites with a branded network of localised websites targeting Greater China and overseas Chinese communities.
4. Tencent's QQ.com is one of the largest web portals in Mainland China.
5. In 1994, the Chinese government adopted a film import quota system, which only allowed a limited number of foreign films to be released in Mainland China per year. The original quota was only ten. This number was increased to twenty in 2001 according to an agreement with the World Trade Organization. However, the State Administration of Radio, Film and Television also released a guideline in 2004, suggesting that the number of Hollywood blockbusters imported each year should be restricted to fourteen. For details, see Cheung et al. (n.d.) and Rosen (2006).
6. See note 3.

CHAPTER 8

Endowing the Fatherhood: The Power Game beyond Chinese Cinema

As the first half of the book detailed, the prefigurative materials surrounding Chow's Hong Kong television and film career and screen images have established his star image as an urban citizen of modern Hong Kong. Although Chow rarely appeared in a pre-modern film before he moved to Hollywood, many scholars have noted that the traditional Chinese cultural code *yi* (altruism and horizontal loyalty between brothers and friends) significantly shaped Chow's pre-1997 star persona (Louie 2002; Williams 1997). The distinctive combination of modern urban citizenship and the traditional Chinese cultural code of *yi* consolidated Chow's star image as a symbol of Hong Kongers' hybrid identity that simultaneously relates to and deviates from the West and China historically, socially and culturally. Signifying Hong Kong's pride, Chow was awarded an honorary doctorate by the City University of Hong Kong in 2001. In 2003, Chow also became the first and only contemporary celebrity to date whose life story had been published in a school textbook in Hong Kong. In a sense, Chow established a star persona as a Hong Konger per se.

In this chapter, I will continue to examine how Chow's star image mediates with the social perception of the Hong Kong identity by focusing on the publicity surrounding his Hollywood films and the recent *huayu dianying* (Chinese-language cinema). Since the beginning of the new millennium, commercial cinema in mainland China has expanded on an unprecedented scale. Annual production increased from thirty-eight films in 2002 to 618 in 2014 (Entgroup 2010: 16; Entgroup 2015: 13). The rapid growth of the mainland Chinese film market and the development of transnational Chinese cinema are currently demanding a large number of film talents, either in front of or behind the camera.

At the same time, however, the production of Hong Kong films has continued to drop. In 2011, the Hong Kong film industry produced only fifty-six films (Zhong 2012: 2), less than half the figure produced in 2000.

Subsequently, many Hong Kong stars and filmmakers, whether they remained in or left Hong Kong in the 1990s, started to work in and even migrated to mainland China from the early 2000s. The timing of Chow's career move to Hollywood and his subsequent return to Chinese cinema not only accords with the rise of *huayu dianying*, but also, as I will argue in this chapter, corresponds well to Hong Kong's complex transition from a British colonial city to the Hong Kong Special Administrative Region (hereafter referred to as HKSAR) after the actual transferral of sovereignty over the city on 1 July 1997.

AN ORPHAN HAS A NEW FATHER

Looking back, one may note that Chow rarely had a father on the big screen from the very early stages of the star's Hong Kong film career, including his characters Woo Viet in *The Story of Woo Viet* (1981), Yip Kim-fay in *Hong Kong 1941* (1984), Mark Gor in *A Better Tomorrow*, and Ah Jong in *The Killer* (1989). Not only is the father absent from Chow's on-screen relationships, but is also missing from Hong Kong mass media's publicity regarding Chow's off-screen relationships. Only on very rare occasions is Chow's real father, or more accurately the absence of his father, mentioned in order to stress the hardship of the star's childhood (Anon. 1987: 51; Lin 1990: 36–37; Pan 1989: 22–3). While the conflict in many of Chow's Hong Kong films is between an individual and the wider environment, the absence of a father creates Chow's star image as an orphan[1] who can rely only on himself, brotherhood or friendship to survive social uncertainty.

Chow's Hollywood action films continued to foreground his screen image as a grown-up orphan, but this time the figure of a foster father is imposed on his on-screen relationships, including as the underworld boss Terence Wei (Kenneth Tsang) in *The Replacement Killers* and Uncle Wong (Kim Chan) – the head of Chinatown's biggest criminal triad Tongs – in *The Corruptor*. In both films, the father figure provides some protection, financial support or convenience to Chow's characters in exchange for their loyalty and services.

Meanwhile, such kinds of protection and support trap Chow's characters in dangerous and immoral situations, as signified by the lawless Chinatown. For instance, *The Replacement Killers* starts with a police raid in which Terence Wei's drug-dealing son is killed. In revenge for his dead son, Wei calls Chow's Lee to murder a seven-year-old boy, the son of the detective who was in charge of the raid. Entrusting Lee to carry out the task, Wei not only intends to release his anger as a Chinese father who has lost an heir, but also seeks a way to maintain his paternal authority through his command of Lee's services. Similarly, Chow's Chen in *The Corruptor*, as the head of the Asian Gang Unit at the New York City Police Department (NYPD), relies on inside information from Uncle Wong and Henry Lee (Ric Young) – the second-in-command of the Tongs, who later takes over Wong's power in the gang – to solve cases and prevent potential gang war. In exchange, Chen accepts the money from Wong and Henry Lee and secretly provides protection for the Tongs' illegal business. Unlike Lee's and Chen's relationships with their late fathers, which are characterised by respect, as conveyed by the two films' narrative and extra features concerning the characters' memories, the foster-father–son relationships between Wei and Lee, and Uncle Benny/Henry Lee and Chen feature constant conflict and defiance.

As the son in the hierarchical relationship, Lee's and Chen's autonomy, independence and selfhood are restricted under the cultural code of *xiao* (filial piety, respect, subordination and vertical loyalty in youngsters to their parents, ancestors and other senior members, such as teachers, mentors, or those who hold a senior position) – a concept I have discussed in Chapter 6. In the Chinese patriarchal social system, a father is endowed with an enormous amount of power and authority over his descendants under the cultural code of *xiao*, even if the son is of age.[2] Lee's and Chen's dilemmas arise when they are caught between their obligations to follow the father figure's orders and their own sense of social justice and moral standards. However, Freudian theory purports that a son will develop a patricidal desire to usurp paternal power (Steinmetz 1991: 15). As a result, the ultimate conflict between Chow's characters and the father figures in the two Hollywood films not only originates from Lee's and Chen's disobedience of their fathers' orders but, more importantly, is a result of the sons' actions of removing their fathers' authority, whether killing Wei in *The Replacement Killers* or convicting Henry Lee for his crimes in *The Corruptor*. In a sense, Chow's screen image has transformed from a fatherless orphan to a rebellious son who negotiates his independence and selfhood through his defiance of the powerful father.

Unlike Chow's Hong Kong action heroes, who often fight to stay in or return to Hong Kong regardless of what the future of the city holds, Lee's and Chen's disobedience and rebelliousness are closely associated with Chinese sons' desire to distance themselves from the China(town) that the father figure symbolises. The attitude of Chow's Hollywood action heroes to China(town) manifests Hollywood and American mainstream media's preconception of China and its post-1997 relationship with Hong Kong city. As the extra features of *The Replacement Killers* DVD reveal, Chow's Lee goes to Wei for help in order to fulfil his father's dying wish of getting the entire family out of China. However, Lee's own situation in Chinatown replicates that of his late father in China. While the relationship between Lee and Wei is comparable to that of Lee's late father and Chairman Mao, the latter serves as an agent inserting a strong political image into the cinematic depiction of a male power conflict between the Chinese father and son.

Unlike the pro-China view that often depicts the country as a loving and suffering mother who has been longing for a century for her long lost son, Hong Kong, to return home (Hu, Li and Ren 1998; Hong and Ling 1997), both Chow's Hollywood films imply that the lawless China(town) is a ruthless father who deprives his son of autonomy and freedom. Hollywood's perception of the father image of China is not unique. As the United States–Hong Kong Policy Act of 1992 (US Department of State n.d.) and the CRS Report for Congress (Martin 2007: 2) clearly state, the United States regards Hong Kong as a separate entity from the rest of China, and hence would continue to treat the city differently after 1997 as long as Hong Kong remained highly autonomous. Meanwhile, both the Act and the Report explicitly urged the US government to be aware that the city's relationship with China might undermine Hong Kong's high degree of autonomy and democracy. In this context, the on-screen relationship of Chow's first two Hollywood roles was embedded in Hollywood's and America's concern about how Hong Kong would maintain its autonomy after the handover.

Like the media publicity for Chow's first two Hollywood screen roles, American media discourse surrounding Chow's career move is also inscribed by America's interpretation of Hong Kongers' post-1997 identity as HKSARers. For instance, in a *Los Angeles Times* interview with Chow, the reporter asserted that many Hong Kong stars, directors and producers had acquired foreign passports as an insurance policy. Repeatedly using terms such as 'the end of something', 'repressed' and 'dying' with regard to Hong Kong cinema (Smith 1995: 10), this interview delivered a somewhat suggestive picture of HKSAR's future being unpredictable due to its subordinate position in the hierarchical relationship with China. Although Chow clearly answered that he was not worried about the city's future and had no intention of obtaining a foreign passport, his career move was presented to the American public as a Hong Kong citizen's rejection of having a new father, the Chinese government. As Joseph Chan Man et al. (2002: 2) argued, the mass media often domesticates its report of international affairs to cater for the domestic market demand. The way that the *Los Angeles Times* presented the interview about Chow's career move thus reinforced America's sceptical view of China's administration of Hong Kong after 1997, and underlined America's local image of Hong Kongers after the 1997 identity crisis. By suggesting that Hong Kong's social system would be suppressed after the city became a Chinese special region, Hollywood and the American mass media deployed Chow's career move and his new Hollywood action roles to confirm the idea that Hong Kongers could only retain their identity as Hong Kongers by leaving Chinese territory, including China(town) and the HKSAR, after the 1997 handover.

FROM FATHER'S SON TO SON'S FATHER

As mentioned earlier Chow has built up a star image as a grown-up orphan in his early Hong Kong films and later became a father's son in his first two Hollywood films. Unlike his action heroes who confront the Chinese father's authority directly, many of Chow's screen roles since the 2000s see him no longer opting to take drastic action to change the institutional rules passed down by a father figure. Instead, the filmic father–son relationship signifies an awareness of compromise. Chow's Li Mubai in *Crouching Tiger, Hidden Dragon*, for instance, is a martial arts master from Wudang (a school of martial arts) who confines his actions (according to the Confucian cultural codes of filial piety) within the *zhongyuan jianghu* (a mythical martial arts world in the central plain), even though he is suffering emotionally from the constraints.[3] Although Li's decision to teach Jen (Zhang Ziyi) *Wudang* martial arts challenges his own master Southern Crane's attitude towards Jade Fox (Cheng Pei-pei), as well as the patriarchal *jianghu*'s discrimination against woman, Li's intention is not to challenge the old tradition but to teach the young martial artist the orthodox way and ethical code of *jianghu*. A similar father–son relationship can be seen in many of Chow's films produced during the first half of the 2000s, such as *Anna and the King* (1999) and *Bulletproof Monk* (2003).

It should be noted here that this was not the first time that Chow played the role of a father. Although Chow's characters rarely had fathers in his Hong Kong films, they did occasionally have a teenage son on the big screen, such as his Ah-Long in *The Story of Ah-Long* and Chung Tin-ching in *Prison on Fire II* (1991). In these Hong Kong films, Chow's characters are men whose wild pasts are blamed for the breakdown of their own families. In compensation for the son's loss, the father attempts to provide the son with better living conditions; thus, the strong paternal love of Ah-Long and Chung Tin-ching often involves the father's self-sacrifice and repentance. While Ah-Long and Chung Tin-ching make every effort to raise their sons in environments that are different from those of their own pasts, the fathers' expectations of the sons are that the boys should become people who are dissimilar from their fathers. Chow's portrayal of paternal love in the Hong Kong cinema thus endows fatherhood with a sense of self-redemption.

Nevertheless, unlike his fatherly roles in Hong Kong films, Chow's father (master) in his post-2000 films is depicted as a man who teaches, inspires and helps youngsters to understand traditional culture and social values, as well as urging youngsters to consider the meaning of responsibility and duty as an adult, a point discussed in Chapter 6. The shifting cinematic depiction of the father–son relationship in Chow's films since the 2000s must be considered in view of the social context of China becoming an increasingly important player in international affairs. After the narrow loss to Sydney to host the 2000

Summer Olympic Games in 1992, Beijing was again shortlisted as a candidate in 2000, and subsequently won the bid to host the 2008 games in 2001. In 2001, after nearly fifteen years of negotiations, China joined the World Trade Organization (hereafter referred to as WTO). As part of the agreement with WTO, the Chinese government doubled the annual number of foreign films that could be released in mainland China under the revenue-share scheme, from ten to twenty (Cheung, Chow and Chow 2002). The deepening trade relationship between mainland China and Hong Kong also lifted the city out of a prolonged recession caused by the Asian financial crisis of 1997 and the outbreak of SARS in 2002 (Martin 2007: 2).

All these high-profile occurrences have gradually reshaped China's image from that of a mythical communist country to an emerging power that participates actively in international affairs on the global stage. China's increasing influence inside and outside Asia not only encourages filmmakers to reconsider the relationship between the East and the West, but also influences Hong Kongers' self-identification. According to a survey conducted by the University of Hong Kong (2015a), the percentage of Hong Kong citizens that identify themselves as Chinese citizens has increased from 18.6 per cent after the handover to 38.6 per cent in 2008. In this context, we can understand not only why fatherly authority is gradually bestowed on Chow's star persona as the star ages, but also why Chow's screen image is increasingly sinicised in films produced since the 2000s.

Like Chow's master and father image in post-2000s martial arts films, many of Chow's new screen roles after his return to Chinese cinema are portrayals of caring and inspiring father figures helping youngsters to understand the traditional values held by the older generation, especially in the films invested in by mainland Chinese studios. One of the examples is Chow's performance of the title character in *Confucius* (2010), a biography of the influential Chinese philosopher and educator. In the film, Chow's Confucius is loyal to his home state Lu even at the time he was exiled as a wandering scholar. More importantly, the film depicts the process whereby Confucius gradually establishes his image as a respected teacher and wise philosopher through his promotion of the ideas of loyalty, love, endurance, and proprieties in accordance with the customs that formed the patriarchal society. In addition to his screen role, Chow also acted accordingly off-screen by performing a bow and even kowtowing to Confucius' descendant, Kong Demao, during Kong's visit to the film set in 2009 and at the film's Beijing premiere in 2010 (Sun 2009a; Wang 2010). In a sense, Chow was selected to play a role as a spokesman who promotes the Confucian codes of filial piety and loyalty.

As the media publicity surrounding the release of *Confucius* indicates, one of the main reasons that the studio selected Chow to play *Confucius* was that the characteristics embodied in Chow's public image, such as his humbleness,

Figure 8.1: still from *Confucius*, film, dir. Hu Mei, China: Dadi Century (Beijing) and China Film Group, 2010.

hard-working attitude, commitment to life-long learning and self-improvement, honour-bound manhood and self-discipline (Li 2009; Sun 2009b; Ni 2009). In fact, the public discourse surrounding Chow's star image at the time of the release of *Confucius* clearly correlates with the message delivered by the City University of Hong Kong's address at a public ceremony where Chow was awarded an honorary doctoral degree in 2001, and with a chapter included in a school textbook in 2003, both of which claimed that it was Chow's 'diligence', 'humility', 'filial respect', 'life-long learning', 'self-improvement' and 'upright character' that made the star a role model for young students (Cheng 2001; *Keys Secondary School Textbook of Chinese* 2003). The qualities highlighted on these occasions correspond strongly with the virtues traditionally appreciated in Chinese culture.

However, we should not overlook the fact that another reason for Chow's casting in these films was his career achievement and transnational presence. As a star who has experience in the global film industry, and a strong fan base in and beyond Asia, Chow was selected by the Chinese cinema as an ideal spokesperson not only for presenting Chinese values to a domestic audience, but also for promoting Chinese films to those overseas audiences who may not be familiar with Chinese culture. The attention paid to Chow's Chineseness is, to some degree, suggestive of China's increasing desire to participate in global affairs and to extend its influence over other cultures and ideologies. In this sense, Chow's sinicised image in *huayu dianying* is comparable to the rapid development of the Confucius Institute since 2004.[4] Whereas the establishment of Confucius Institutes intends to promote Chinese culture and language overseas through the government-sponsored educational pro-gramme, the casting of Chow as Confucius and the recognition of Chinese virtues in Chow's transnational stardom aim to improve cross-cultural under-standing of the cultural identification of Chinese men through the image of a popular icon.

FATHER'S TWO FACES

As Guo Xiaoqin (2003: 44) and Zheng Yongnian (2010: 168) pointed out, one of the primary concerns of the Chinese central government at present is to maintain the country's unity and stability and to reinforce the one-party policy during a period in which China has undergone rapid economic growth. Whilst Confucianism served the ruling society well for over a thousand years of Chinese history, the Chinese government has also started to re-imbibe and re-promote Confucianism in recent years. To some degree, the paternal power endowed on Chow's recent screen roles is deployed to defend the legitimacy of the ruling party in the name of maintaining social stability and harmony. Whereas Chow's portrayal of the frightening Emperor Ping in *Curse of the Golden Flower* (2006) suggests that a father's power is too strong to be chal-lenged, Chow's later roles increasingly suggest that the star has been chosen by the Chinese cinema as the face of emerging China, which intends to establish an image as a powerful but peaceful nation.

The refocused cinematic and media construction of Chow's star image from a rebellious son to a venerable father is not only evident in Chow's per-formance in films like *Confucius* and its publicity, as detailed in the previous section, but is also demonstrated by the Chinese cinema's effort to change the popular perception of controversial paternal figures, such as Cao Cao and the Jade Emperor. Cao Cao, a historical figure, is often vilified as a cruel and suspicious tyrant in Chinese literature and theatrical drama, as in *Romance of the Three Kingdoms*.[5] However, in *The Assassins* (2012), Chow's Cao Cao is no longer an ambitious man who wants to conquer other kingdoms. Instead, he is presented as a man who pursues love, peace and humanity, and as a hero who seeks a way to stop the war between different states in China, as the film's director Zhao Linshan emphasised (cited in Chen 2011).

Similarly, as a ruler of Heaven, Earth and Hell, the Jade Emperor is a symbol of paternal authority in the well-known Chinese classical novel *Journey to the West*, which was written by Wu Cheng'en in the sixteenth century. In the novel, and in many theatrical and screen adaptations, especially in the 'Havoc in heaven' act,[6] the Monkey King often embodies freedom, independence, and a rebellious force, while the Jade Emperor is one of the highest gods who suppresses the Monkey King's challenges and defends his ruling position and the existing social order across the three universes. However, the media publicity for Chow's *The Monkey King* (2014) portrays the young Monkey King (Donnie Yen) as a mischievous character who has been misled by the Bull Demon King (Aaron Kwok), while Chow's Jade Emperor is reinterpreted as a tolerant and wise god who only uses his power when the world's peace, unity, and social order are under threat, and it is through the Jade Emperor that the young Monkey King learns an important lesson about maintaining harmony across the different worlds (Zhao 2011; Bai 2010).

In line with the media emphasis on the powerful yet peaceful fatherliness of Chow's new screen roles, the media publicity surrounding Chow's star persona is also intended to endow the star with similar characteristics. On one hand, Chow is presented as a highly influential and respected veteran star of whose experience of the industry, professional reputation and perceived global fame young actors and filmmakers are in awe (*Sichuan Daily* 2006; Sun 2009b; Zhao 2011; Zhu 2011). On the other hand, Chow's star persona as a friendly and easy-going man is highlighted in various media publicity for Chow's latest films (Li 2009; Sun 2009a; Zhao 2011). The combination of the two elements in the Chinese media accordingly portrayed the star as a man who is authoritative but not threatening, humble but not weak. As a result, Chow's public image corresponds strongly to the ideal of manhood in the Confucian codes that are traditionally appreciated in Chinese patriarchal society.

Defending authority and institutional power, Chow's star image as a powerful yet peace-loving father on and off the Chinese big screen seems to be particularly timely in conformance with the resurgent fear of mainland China's threat to Hong Kong's local identity along with mainland China's continuously growing power. According to a survey (University of Hong Kong 2015b), Hong Kongers' confidence in the city's future grew from 62.1 per cent in the second half of 1998 to 80.2 per cent in 2007. However, this figure has gradually dropped back to 47.1 per cent in 2015, nearly 15 per cent lower than the figure in 1998. These figures are a good reflection of the complex relationship between Hong Kong and mainland China nearly twenty years after the city's return to China. The deepening economic ties and relaxed border controls, such as the Closer Economic Partnership Agreement (CEPA) and the Individual Visit Scheme, have indeed been beneficial to Hong Kong's recovery from recession and its economic development. However, there is also growing concern regarding the preservation of Hong Kong's local culture, as the relaxed border controls have resulted in an influx of mainland Chinese into Hong Kong as tourists, migrants, highly skilled workers, investors and others. Among the concerns is the worry that the high purchase demand of mainlanders overstretches local resources as shown in a number of occurrences, such as the case of lowered quality of maternal care due to the large number of pregnant women flocking into Hong Kong to deliver babies in order to get Hong Kong citizenship, local Hong Kong parents' frustration with the shortage of baby formula milk because of mainland parents' panic-buying since tainted milk was found in mainland China, and sustained high mortgages being pushed up by mainland Chinese investors' demand for local housing.

The dispute between Hong Kong's citizens and mainlanders is further escalated by a series of incidents, including but not limited to the provoking remarks made by Peking University professor Kong Qingdong, who called Hong Kongers *zougou* (puppets, running dogs) of British imperialists (Watts 2012); the Hong Kong Education Bureau's proposal to replace moral and civic education with moral and national education – a school curriculum that aims to strengthen the education on patriotism – and the restrictions imposed by the central government on Hong Kong's electoral system. All of these incidents have sparked a number of anti-mainland China protests in Hong Kong since 2012, including the anti-parallel trading protests and the Umbrella Movement. Nevertheless, the large scale of Hong Kong citizens' protests have in turn angered many mainlanders, including Lu Ping – former director of the State Council's Hong Kong and Macau Affairs Office – who regarded the anti-mainland sentiment in Hong Kong as having been stirred up by some arrogant Hong Kongers who are disloyal to China and fear losing their sense of superiority over mainlanders (Cheung and Lau 2012). The conflict between Hong Kong citizens and mainlanders is in fact putting 'One Country, Two Systems' in doubt on both sides.

In this context, Chow's screen image as a respected Chinese father reveals Chinese commercial cinema's embrace of the central government's promotion of the ideas of social stability, unity and harmony, as well as faith in the ruling party. Sabrina Yu (2012: 234–5) convincingly pointed out that, in the post-socialist period, 'patriotism' has become:

> a basic criterion Chinese actors have to meet if they want to establish their stardom in the PRC . . . For Hong Kong and Taiwan stars, it is even more important to package themselves as patriotic stars in order to consolidate their star status and expand their fan base on the mainland.

Whilst these films, mainly produced by state-owned studios, chose Chow – a native Hong Kong star – to play characters endorsing the father's power, Chow's performances and star persona also become an illustration of a Hong Kong son's loyalty and obedience to his Chinese father's authority.

Even in the latest films produced by Hong Kong filmmakers, such as Wong Jing's *The Last Tycoon* (2012), *From Vegas to Macau* I and II (2014 and 2015), Chow plays roles that embody the notion of *xiao*. In *The Last Tycoon*, Chow played middle-aged Cheng Daqi, a patriotic gang lord, who not only pays filial piety to his master Hong Shouting (Sammo Hung), but also fights against traitors and Japanese enemies in order to retain his moral integrity for being loyal to his home country, China. In *From Vegas to Macau* I and II, Chow's Ken, a semi-retired gambling master, is a caring and protective father who assists the Chinese police and Interpol to fight against an international crime organisation's financial fraud and other crimes. Accordingly, Chow's screen image not only embodies China's attempt to shape the way in which the country and its ruling party are perceived domestically and globally, but also reinforces the dependent status of Hong Kong as a special Chinese region on the Chinese big screen.

Of course, not all of Chow's latest roles fit neatly within this paradigm of the relationship between a loving father and a respectful son. Unlike his role in Wong Jing's films, Chow's character Ho Chung-ping in Johnnie To's *Office* (2015) bears a similarity to his role as Emperor Ping in *Curse of the Golden Flower*. Representing the most powerful point of a hierarchical structure, Ho is the powerful boss of a trading company that is caught in the 2008 global financial crisis triggered by the bankruptcy and liquidation of Lehman Brothers. While every character in the film is caught in the giant machine of office politics, the company also mirrors a ruthless social system that could destroy an individual's integrity and dreams.

The promotional materials for *Office* stress the reunion of the director Johnnie To and the two stars, Sylvia Chang and Chow, more than twenty-five years after their collaboration in *All about Ah-Long* (1989)[7] and *The Fun, the Luck & the Tycoon* (1990) (CCTV, 2015). In *All about Ah-Long*, Chow's Ah-Long is a loving but flawed father who is imprisoned for illegal racing shortly before the birth of his son. Also guilty of assaulting his son's mother, he is somehow left to raise the child on his release from prison, and makes an honest effort to mend his ways. Ah-Long dies in a racing accident at the end of the film, ensuring the father's redemption. By contrast, Chow's Ho in Office is a winner. By defeating the upper- and middle-ranking employees whose actions threaten the company's stability and fortunes, as well as Ho's own position, Chow's character manages to retain fatherly control and absolute power. In other words, the father punishes the son in the power game. The father's power embodied in Chow's screen image reinforces Johnnie To's claim that the film allows audiences to see the harsh reality of modern society and urges individuals to have a clear vision of their own value and position in the office (and in society, to some degree). In an interview about the release of *Office*, To admitted that he would have changed the ending of *All about Ah-Long* if he had filmed it twenty-five years later. Rather than letting Ah-Long die, he would probably have killed Ah-Long's son instead (He 2015, Xiao 2015). Although To's comment appears to be a light-hearted joke, his remark, together with

Chow's image in the latest Hong Kong films, suggests that Hong Kong cinema begrudges the power of the Chinese father in the new *huayu dianying*.

CONCLUSION

Since Chow transformed from being a Hong Kong megastar to a transnational Chinese icon, his star image and career trajectory provide a flexible site, through which Hong Kong and Hong Kongers' post-1997 identity are contested. In comparison to the cultural code of *yi* incorporated in Chow's Hong Kong stardom, Chow's post-1997 star image has become increasingly involved in the cinematic debate surrounding the Confucian code *xiao*, a notion that plays a significant role in maintaining the stability and the continuity of the father's authority in a Chinese patriarchal society. As detailed in this chapter, Chow's screen image has gradually changed since the 2000s from that of a son who negotiates his independence in his early films to a father who negotiates his authority. Despite the two different types of fatherhood that Chow portrayed, the aloof father and the peace-loving father, Chow's on- and off-screen performances, as well as the media publicity surrounding these films, all confirm that the father's absolute power is unchallengeable.

Behind Chow's shifting screen image, however, is the complex and constant negotiation between resistance to and embrace of China's growing power across borders. As a native Hong Konger, Chow and his shifting star image since his return to the Chinese film industry reveal the way in which the flexibility and adaptability of (expatriate) Hong Kong stardom is deployed as a site where Hong Kong's post-1997 identity is interrogated and constructed. Whilst Chow has had a strong star persona as a Hong Konger per se, his casting and performance as a Chinese father indicate the submissive status of Hong Kong cinema in the rising *huayu dianying* that is dominated to some extent by mainland Chinese investment and central government control of the profitable mainland film market.

NOTES

1. Although a restricted definition of the word 'orphan' refers only to those children who have lost both parents, in Chinese patriarchal society the word is also frequently used to refer those who have no father, such as the way it is used in the phrase *gu'er guamu* (orphan and widowed mother).
2. *The Analects of Confucius* asserts that a filial son should not complain about or challenge his father's actions directly, even though he may not agree with his father. As Confucius argues, even if the father's conduct is wrong, a filial son should conceal them for his father, rather than defying his father publicly (Legge trans. 1861).

3. In the context of martial arts films, the word *zhongyuan* mainly refers to the mainland area of China where the majority of residents are Han people. Han is the largest ethnic group in China, accounting for over 90 per cent of its population. *Jianghu* is a mythical martial arts world that shares some ethical codes with civic society. For further discussions about *jianghu*, please see Song (2007).

4. The first Confucius Institute was found in Uzbekistan in June 2004. By September of 2013, over three hundred Confucius Institutes had been established in ninety countries and regions around the world. For details, see Mohamedbhai (2012).

5. Written in the fourteenth and sixteenth centuries respectively, the *Romance of the Three Kingdoms* and *Journey to the West* are acclaimed as two of the Four Great Classical Novels of Chinese literature. The other two are *Water Margin* and *Dream of the Red Chamber*. The four novels are commonly regarded as the greatest and most influential pre-modern Chinese novels.

6. The literal meaning of the film *The Monkey King*'s (2014) Chinese title *danao tiangong* is havoc in heaven, or uproar in heaven.

7. Both Chow Yun-fat and Sylvia Chang are credited for contributing to the story of *All about Ah-Long*.

Conclusion

The discussion of a star as a public figure whose image appears both on the big screen and across various mass media channels provides an accessible topic through which people can express and exchange their understanding of cultural identification. In 1979, Richard Dyer published his influential book on the star phenomenon, which fundamentally challenged the way in which the extent of star studies could be understood across disciplines and media texts. What is particularly valuable in Dyer's work is his effort to contextualise the interpretation of star images and his recognition of stardom as a phenomenon of both production and consumption. Rather than restricting the star persona to the big screen, Dyer demonstrated how the discourses surrounding a star's off-screen life could impact on the construction of stardom. By so doing, Dyer recognised that star image is not just a simple reflection of social type, but that star image is instead a site where different social and cultural perceptions negotiate with each other. However, seeing films as 'the most important of the texts' (Dyer 1998: 61), Dyer reduced other media texts, such as a film's promotional materials, media publicity and the audiences' reviews, to the status of auxiliary or secondary tools. As such, Dyer's emphasis on a star's symbolic meaning and charisma has invited criticism. For instance, Barry King (1987: 147) argued that Dyer has 'apparent "proneness" to star-worship'. For King, Dyer's studies of the representation of star image do not fully engage with the specific market conditions through which stardom is mediated.

Responding to the inadequate attention to the market specifications of star image, a number of film scholars, including Dyer himself (2004), started to seek solutions in reception studies by investigating the role of audiences. This analysis of reception catalysed a debate concerning spectatorship and the viewing experience. Analysing the star–audience relationship, Jackie Stacey (1991: 159) argued that the study of audiences distinguishes 'the cinematic identification, which refers to the viewing experience' from the 'extra-cinematic identification, referring to the use of stars' identities in a different cultural time and space'. While criticising most representation studies as tending to 'emphasise the presence of the star and de-emphasise the identity of the spectator', Stacey (1991: 159–60) stressed that the processes of constructing star–audience identification does not simply involve a passive reproduction, but rather 'an active engagement and production of changing identities'. In light of this, many reception studies often regard the stars' public appearances and their performances in films as raw material that regulates the potential range of experiences and meanings with which an audience may be associated.

Considering this from the audience's perspective, many film scholars who adopt reception approaches particularly emphasise the incoherent meaning of star image, and argue that various interpretations of star image largely depend on the viewers' membership of specific cultural communities (Jancovich 2004: 67; Brooker and Jermyn 2003: 275; Staiger 2005: 3; Nowell-Smith 2000: 10–11). For instance, Rachel Moseley (2002: 218) and Tessa Perkins (2000: 87) have argued that an audience's social class, race, sexual orientation, generation, and educational background are key factors in determining the nature of the relationships between audience members and star texts. Calling for more attention to be paid to the connection between an individual audience's or fan's personal background and viewing experiences, the scholarly emphasis on an audiences' active participation has, in a sense, transformed star image from an industrial product to a market commodity.

Nevertheless, while reception theory and audience research criticise the tendency in representation studies to generalise the social context and to disconnect from an audience member's personal experiences during the process of encountering a star image, their assumption that an audience generates the meaning of star image also raises concerns regarding how the interview scripts of an audience's answers or questionnaire feedback engage with the social context in which the star image is constructed. One of the concerns is the shifting nature of audiences' personal experiences, tastes and circumstances. This suggests that audiences' understanding and interpretation of star images may change over time. In addition, the emphasis on audiences' active interpretations does not always tell us how their points of view are shaped by films and numerous media texts constructed around the star. In this regard, it is understandable why some film scholars, such as Janet Staiger (2000: 23), Henry Jenkins (2000: 169) and Thomas Austin (2002: 27), have urged that a historical materialist approach should be adopted when conducting reception research, and have argued that reception studies should acknowledge the significance of a film's promotional materials.

As illustrated above, neither the textual analysis of a film nor the research into an audience's response to star image in a film is adequate to explain how stardom articulates its specific cultural, historical and social experiences.

However, despite the fact that they approach star images from two different angles, namely from the perspective of production and consumption respectively, these studies have raised a common concern in terms of the constitution of the star image; that is to say, the importance of a star's presence in the media texts circulating beyond the big screen. Christine Gledhill (1991: xv) has argued from a star production perspective that:

> the fragmentary, extra-cinematic circulation of the star image acts as an inducement to the consumption of films for their promise to the viewer of completion both of star image and self image through the structure of identification offered by classic narrative.

Similarly, Jenkins (2000: 169) and Austin (2002: 13) have argued via the lens of star consumption that a star's presence in advertisements, film trailers, newspaper reviews and other textual activators shapes audience expectations. On both sides, the attention placed on a star's presence in the media texts apart from film helps to construct critical engagement between the star's image and specific social contexts. In this sense, the prefigurative texts, as analysed in this book, provide a valuable link through which the production and consumption of the star image are interacted.

As one of the most successful Hong Kong stars, Chow Yun-fat has enjoyed huge popularity in East Asia and beyond. His long screen career provides a sound case for the study of stardom, as it vividly illustrates the transformation of Hong Kong cinema and society since the 1970s, as well as delineating the formation of transnational Chinese cinema in the last three decades. Through the media publicity surrounding Chow's films, TV programmes, music albums and the public discourse of Chow's stardom circulated via various media texts, this book has explored the plural territories of Chow's star image as a modern *xiaosheng*, star actor, fashion and lifestyle icon, comedic actor, Asian hero, ageing master and more. While the different territories of Chow's public image suggest that the star is both a versatile actor and a renowned celebrity, they also demonstrate that star image shifts constantly, not only over time but also across different historical, social and cultural spaces.

As illustrated in the first half of the book, Chow's Hong Kong career before 1995 can be seen as expressing a larger representation of the social mobility in Hong Kong's local society during its metropolitan history. In comparison to other stars of Hong Kong cinema, Chow's star persona has a particular connection to Hong Kongers' self-identification. This is not only because of his early star persona established in the local TV industry (as detailed in Chapter 1), but also because of the presentation of his off-screen life and career path across different media platforms in Hong Kong. Unlike mainland Chinese-born Jet Li and Malaysian-born Michelle Yeoh, who became Hong Kong citizens as adults, Chow is a locally born Hong Kong citizen whose image is closely linked to local community. Also, unlike Jackie Chan and Sammo Hung who started acting in Mandarin cinema, Chow began his acting career on TVB, the prime commercial terrestrial channel in Hong Kong in the mid-1970s. Whereas Chan and Hung achieved their initial fame in martial arts films set in Chinese agricultural society, such as *The Iron-fisted Monk* (1977) and *Snake in the Eagle's Shadow* (1978), Chow gained his fame by playing a number of urban young men in localised Cantonese television dramas set in modern Hong Kong, such as *The Good, the Bad, and the Ugly* (1979) and *Family Feelings* (1980). Even after Chow moved his career from the small screen to the big screen, the prefigurative materials surrounding Chow's screen career and performances continued to stress the star's connection with the city of Hong Kong.

As the four chapters in the first part of the book have illustrated, the construction of Chow's star image as a *xiaosheng*, a sentimental man, a fashion and lifestyle icon and a cosmopolitan citizen has incorporated a social and industrial understanding of the importance of Hong Kong's cross-border communication with the rest of the world. Whereas the Chinese cultural codes, such as *yi*, have never been removed from Chow's stardom, public discourses surrounding Chow's star image have particularly emphasised the influences of global contact, Western culture and modernisation. Such connotations illustrate that the construction of Hong Kong identity is not self-contained, and is open to influences from different cultures. In a sense, Chow's star image is that of a proud local Hong Konger as a cosmopolitan citizen.

In comparison, Chow's cross-border stardom reveals the complex social perception of expatriate Hong Kong stardom. As the second half of the book discusses, audiences' perceptions of overseas Hong Kong stars' screen images are often associated with their ethnic Chinese backgrounds. This raises the question of how expatriate Hong Kong stars negotiate their political identity through, rather than against, their ethnic identity. In conjunction with Chow's career moves from Hong Kong to Hollywood and then to transnational Chinese cinema, the media focus on the cultural identifications embodied in his star image have gradually shifted to Orientalism, Chineseness, and Asianness. Unlike Jackie Chan or Jet Li, who were portrayed as less 'Chinese' and who adopted a modern look within modern urban settings when they moved to Hollywood and entered the global film market,[1] Chow has become increasingly involved with the production of those films set in historical Asia, including *Anna and the King* (1999), *Crouching Tiger, Hidden Dragon* (2000), *Curse of the Golden Flower* (2006), *Confucius* (2008), and *The Assassins* (2012). This shift not only differentiates Chow from many other Chinese stars who extended their career beyond Asia during a similar period, but also distinguishes Chow's transnational star status from his modern and Westernised look developed during his early acting career in Hong Kong.

In comparison to Chow's Hong Kong screen image, Chow's post-1997 screen image is indeed very versatile in terms of his characters' ethnicities, nationalities and personal backgrounds. Chow plays a Chinese hitman in *The Replacement Killers*, a second-generation Hong Kong migrant in *The Corruptor*, a Siamese king in *Anna and the King*, a Chinese martial artist in *Crouching Tiger, Hidden Dragon*, a Tibetan monk in *Bulletproof Monk*, a Singaporean pirate in *At World's End*, a Chinese philosopher in *Confucius*, a mythological god in *The Monkey King*, an expatriate Hong Kong gambler residing in Macau in *From Vegas to Macau*, and many more. Chow's screen portrayals of different Asian ethnicities, especially the roles that he played in Hollywood films, attracted criticism from Julian Stringer (2003b: 233) for signifying an arbitrary otherness, with little distinction between the subtle differences in Asian ethnicities.

However, there are other voices in the film industry. Director John Woo and producer Terence Chang, both from Hong Kong and working in the Hollywood since mid-1990s before their return to Chinese cinema, have claimed that Chow belongs to the category of actors whose faces transcend race and nationality (Coker 1997: 8). As a professional actor whose job is to act, to impersonate, and to become someone else on the big screen, Chow thus embodies the flexibility and adaptability of Hong Kong stardom, professionally, ethnically and culturally. While the hybridity and adaptability of Chow's on- and off-screen image allows the star to link and cross various ethnic, national/regional and cultural borders, it also suggests that a Hong Kong star could simultaneously hold multiple identities as a Hong Konger, HKSARer, overseas Chinese, expatriate Hong Konger, diasporic Chinese and Asian. In this regard, Chow's star image – whether in Hong Kong, Hollywood or in the transnational Chinese cinema – constitutes a public site where various social perceptions of Hong Kong identity across a variety of different cultural locations contest each other.

Meanwhile, throughout various stages of Chow's screen career, the prefigurative materials investigated in this book have been shown to select and modify different territories of Chow's star image in order to cater for different social perceptions of Hong Kong's cultural identities across specific cultural locations. In Hong Kong, the media discourse on Chow's star image focuses on the star's impersonation of local citizens' growing awareness of self-identity and pride in Hong Kong in the context of the city's cosmopolitan history. In comparison, Hollywood and American mass media's discourse endows Chow with the ambiguity of Asianness and Orientalism, while using Chow's career move to suggest that a Hong Konger and a mainland Chinese person have different political identities. However, Chow's star image changed again when the star moved to transnational Chinese cinema. The selective emphasis on traditional Chinese values and cultural code *xiao* sinicised Chow's star image, and to some degree illustrates the ever-changing relationship between Hong Kong and mainland China, politically, economically and culturally.

Indeed, it was not until very recently that film scholars started to pay attention to Hong Kong stars from non-action cinema, such as Leslie Cheung and Tony Leung Chiu-wai. However, this kind of study is far from sufficient. As a response to the scarcity of studies of Hong Kong stars, this book's examination of the various territories that have become articulated within Chow's stardom has expanded our understanding of Chow's star image, as well as of Hong Kong stardom beyond action cinema. In addition, this book has demonstrated that an interpretation of Hong Kong stardom can no longer be restricted to film texts alone. Instead, an intertextual approach helps to reveal the complex relationships between the construction of star image and social perceptions of Hong Kongers' cultural identity within its specific historical, social and cultural contexts. Finally, I want to stress here that the analysis of Chow's star image in this book is by no means conclusive. The scope of my discussion of Chow's stardom is largely restricted to the Hong Kong, American and Chinese film industries and markets. However, Chow, as many other Hong Kong and Chinese stars, has also acted in a range of films co-produced by different countries, such as Chow's *Children of Huang Shi* (2007), a co-production by Chinese, German and Australian companies. The construction and circulation of the star images of Chow and other Hong Kong stars beyond the parameters of America and China is an area for future research.

NOTE

1. Since the two stars moved to Hollywood in the 1990s, their Hollywood-produced films, including Chan's *Rush Hour III* (2007) and *The Spy Next Door* (2010), and Li's *Danny the Dog* (2005), *War* (2007), and *The Expendables* (2010), reshaped their star images as modern urban men. It was not until Jackie Chan and Jet Li partially moved their careers back to Chinese-language cinema in the 2000s that they reappeared as pre-modern Chinese characters in transnational Chinese-language films, such as Chan's *The Forbidden Kingdom* (2008) and *Little Big Soldier* (2010), and Li's *Hero* (2002) and *Fearless* (2006).

Appendix I
General Filmography

A Better Tomorrow/英雄本色, dir. John Woo, Hong Kong, Cinema City & Films Co., 1986.

A Touch of Zen/侠女, dir. King Hu, Taiwan, International Film Company and Union Film Company, 1971.

All about Ah–Long/阿郎的故事, dir. Johnnie To, Hong Kong, Cinema City & Films Co., 1989.

American Beauty, dir. Sam Mendes, USA, DreamWorks Pictures, 1999.

An Autumn's Tale/秋天的童话, dir. Mabel Cheung, Hong Kong, D&B Films, 1987.

Anna and the King, dir. Andy Tennant, USA, 20th Century Fox, 1999.

Bed for Day, Bed for Night/床上的故事, dir. Cheung Sum, Hong Kong, Goldig Films (HK) Ltd, 1977.

Bulletproof Monk, dir. Paul Hunter, USA, Metro-Goldwyn-Mayer, 2003.

Children of Huang Shi, dir. Roger Spottiswoode, Australia, PRC and German, Australian Film Finance Corporation (AFFC), Ming Productions and Bluewater Pictures, 2007.

City on Fire/龙虎风云, dir. Ringo Lam, Hong Kong, Cinema City & Films Co., 1987.

Confucius/孔子, dir. Hu Mei, PRC, Beijing Dadi Century Limited and China Film Group, 2008.

Crouching Tiger, Hidden Dragon/卧虎藏龙, dir. Ang Lee, Taiwan, Hong Kong, USA and PRC, Asia Union Film & Entertainment Ltd, China Film Co-Production Corporation, Columbia Pictures Film Production Asia, and Edko Films, 2000.

Curse of the Golden Flower/满城尽带黄金甲, dir. Zhang Yimou, PRC, Beijing New Picture Film Co. and Edko Film, 2006.

Danny the Dog (a.k.a. *Unleashed*), dir. Louis Leterrier, France, USA and UK, EuropaCorp and TF1 Films Production, 2005.

Dragon Gate Inn/龙门客栈, dir. King Hu, Taiwan, Union Film Company, 1967.

Dream Lovers/梦中人, dir. Tony Au, Hong Kong, D&B Films, 1986.

Drunken Master/醉拳, dir. Woo-Ping Yuen, Hong Kong, Seasonal Film Corporation, 1978.

Empress Wu Tse-tien/武则天, dir. Li Han-hsiang, Hong Kong, Shaw Brothers, 1963.

Evening Bell/晚钟, dir. Wu Ziniu, PRC, August 1st Film Studio and Beijing Film Studio, 1989.

Farewell China/爱在别乡的季节, dir. Clara Law, Hong Kong, Golden Harvest and Precision Laboratory, 1990.

Farewell My Concubine/霸王别姬, dir. Chen Kaige, Hong Kong and PRC, Beijing Film Studio, Tomson Films and China Film Co-Production Corporation, 1993.

Fearless/霍元甲, dir. Ronny Yu, PRC and Hong Kong, Beijing Film Studio, China Film Co-Production Corporation and China Film Group, 2006.

From Vegas to Macau I (a.k.a. *The Man From Macau I*)/赌城风云I, dir. Jing Wong, PRC and Hong Kong, Bona International Film Group, Mega-Vision Project Distribution, Sun Entertainment Culture, and Media Asia Films, 2014.

From Vegas to Macau II (a.k.a. *The Man From Macau II*)/赌城风云II, dir. Jing Wong, PRC and Hong Kong, Bona International Film Group, Mega-Vision Project Distribution, Sun Entertainment Culture, and Media Asia Films, 2015.

Full Contact/侠盗高飞, dir. Ringo Lam Hong Kong, Golden Princess Film Production, 1992.

Golden Swallow/金燕子, dir. Chang Cheh, Hong Kong, Shaw Brothers, 1968.

Games Gamblers Play/鬼马双星, dir. Michael Hui, Hong Kong, Golden Harvest, 1974.

God of Gamblers/赌神, dir. Wong Jing, Hong Kong, Win's Movie Productions, 1989.

God of Gamblers II/赌神 II, dir. Wong Jing, Hong Kong, Win's Movie Productions, 1991.

Hard Boiled/辣手神探, dir. John Woo, Hong Kong, Golden Princess Film Production, 1992.

Hero/英雄, dir. Zhang Yimou, PRC and Hong Kong, Beijing New Picture Film Co., China Film Co-Production Corporation and Elite Group Enterprises 2002.

Heroes among Heroes/苏乞儿, dir. Chan Chin-chung and Yuen Woo-ping, Hong Kong, Art Sea Films, 1993.

Hong Kong 1941/等待黎明, dir. Leong Po-chih, Hong Kong, D&B Films, 1984.

Kids from Shaolin/少林小子, dir. Chang Hsin-yen, Hong Kong, Chung Yuen Motion Picture Co., 1984.

Kingdom and the Beauty/江山美人, dir. Li Han-hsiang, Hong Kong, Shaw Brothers, 1959.

Lethal Weapon 4, dir. Richard Donner, USA, Warner Bros., 1998.

Little Big Soldier/大兵小将, dir. Sheng Ding, PRC and Hong Kong, Beijing Dragon Garden Culture & Art, Jackie & JJ Productions and Beijing Universe Starlight Culture Media, 2010.

Love in a Fallen City/倾城之恋, dir. Ann Hui, Hong Kong, Shaw Brothers, 1984.

Love Unto Waste/地下情, dir. Stanley Kwan, Hong Kong, D&B Films, 1986.

Massage Girls/池女, dir. Cheung Sum, Hong Kong, Goldig Films (HK) Ltd, 1976.

Miss O/O女, dir. Cheung Sum, Hong Kong, Goldig Films (HK) Ltd, 1978.

New Dragon Gate Inn/新龙门客栈, dir. Raymond Lee, Hong Kong, Film Workshop and Seasonal Film Corporation, 1992.

New Police Story/新警察故事, dir. Benny Chan, Hong Kong and PRC, China Film Group and JCE Entertainment Ltd, 2004.

Now You See Love, Now You Don't/我爱扭纹柴, dir. Mabel Cheung and Alex Law, Hong Kong, Golden Princess Film Production, 1992.

Office/华丽上班族, dir. Johnnie To, PRC and Hong Kong, Edko Films, Media Asia Films, and Milky Way Image Company, 2015.

Once a Thief/纵横四海, dir. John Woo, Hong Kong, Golden Princess Film Production, 1991.

Once Upon a Time in China I/黄飞鸿I, dir. Hark Tsui, Hong Kong, Golden Harvest and Film Workshop, 1991.

Once Upon a Time in China II/黄飞鸿II: 男儿当自强, dir. Hark Tsui, Hong Kong, Golden Harvest and Film Workshop, 1992.

Once Upon a Time in China III/黄飞鸿III: 狮王争霸, dir. Hark Tsui, Hong Kong, Golden Harvest and Film Workshop, 1993.

Pirates of the Caribbean I: The Curse of the Black Pearl, dir. Gore Verbinski USA, Walt Disney Pictures, 2003.

Pirates of the Caribbean II: Dead Man's Chest, dir. Gore Verbinski USA, Walt Disney Pictures, 2006.

Pirates of the Caribbean III: At World's End, dir. Gore Verbinski USA, Walt Disney Pictures, 2007.

Prison on Fire/监狱风云, dir. Ringo Lam, Hong Kong, Cinema City & Films Co., 1987.

Prison on Fire II/监狱风云 II: 逃犯, dir. Ringo Lam, Hong Kong, Cinema City & Films Co. and Golden Princess Film Production, 1991.

Red Sorghum/红高粱, dir. Zhang Yimou, PRC, Xi'an Film Studio, 1988.

Rumble in the Bronx/红番区, dir. Stanley Tong, Hong Kong, Golden Harvest, 1995.

Rush Hour III, dir. Brett Ratner, USA, New Line Cinema, 2007.

Security Unlimited/摩登保镖, dir. Michael Hui, Hong Kong, Golden Harvest, 1981.

Shanghai, dir. Mikael Håfström, USA, Phoenix Pictures, 2010.

Shinjuku Incident/新宿事件, dir. Yee Tung-shing, Hong Kong, Emperor Dragon, Jackie Chan Productions and JCE Movies, 2009.

Snake in the Eagle's Shadow/蛇形刁手, dir. Yuen Woo-ping, Hong Kong, Seasonal Film Corporation, 1978.

Song of the Exile/客途秋恨, dir. Ann Hui, Hong Kong and Taiwan, Cos Group and Central Pictures Corporation, 1990.

The Assassins/铜雀台, dir. Zhao Linshan, PRC, Changchun Film Studio, 2012.

The Big Brawl, dir. Robert Clouse, Hong Kong and USA, Golden Harvest and Warner Bros, 1980.

The Blue Kite/蓝风筝, dir. Tian Zhuangzhuang, PRC, Beijing Film Studio, 1993.

The Bridges of Madison County, dir. Clint Eastwood, USA, Warner Bros, 1995.

The Cannonball Run, dir. Hal Needham, Hong Kong and USA, Golden Harvest Company and Eurasia Investments, 1981.

The Corruptor, dir. James Foley, USA, New Line Cinema, 1999.

The Diary of a Big Man/大丈夫日记, dir. Chor Yuen, Hong Kong, Cinema City & Films Co., 1988.

The Eighth Happiness/八星报喜, dir. Johnnie To, Hong Kong, Cinema City & Films Co., 1988.

The Expendables I, dir. Sylvester Stallone, USA, 2010.

The Expendables II, dir. Simon West, USA, 2012.

The Expendables III, dir. Patrick Hughes, USA, 2014.

The Forbidden Kingdom/功夫之王, dir. Rob Minkoff, USA and PRC, Casey Silver Productions, China Film Co-Production Corporation and Huayi Brothers Media, 2008.

The Fun, the Luck & the Tycoon, dir. Johnnie To, Hong Kong, Cinema City & Films Co., 1990.

The Good Earth, dir. Sidney Franklin, USA, Metro-Goldwyn-Mayer, 1937.

The Greatest Lover/公子多情, dir. Clarence Fok Yiu-leung, Hong Kong, Golden Harvest, 1988.

The House of 72 Tenants/七十二家房客, dir. Wang Weiyi, PRC and Hong Kong, Pearl River Film Studio and Hongtu Film Company, 1963.

The House of 72 Tenants/七十二家房客, dir. Chor Yuen, Hong Kong, Shaw Brothers, 1973.

The Hunter, the Butterfly and the Crocodile/捞家邪牌姑爷仔, dir. Yeung Kuen, Hong Kong, Goldig Films (HK) Ltd, 1976.

The Iron-fisted Monk/三德和尚与舂米六, dir. Simon Hung, Hong Kong, Golden Harvest, 1977.

The Killer/喋血双雄, dir. John Woo, Hong Kong, Film Workshop and Golden Princess Film Production, 1989.

The King and I, dir. Walter Lang, USA, 20th Century Fox, 1956.

The Last Affair/花城, dir. Tony Au, Hong Kong, Pearl City Films, 1983.

The Last Tycoon/大上海, dir. Wong Jing, Hong Kong and PRC, Bona Film Group, 2012.

The Lunatics/癫佬正传, dir. Yee Tung-shing, Hong Kong, D&B Films, 1986.

The Matrix, dir. Andy Wachowski and Lana Wachowski, USA, Warner Bros, 1999.

The Monkey King/大闹天宫, dir. Cheang Pou-Soi, Hong Kong and PRC, China Film Group, Mandarin Films Distribution, Filmko Pictures and Global Star Productions, 2014.

The Mummy: Tomb of the Dragon Emperor, dir. Rob Cohen, USA, Universal Pictures, 2008.

The One, dir. James Wong, USA, Revolution Studios and Hard Eight Pictures, 2001.

The Postman Strikes Back/巡城马, dir. Ronny Yu, Hong Kong, Golden Harvest, 1982.

The Replacement Killers, dir. Antoine Fuqua, USA, Columbia Pictures, 1998.

The Shaolin Temple/少林寺, dir. Chang Hsin-yen, Hong Kong, Chung Yuen Motion Picture Co., 1982.

The Spy Next Door, dir. Brian Levant, USA, Relativity Media and Robert Simonds Production, 2010.

The Story of Qiu Ju/秋菊打官司, dir. Zhang Yimou, Hong Kong and PRC, Sil-Metropole Organisation and Youth Film Studio of Beijing Film Academy, 1992.

The Story of Woo Viet/胡越的故事, dir. Ann Hui, Hong Kong, Pearl City Films, 1981.

The Tuxedo, dir. Kevin Donovan, USA, DreamWorks Pictures, 2002.

The Warlords/投名状, dir. Peter Chan and Wai Man Yip, Hong Kong and PRC, Media Asia Films, Morgan & Chan Films and China Film Group, 2007.

Their Private Lives/爱欲狂潮, dir. Yeung Kuen, Hong Kong, Goldig Films (HK) Ltd, 1978.

War, dir. Philip G. Atwell, USA, Liongate, 2007.

Waterloo Bridge, dir. Mervyn LeRoy, USA, Metro-Goldwyn-Mayer, 1940.

Women/女人心, dir. Stanley Kwan, Hong Kong, Pearl City Films and Shaw Brothers, 1985.

Appendix II
Chow Yun-fat's Filmography

2015   *Office*/华丽上班族, dir. Johnnie To, Hong Kong (as Ho Chung-ping/何仲平)

2015   *From Vegas to Macau II*/赌城风云II, dir. Wang Jing, Hong Kong (as Ken/石一坚 and Ko Chun/高进)

2014   *From Vegas to Macau I* (a.k.a. *The Man from Macau*)/赌城风云, dir. Wang Jing, HK (as Ken/石一坚)

2014   *The Monkey King*/大闹天宫, dir. Cheang Pou-soi, PRC and Hong Kong (as Jade Emperor/玉帝)

2012   *The Last Tycoon*/大上海, dir. Wong Jing, PRC and Hong Kong (as Cheng Daqi/成大器)

2012   *The Assassins*/铜雀台, dir. Zhao Linshan, PRC (as Cao Cao/曹操)

2011   *The Founding of a Party*/建党伟业, dir. Huang Jianxin and Han Sanping, PRC (as Yuan Shikai/袁世凯)

2010   *Let the Bullets Fly*/让子弹飞, dir. Jiang Wen, PRC (as Huang Silang/黄四郎)

2010   *Shanghai*, dir. Mikael Håfström, USA (as Anthony Lan-ting/安东尼·兰廷)

2010   *Confucius*/孔子, dir. Hu Mei, PRC (as Confucius/孔子)

2009   *Dragonball Evolution*/七龙珠, dir. James Wong, USA (as Master Roshi/龟仙人)

2007   *Children of Huang Shi*/黄石的孩子, dir. Roger Spottiswoode, Australia, Germany and PRC (as Chen Hansheng/陈汉生)

2007   *Pirates of the Caribbean III: At World's End*/加勒比海盗3: 世界的尽头, dir. Gore Verbinski, USA (as Capitan Sao Feng/啸风船长)

2006   *Curse of the Golden Flower*/满城尽带黄金甲, dir. Zhang Yimou, PRC (as Emperor Ping/大王)

2006   *The Postmodern Life of My Aunt*/姨妈的后现代故事, dir. Ann Hui, Hong Kong and PRC (as Pan Zhichang/潘知常)

2004   *Waiting Alone*/独自等待, dir. Dayyan Eng, PRC (as Fa Ge/Chow Yun-fat himself/发哥)

2003   *Bulletproof Monk*/防弹武僧, dir. Paul Hunter, USA (as Monk with no name/无名僧)

2000   *Crouching Tiger, Hidden Dragon*/卧虎藏龙, dir. Ang Lee, Taiwan, Hong Kong, USA and PRC (as Li Mubai/李慕白)

1999   *Anna and the King*/安娜与国王, dir. Andy Tennant, USA (as King Mongkut)

1999   *The Corruptor*/再战边缘, dir. James Foley, USA (as Nick Chen)

1998   *The Replacement Killers*/替身杀手, dir. Antoine Fuqua, USA (as John Lee)

1995   *Peace Hotel*/和平饭店, dir. Wai Ka-fai, Hong Kong (as The Killer Ping/杀人王)

1994   *God of Gamblers Return*/赌神II, dir. Wong Jing, Hong Kong (as Ko Chun, a.k.a. 'The God of Gamblers'/高进)

1994   *Treasure Hunt*/花旗少林, dir. Jeffrey Lau, Hong Kong (as Chang Ching/张正)

1992   *Full Contact*/侠盗高飞, dir. Ringo Lam, Hong Kong (as Gao Fei/高飞)

1992   *Hard Boiled*/辣手神探, dir. John Woo, Hong Kong (as Inspector Yuen/Tequila)

1992   *Now You See Love, Now You Don't*/我爱扭纹柴, dir. Mabel Cheung, Hong Kong (as Ng Shan-shui/吴山水)

1991   *Prison on Fire II: Tao Fan*/监狱风雨II: 逃犯, dir. Ringo Lam, Hong Kong (as Chung Tin-ching/钟天正)

1991   *Once a Thief*/纵横四海, dir. John Woo, Hong Kong (as Joe, a.k.a. Red Bean Pudding/砵仔糕)

1990   *The Fun, the Luck & the Tycoon*/吉星高照, dir. Johnnie To, Hong Kong (as Lam Bo-sun/林宝生)

1989   *God of Gamblers*/赌神, dir. Wong Jing, Hong Kong (as Ko Chun, a.k.a. 'The God of Gamblers'/高进)

1989   *A Better Tomorrow III: Love and Death in Saigon*/英雄本色3: 夕阳之歌, dir. Hark Tsui, Hong Kong (as Mark Gor/小马哥)

1989   *Triads: The Inside Story*/我在黑社会的日子, dir. Taylor Wong, Hong Kong (as Li Man-ho/李万豪)

1989   *The Killer*/喋血双雄, dir. John Woo, Hong Kong (as Ah Jong/小庄)

1989   *Wild Search*/伴我闯天涯, dir. Ringo Lam, Hong Kong (as Lau Chung-pong, a.k.a. 'Mew-Mew'/刘振邦)

1989   *All about Ah-Long*/阿郎的故事, dir. Johnnie To, Hong Kong (as Ah-Long/阿郎)

1988   *City War*/义胆红唇, dir. Chung Sun, Hong Kong (as Officer Chiu Lee/李志超)

1988   *Goodbye, My Friend*/再见英雄, dir. Ho Lien-chou, Hong Kong (as Hung/阿雄)

1988   *Cherry Blossoms*/郁达夫传奇, dir. Eddie Fong Ling-ching, Hong Kong (as adult Yu Dafu/成年郁达夫)

1988   *The Greatest Lover*/公子多情, dir. Clarence Fok Yiu-leung, Hong Kong (as Locomotive/周前进)

1988   *The Diary of a Big Man*/大丈夫日记, dir. Chor Yuen, Hong Kong (as Chow Chen-fat/周定发)

1988   *Fractured Follies*/长短脚之恋, dir. Wang Chung, Hong Kong (as Joe/梁少祖)

1988   *Tiger On Beat*/老虎出更, dir. Lau Kar-leung, Hong Kong (as Sgt Francis Li/阿辉)

1988   *The Eighth Happiness*/八星报喜, dir. Johnnie To, Hong Kong (as 'Handsome' Long/方剑郎)

1987   *A Better Tomorrow II* (英雄本色 2), dir. John Woo, Hong Kong (as Ken/阿健)

1987   *Prison on Fire*/监狱风云, dir. Ringo Lam, Hong Kong (as Chung Tin-ching, a.k.a. 41671/钟天正)

1987   *Spiritual Love*/鬼新娘, dir. David Lai and Taylor Wong, Hong Kong (as Pu Yongcai/阿搏)

1987   *Flaming Brothers*/江湖龙虎斗, dir. Joe Cheung Tung-cho, Hong Kong (as Chang Ho-tien/阿天)

1987   *An Autumn's Tale*/秋天的童话, dir. Mabel Cheung, Hong Kong (as Samuel Pang, a.k.a. Boat-head/船头尺)

1987   *The Romancing Star*/精装追女仔, dir. Wong Jing, Hong Kong (as Wong Yat-fat/王日发)

1987   *Rich and Famous*/江湖情, dir. Taylor Wong, Hong Kong (as Li Ah-chai/李阿济)

1987   *Code of Honour*/义本无言, dir. Billy Chan, Hong Kong (as Hui/阿辉)

1987   *Scared Stiff*/小生梦惊魂, dir. Lau Kar-wing, Hong Kong (as detective Chow/周探长)

1987 *Tragic Hero*/英雄好汉, dir. Taylor Wong, Hong Kong (as Li Ah-chai/李阿济)

1987 *City on Fire*/龙虎风云, dir. Ringo Lam, Hong Kong (as Ko Chow/高秋)

1986 *My Will, I Will!*/你情我愿, dir. Jamie Luk, Hong Kong (as Fong Yali/周正)

1986 *A Hearty Response*/义盖云天, dir. Norman Law Man, Hong Kong (as Ho Ting-bon/何定邦)

1986 *The Seventh Curse*/原振侠与卫斯里, dir. Ngai Kai-choi, Hong Kong (as Wei Sili/卫斯里)

1986 *Love Unto Waste*/地下情, dir. Stanley Kwan, Hong Kong (as Detective Lan/蓝探长)

1986 *A Better Tomorrow*/英雄本色, dir. John Woo, Hong Kong (as Mark Gor/小马哥)

1986 *100 Ways to Murder Your Wife*/杀妻二人组, dir. Kenny Bee, Hong Kong (as Football Fat/大脚发)

1986 *The Lunatics*/癫佬正传, dir.Yee Tung-shing, Hong Kong (as Chung/阿松)

1986 *The Missed Date*/初一十五, dir. Teresa Woo, Hong Kong (as Peter/彼得)

1986 *Dream Lovers*/梦中人, dir. Tony Au, Hong Kong (as Song Yu/宋羽)

1986 *The Witch from Nepal*/奇缘, dir. Ching Siu-tung, Hong Kong (as Joe/祖)

1985 *Why Me?!*/何必有我. dir. Kent Cheng, Hong Kong (as Mr Chow/周主任)

1985 *Women*/女人心, dir. Stanley Kwan, Hong Kong (as Derek/孙子威)

1985 *Story of Rose*/玫瑰的故事, dir. Yonfan, Hong Kong (as Charles Wong Chun-wah/黄振华 and Ga-ming/傅家明)

1984 *Hong Kong 1941*/香港1941, dir. Leong Po-chih, Hong Kong (as Yip Kim-fay/叶剑飞)

1984 *The Occupant*/灵气逼人, dir. Ronny Yu, Hong Kong (as Valentino Chow/周发)

1984 *Love in a Fallen City*/倾城之恋, dir. Ann Hui, Hong Kong (as Fan Liuyuan/范柳原)

1983 *The Last Affair*/花城, dir. Tony Au, Hong Kong (as Kwong-ping/广平)

1983 *Bloody Money*/血汗金钱, dir. Wong Shee-tong, Hong Kong (as Bullet/子弹)

1983 *The Bund II*/上海滩II, dir. Chiu Chun-keung, Hong Kong (as Hui Man-keung/许文强)

1983 *The Bund*/上海滩, dir. Chiu Chun-keung, Hong Kong (as Hui Man-keung/许文强)

1982 *Head Hunter*/猎头, dir. Lau Shing-hon, Hong Kong (as Yuen Lik/阮力)

1982 *The Postman Strikes Back*/巡城马, dir. Ronny Yu, Hong Kong (as Fu Jun/傅俊)

1981 *The Story of Woo Viet*/胡越的故事, dir. Ann Hui, Hong Kong (as Woo Viet/胡越)

1981 *The Executor*/执法者, dir. Chuen Chan and Ngai Hung-chik, Hong Kong (as Ng To/吴滔)

1981 *Soul Ash*/灰灵, dir. Wong Ying-kit, Hong Kong

1980 *Police Sir*/系咁先, dir. Wong Fung, Hong Kong (as Chu Ka-wah/朱嘉华)

1980 *Pembunahan Pursuit*/懵佬, 大贼, 傻侦探, dir. Wang Tianlin (as Liang Biao/梁标)

1980 *Joy To The World*/喜剧王, dir. Giam Yam, Hong Kong (as Yam Chung-lung/任中龙)

1980 *See-Bar*/师爸, dir. Dennis Yu, Hong Kong (as Chieh/阿杰)

1978 *Miss O*/O女, dir. Cheung Sum, Hong Kong (as Kuan Yen-ping/管严平)

1978 *Their Private Lives*/爱欲狂潮, dir. Yeung Kuen, Hong Kong (as Ko Ming-chung/柯明宗)

1977 *Hot Blood*/入册, dir. Yeung Kuen, Hong Kong (as Ho Cheng/何志成)

1977 *Bed for Day, Bed for Night*/床上的故事, dir. Cheung Sum, Hong Kong (as Zhou Zhiqiang/周志强)

1976 *The Hunter, the Butterfly and the Crocodile*/捞家邪牌姑爷仔 (a.k.a. 神鹰, 蝴蝶, 鳄鱼头), dir. Yeung Kuen, Hong Kong (as Lau Tai-kong/刘大光)

1976 *Massage Girls*/池女, dir. Cheung Sum, Hong Kong (as Ah Gin/阿锦)

1976 *Learned Bride Thrice Fools the Bridegroom*/苏小妹三难新郎, dir. Yeung Kuen, Hong Kong (as Wang Pang/王雱)

1976 *The Reincarnation*/投胎人, dir. Cheung Sum, Hong Kong (as Hsiang-ying's brother/湘莹的哥哥)

Appendix III
Chow Yun-fat's TV Works

1985   *The Yang's Saga* (杨家将), 5 episodes, TVB, HK (as Lü Dongbin/吕洞宾)

1985   *Police Cadet '85* (新扎师兄2), 30 episodes, TVB, HK (as Ging Shing/张竟成)

1985   *The Battle among the Clans* (大香港), 20 episodes, TVB, HK (as Lok Chong-hing/骆中兴)

1984   *The Smiling Proud Wanderer* (笑傲江湖), 20 episodes, TVB, HK (as Linghu Chong/令狐冲)

1983   *Angels and Devils* (北斗双雄), 20 episodes, TVB, HK (as Yu Fan/于凡)

1982   *Radio Tycoon* (播音人), 30 episodes, TVB, HK (as Wai Yip-cheung/韦业昌)

1982   *Super Power* (天降财神), 20 episodes, TVB, HK (as Tian Ri/天日)

1982   *The Legend of Master So* (苏乞儿), 20 episodes, TVB, HK (as So Chian, a.k.a. Beggar So/苏灿)

1982   *The Lone Ranger* (孤城客), 20 episodes, TVB, HK (as Liu Chi/柳迟)

1981   *The Fate* (火凤凰), 20 episodes, TVB, HK (as Ngai Chun/倪骏)

1981   *The Good Old Times* (鳄鱼潭), 20 episodes, TVB, HK (as Ouyang Han/欧阳汉)

1981   *The Shell Game II* (千王群英会), 20 episodes, TVB, HK (as Lung/阿龙)

1980   *Seekers* (英雄血路, a.k.a. 前路), 20 episodes, TVB, HK (as Fu Guozhao/傅国兆)

1980   *The Bund* (上海滩), 25 episodes, TVB, HK (as Hui Man-keung/许文强)

1980   *Family Feelings* (亲情), 75 episodes, TVB, HK (as Shi Hui/石晖, a.k.a. 木咀晖)

1979–80   *The Good, the Bad, and the Ugly* (网中人), 80 episodes, TVB, HK (as Ching Wai/程纬)

1979   *The Landlord* (有楼收租), 13 episodes, TVB, HK (as Ah-Long/阿龙)

1979   *Man from Hong Kong* (龙潭群英), 13 episodes, TVB, HK

1979   *When a Woman is 30* (女人三十之空), TVB, HK

1978   *Mystery Beyond* (幻海奇情), 54 episodes, TVB, HK
– 'Realm of Death' (死之境界) (as Ah Niu/阿牛)
– 'Reappearance' (重现) (as Mr Chen/陈会计)

1978   *Conflict* (奋斗), 80 episodes, TVB, HK (as Xu Chengxi/徐承熙)

1978   *The Giants* (强人), 110 episodes, TVB, HK (as Lei Xuewen/雷学文)

1978   *Vanity Fair* (大亨), TVB, HK

1978   *The Heated Wave of Youth*, a.k.a. *Disco Fever* (青春热潮), 8 episodes, TVB, HK

1977   *A House is not a Home* (家变), 110 episodes, TVB, HK (as He Yanming/何严明)

1976   *Big River South North* (大江南北), 20 episodes, TVB, HK (as Lü Gang/吕刚)

1976   *Hotel* (狂潮), 128 episodes, TVB, HK (as Shao Huashan/邵华山)

1976   *The Itinerant Boy* (江湖小子), 20 episodes, TVB, HK (as Ah Wei/阿伟)

1976   *Lady Yang/Concubine Yang* (杨贵妃), TVB, HK (as Li Linfu/李林甫)

1976   *Dragon, Tiger and Leopard* (龙虎豹), TVB, HK (as Yu Dawei/余大为)

1976   *Seven Women* (七女性), TVB, HK (as Benny)

1976   *Let it Be* (睇開啲啦), 13 episodes, TVB, HK

1976   *Social Worker* (北斗星), 14 episodes, TVB, HK

1976   *Below the Lion Rock Series* (狮子山下), RTHK, HK:
   – 'Rebirth' (重生) (as Chen Tai/陈泰)
   – 'Rest of His Life' (他的下半生) (as Gen/根)
   – 'Target' (目标) (as Zongwei/宗伟)
   – 'Mo Qi Shui' (莫欺水) (as lifeguard/救生员)
   – 'Mother' (母亲) (as Ah Ming/阿明)
   – 'A Story of Beach' (海滩的故事) (as lifeguard/救生员)

1975   *Tung Siu Yuen* (董小宛), 40 episodes, TVB, HK (as Fang Mizhi/方密之)

1975   *Little Women* (小妇人), TVB, HK

1975   *Beautiful Ladies* (千娇百媚俏佳人), TVB, HK

1975   *God of River Lok* (洛神), 7 episodes, TVB, HK (as Xu Huang/徐晃)

1975   *Dream of the Red Chamber* (红楼梦), 5 episodes, TVB, HK (as Jiang Yuhan/蒋玉菡)

1974–6   *Chinese Folklore* (民间传奇), 132 episodes, TVB, HK
   – 'Song Jingshi' *(*宋景诗) (as Yang Dianyi/杨殿乙)
   – 'Wangjiang Pavilion' (望江亭) (as a police officer/衙差)
   – 'Magistrate Teng Settles the Case of Inheritance with Ghostly Cleverness' (滕太尹鬼断家私) (as a servant/仆人)
   – 'Jiang Zhenqing Gain a Wife in a Few Words' (蒋震卿片言得妻) (as Zhang Jiajun/张家骏)
   – 'The Emerald Hairpin' (碧玉簪) (as a guest/宾客)
   – 'Magistrate Qiao's Careless Matching' (乔太守乱点鸳鸯谱) (as a guest/宾客)
   – 'The Old Man and The Fairy' (秋翁遇仙记) (as a villager/村民)
   – 'Four Scholars' (四进士) (as police officer/衙差)
   – 'The Story of Incense' (焚香記) (as Niu Tou/牛头)
   – 'Two Happy Events Come at the Same Time'/双喜临门 (as a guest/宾客)
   – 'Lady With The Lute' (赵五娘) (as a scholar/书生)
   – 'The Purple Hairpin' (紫钗記) (as a military officer/将士)
   – 'The Bride Napping' (花田错) (as a servant/随从)
   – 'The Pavilion of Moon-Worship' (拜月亭) (as a villager/村民)
   – 'Lü Mengzheng'/吕蒙正
   – 'Over Fifteen Strings of Cash'/十五贯 (as a police officer/衙差)
   – 'Taming of the Princess'/醉打金枝 (as a servant)
   – 'Censor Chen Ingeniously Solves the Case of the Gold Hairpins and Brooches'/陈御史巧勘金钗钿 (as a police officer/衙役)
   – 'The Lion Roars' (狮吼记) (as a servant/仆人)
   – 'The Legend of Yuk Tong Chun' (三司会审玉堂春) (as a villager/村民and a police officer/衙差).

English–Chinese Glossary

Ah, Chian　阿灿
Anti-parallel trading protests　反水货客示威
Anti-rightist Movement　反右运动
Asia Television Limited (ATV)　亚洲电视有限公司 (亚视)
Asian Pacific Film Festival　亚太影展
Bak, Sheut-sin (Bai Xuexian)　白雪仙
bao　包
bianfu dadao　蝙蝠大盗
boluo bao　菠萝包
Cao Cao　曹操
Cao Yu　曹禺
Chan, Idy Yuk-lin (Chen Yulian)　陈玉莲
Chan, Jackie (Cheng Long)　成龙
Chan, Kim (Chen Jinxiang)　陈锦湘
Chan, Lap-ban (Chen Lipin)　陈立品
Chang, Cheh (Zhang Che)　张彻
Chang, Chen (Zhang Zhen)　张震
Chang, Sylvia (Zhang Aijia)　张艾嘉
Chang, Terence (Zhang Jiazhen)　张家振
changshan　长衫
Chen, Joan (Chen Chong)　陈冲
Chen, Kaige　陈凯歌
Cheng, Adam (Zheng Shaoqiu)　郑少秋
Cheng, Carol (Zheng Yuling)　郑裕玲
Cheng, Pei-pei (Zheng, Peipei)　郑佩佩
Cheung, Leslie (Zhang Guorong)　张国荣
Cheung, Maggie (Zhang Manyu)　张曼玉
Cheung, Ying (Zhang Ying)　张瑛
China Film Group　中国电影集团
China Radio International　中国国际广播电台
China.com　中华网
Chinanews.com　中国新闻网
Chor, Yuen (Chu Yuan)　楚原

chou   丑
Chow Yun-fat (Zhou Runfa)   周润发
Chow, Stephen (Zhou Xingchi)   周星驰
Chun, Paul (Qin Pei)   秦沛
Chung, Cherie (Zhong Chuhong)   钟楚红
Cinema City & Films Co.   新艺城影业公司
Cinepoly Record Co. Ltd   新艺宝
City Entertainment   电影双周刊
City University of Hong Kong   香港城市大学
Closer Economic Partnership Agreement (CEPA)   内地与港澳关于建立更紧密经贸关系的安排
Commercial Television (CTV)   佳艺电视有限公司 (佳艺)
Confucius (Kongzi)   孔子
Cong, Shan   丛姗
CRI Online   (中国国际广播电台）国际在线
Cultural Revolution   文化大革命
D&B Films Co. Ltd (D&B)   德宝电影公司 (德宝)
Dadi Century (Beijing) Ltd   大地时代文化传播有限公司
dan   旦
Dickson Concepts (International) Limited (Dickson Concepts)   迪生创建(国际)有限公司
   (迪生创建)
Dream of the Red Chamber   《红楼梦》
erhu   二胡
gangren zhi gang   港人治港
Golden Harvest   嘉禾
Golden Horse Awards   金马奖
Goldig Films (HK) Ltd   协利电影(香港)有限公司
Gong, Li   巩俐
Gu, Changwei   顾长卫
gu'er guamu   孤儿寡母
hanbao bao   汉堡包
Hengdian Group   横店集团
Hong Kong Economic Times   香港经济日报
Hong Kong Film Awards   香港电影金像奖
(Hong Kong) New Wave   (香港) 新浪潮
Hu, King (Hu Jinquan)   胡金铨
Hu, Mei   胡玫
huadan   花旦
huangmei diao   黄梅调
huayu dapian   华语大片
huayu dianying   华语电影
Hui Brothers   许氏兄弟
Hui, Ann (Xu Anhua)   许鞍华
Hung, Sammo (Hong Jinbao)   洪金宝
Individual Visit Scheme   自由行
Jade Emperor   玉帝
Jeet Kune Do   截拳道
ji   机
jiandao   剑道
jiande   剑德

jianghu   江湖
jing   净
jiwei bao   鸡尾包
Journey to the West   《西游记》
Kong, Demao   孔德懋
Kong, Qingdong   孔庆东
kongzhong feiren   空中飞人
Kwok, Aaron (Guo Fucheng)   郭富城
Lam, Ringo (Lin Lingdong)   林岭东
Lamma Island   南丫岛
Lau, Andy (Liu Dehua)   刘德华
Lau, Damian Chung-yan (Liu Songren)   刘松仁
Lee, Ang (Li An)   李安
Lee, Bruce (Li Xiaolong)   李小龙
Lee, Danny (Li Xiuxian)   李修贤
Lee, Harold Hsiao-wo (Li Xiaohe)   利孝和
Lee, Heung-kam (Li Xiangqin)   李香琴
Lee, Waise (Li Zixiong)   李子雄
Leung, Tony Chiu-wai (Liang Chaowei)   梁朝伟
Leung, Tony Ka-fai (Liang Jiahui)   梁家辉
Li, Cheuk-to (Li Zhuotao)   李焯桃
Li, Han-hsiang (Li Hanxiang)   李翰祥
Li, Jet (Li Lianjie)   李连杰
Lo, Lieh (Luo Lie)   罗烈
Lü, Dongbin   吕洞宾
Lu, Ping   鲁平
Lung, Sihung (Lang Xiong)   朗雄
Maka, Karl (Mai Jia)   麦嘉
Mao, Zedong   毛泽东
Mark, Sin-sing (Mai Xiansheng)   麦先声
Miao, Cora (Miao Qianren)   缪骞人
miaoshou huakui   妙手花魁
Ming Pao   明报
Ming Pao Weekly   明报周刊
Miu, Michael Kiu-wai (Miao Qiaowei)   苗侨伟
mo   末
Mui, Anita (Mei Yanfang)   梅艳芳
naiyou bao   奶油包
Ng, Cho-fan (Wu Chufan)   吴楚凡
Ng, Lawrence Wai-kwok (Wu Weiguo)   伍卫国
One Country, Two Systems   一国两制
Peng, Cao   蓬草
People's Daily   人民日报
PolyGram   宝丽金
Poon, Dickson Dik-sang (Pan Disheng)   潘迪生
QQ.com   腾讯网
Rediffusion Television (RTV)   丽的电视有限公司 (丽的)
Romance of the Three Kingdoms   《三国演义》
Shanghai Dagong Comedy Theatre   上海大公滑稽剧团

Shaw Brothers   邵氏兄弟(香港)有限公司
Shaw, Run Run (Shao Yifu)   邵逸夫
sheng   生
shizhuang ju   时装剧
Shum, Lydia (Shen Dianxia)   沈殿霞
Sina   新浪
Sing Tao Daily   星岛日报
Sohu   搜狐
State Administration of Radio, Film and Television   中国国家广播电影电视总局
Ta Kung Pao   大公报
Television Broadcast Ltd (TVB)   电视广播有限公司 (无线)
Tencent   腾讯
The Analects of Confucius   《论语》
The Great Leap Forward   大跃进
Thunderstorm   《雷雨》
Ti, Lung (Di Long)   狄龙
Tian, Zhuangzhuang   田壮壮
tianya langzi   天涯浪子
To, Johnnie (Du Qifeng)   杜琪峰
Tong, Kent (Tang Zhenye)   汤镇业
Tsang, Kenneth (Zeng Jiang)   曾江
Tse, Patrick (Xie Xian)   谢贤
Tsui, Hark (Xu Ke)   徐克
TVB Five Tigers   无线五虎
Umbrella Movement   雨伞运动
Up to the Mountains and Down to the Countryside Movement   上山下乡运动
Wang, Ji   王姬
Water Margin Great Classical Novel   《水浒传》
wei   危
Wen Wei Po   文汇报
Wong, Anna May (Huang Liushuang)   黄柳霜
Wong, Felix Yat-wa (Huang Rihua)   黄日华
Wong, Jing (Wang Jing)   王晶
Wong, Joey (Wang Zuxian)   王祖贤
Wong, Wan-choi (Huang Yuncai)   黄允财
Wong, Yuen-san (Huang Yuanshen)   黄元申
Woo, John (Wu Yusen)   吴宇森
Wu, Cheng'en   吴承恩
Wu, Jacklyn Chien-lien (Wu Qianlian)   吴倩莲
Wu, Vivian (Wu Junmei)   邬君梅
Wu, Ziniu   吴子牛
Wudang   武当
xiake   侠客
xiao (kŏ)   孝
xiaosheng   小生
Yam, Kim-fai (Ren Jianhui)   任剑辉
yangren   洋人
Yee, Tung-shing (Er Dongsheng)   尔冬升
Yeh, Sally (Ye Qianwen)   叶倩文

Yen, Donnie (Zhen Zidan) 甄子丹

Yeoh, Michelle (Yang Ziqiong) 杨紫琼

yi 义

yiren 艺人

Yu, Hai 于海

Yu, On-on (Yu An'an) 余安安

Yuen, Siu-tien (Yuan Xiaotian) 袁小田

Yuen, Woo-ping (Yuan, Heping) 袁和平

yuliu bao 鱼柳包

Zhang, Tielin 张铁林

Zhang, Yimou 张艺谋

Zhang, Yu 张瑜

Zhang, Ziyi 章子怡

Zhao, Linshan 赵林山

zhongyuan 中原

zougou 走狗

Bibliography

Addison, Heather (2000), 'Hollywood, consumer culture, and the rise of "body shaping"', in David Desser and Garth S. Jowett (eds), *Hollywood Goes Shopping*, Minneapolis: University of Minnesota Press, pp. 3–33.

Ah, Mei (1999), 'The rumour of Ang Lee replacing the cast is collapsed: Chow Yun-fat going to the north to practice martial arts and get his hair shaved' [*Li An yijue chuanwen bugongzipo: Zhou Runfa beishang liangong titou*], *Ming Pao*, 17 July, C01.

Anon. (1987), 'Piteous Chow Yun-fat' [*kelian de Zhou Runfa*], *Cinemart*, no. 212, p. 51.

Anon. (1999), 'Stars of highest market value' [*zui ju shichang jiazhi de mingxing*], *Hong Kong Economic Times*, 4 June, A12.

Anon. (2000), 'Extramarital affairs in films' [*dianying zhong de hunwaiqing*], *Hong Kong Economic Times*, 3 October, C01.

Ansari, Zarminae (2000), '*Anna and the King*, etcetera, etcetera, etcetera', *The Tech*, vol. 119, issue 68, <http://tech.mit.edu/V119/N68/Anna__King.68a.html> (last accessed 15 October 2015).

Arber, Sara and Jay Ginn (1991), *Gender and Later Life: A Sociological Analysis of Resources and Constraints*, London: Sage Publications.

Armitage, Beth (n.d.), '*Anna and the King* (1999): knocking on Siam's door', *Popmatters*, <http://www.popmatters.com/review/anna-and-the-king/> (last accessed 15 October 2015).

Arnold, William (1999), '"Anna" doesn't compare as well to older versions', *Seattle Post-Intelligencer*, 17 December, <http://www.seattlepi.com/movies/annaq.shtml> (last accessed 10 September 2009).

Associated Press (2005), 'Chow returns to Hong Kong, star to appear in Hui's *Aunt's Postmodern Life*', *Variety*, 18 July, <http://www.variety.com/article/VR1117926113.html> (last accessed 27 October 2006).

Austin, Thomas (2002), *Hollywood, Hype and Audiences: Selling and Watching Popular Film in the 1990s*, Manchester: Manchester University Press.

Bai, Ying (2010), 'Chow Yun-fat and Donnie Yen joined 3D film *Monkey King*' [*3D dianying danao tiangong zhujue jiemi Zhou Runfa Zhen Zidan deng jiameng*], *Xinhuanet*, 12 December, <http://news.xinhuanet.com/2010–12/12/c_13645880.htm> (last accessed 28 October 2015).

Barker, Martin (2006), 'News, reviews, clues, interviews and other ancillary materials – a critique and research proposal', *Scope: On-line Film Studies Journal*, <http://www.

nottingham.ac.uk/scope/documents/2004/february-2004/barker.pdf > (last accessed 3 November 2015).

Beijing News (2006), 'Zhang Yimou tutoring Gong Li: Chow Yun-fat learning Mandarin from Ni Dahong' [*Zhang Yimou gei Gong Li 'kai xiaozao', Zhou Runfa xiang Ni Dahong xuexi*], Sina.com, 22 February, <http://ent.sina.com.cn/m/c/2006-02-22/2345994449.html> (last accessed 19 August 2006).

Bernard, Jami (1999), '"Anna and the King" get along royally', *New York Daily News*, 17 December, <http://www.nydailynews.com/archives/nydn-features/anna-king-royally article-1.845699> (last accessed 15 October 2015).

Berry, Chris (2003), '"What's big about the Big Film?": "De-Westernizing" the blockbuster in Korea and China', in Julian Stringer (ed.), *Movie Blockbusters*, London: Routledge, pp. 217–29.

Berry, Chris and Mary Farquhar (2006), *China on Screen*, New York: Columbia University Press.

Berry, Michael (2005), *Speaking in Image, Interviews with Contemporary Chinese Filmmakers*, New York: Columbia University Press, pp. 423–39.

Berry, Sarah (2000), *Screen Style: Fashion and Femininity in 1930s' Hollywood*, Minneapolis: University of Minnesota Press.

Bonner, Frances (2005), 'The celebrity in the text', in Jessica Evans and David Hesmondhalgh (eds), *Understanding Media: Inside Celebrity*, Maidenhead: Open University Press, pp. 58–96.

Bordwell, David (2000), *Planet Hong Kong: Popular Cinema and the Art of Entertainment*, London: Harvard University Press.

Box Office Moji (2015), 'Total grosses of all movies released in 1999', <http://www.boxofficemojo.com/yearly/chart/?yr=1999&p=.htm> (last accessed 4 September 2015).

Brook, Tom (2001), 'Hollywood's ageing he-men', BBC, 27 April, <http://news.bbc.co.uk/1/hi/entertainment/film/1300739.stm> (last accessed 21 October 2015).

Brooker, Will and Deborah Jermyn (2003), 'Interpretive communities, nation and ethnicity', in Will Brooker and Deborah Jermyn (eds), *The Audience Studies Reader*, London: Routledge, pp. 275–8.

Bruzzi, Stela (2005), *Bringing Up Daddy: Fatherhood and Masculinity in Post-War Hollywood*, London: BFI Publishing.

Bulag, Uradyn Erden (2002), *The Mongols at China's Edge: History and the Politics of National Unity*, Lanham: Rowman & Littlefield.

Butler, Jeremy G. (1991), 'Introduction', in Jeremy G. Butler (ed.), *Star Texts, Image and Performance in Film and Television*, Detroit: Wayne State University Press, pp. 7–16.

Carrell, Severin (2011), 'Middle-aged men at risk of "addiction" to plastic surgery', *Independent*, 7 April, <http://www.independent.co.uk/life-style/health-and-families/health-news/middle-aged-men-at-risk-of-addiction-to-plastic-surgery-5542431.html> (last accessed 21 October 2015).

Cavell, Stanley (2004), 'Reflections on the ontology of film', in Pamela Robertson Wojcik *(ed.), Movie Acting, The Film Reader*, London: Routledge, pp. 29–35.

CCTV (2015), 'Johnnie to back with Chow Yun-Fat in new film', video clip, 26 June, <http://english.cntv.cn/2015/06/26/VIDE1435291575607476.shtml> (last accessed 25 September 2015).

Chan, Gordon, Cheung Chi-shing, Kam Kwok-leung, Lai Kit, Lam Chiu-wing, Li Cheuk-to and Sek Kei [1990] (2000), 'Views on New Hong Kong films 1989–90', in Li Cheuk-to (ed.), *The 24th HK International Film Festival: Hong Kong Cinema '79–'89*, combined edition, Hong Kong: Leisure and Cultural Services Department, pp. 118–28.

Chan, Jachinson (2001), *Chinese American Masculinities: From Fu Manchu to Bruce Lee*, New York: Routledge.

Chan, Joseph Man, Lee Chin-chuan, Pan Zhong-Dang and So Clement Y. K. (2002), 'Domesticating international news: a comparative study of the coverage on the Hong Kong handover', *Mass Communication Research*, no. 73, pp. 1–27.

Chang, Justin (2005), 'Reggie Lee', *Variety*, 17 August, <http://www.variety.com/article/VR1117927662.html> (last accessed 18 November 2006).

Chen, Bin (2011), 'Chow Yun-fat plays the role of Cao Cao' [*Zhou Runfa yan Cao Cao*], *Beijing Evening News*, 13 September, <http://news.163.com/11/0913/15/7DRDTRCN00014AED.html> (last accessed 9 September 2015).

Chen, Yaocheng (1982), 'From the nightmare of nostalgia to the affliction of rootlessness – rethinking Ann Hui' [*cong huaijiu zhi yan dao wugen zhi yuan – sansi Xu Anhua*], *City Entertainment*, no. 98, pp. 22–6.

Chen, Yaocheng (1984), 'Hui's stiff interpretation of *Love in a Fallen City*' [*qing cheng zhi lian – Xu Anhua ying yi ji*], *City Entertainment*, no. 143, pp. 30–3.

Cheng, Che-ching (2001), 'Honorary Doctor of Letters: Mr Chow Yun-fat', *Address at 16th Congregation*, City University of Hong Kong, 14 November, <https://www.cityu.edu.hk/cityu/about/honorary/doc/chow-en.pdf> (last accessed 5 November 2015).

Cheng, Scarlet (2000), 'Art and action kick it up', *Los Angeles Times*, home edition, 12 November, p. 1.

Cheng, Yu (1985), 'The world according to everyday man – the ideology of Cantonese comedies' [*xiao renwu kan shijie – yueyu xijupian de yishi xingtai*], in Hong Kong Urban Council (ed.), *The 9th Hong Kong International Film Festival: The Traditions of Hong Kong Comedy*, Hong Kong: Hong Kong Urban Council, pp. 36–45.

Cheng, Yu (1988), 'The gambling streak as seen in Hong Kong movies', in Hong Kong Urban Council (ed.), *The 12th Hong Kong International Film Festival: Changes in Hong Kong Society through Cinema*, Hong Kong: Hong Kong Urban Council, pp. 29–33.

Cheng, Yu [1988] (2002), 'Uninvited guest: investigating the image of mainlander Chinese in 1980s Hong Kong cinema' [*bu su zhi ke: bashi niandai xianggang dianying de dalu laike xingxiang chutan*], in Wu Junxiong and Zhang Zhiwei (eds), *Reading Hong Kong Popular Cultures 1970–2000*, Hong Kong: Oxford University Press (China), pp. 181–6.

Cheuk, Pak Tong (2008), *Hong Kong New Wave Cinema 1978–2000*, Bristol: Intellect.

Cheung, Gary and Stuart Lau (2012), 'Love China or leave, Lu Ping tells Hong Kong's would-be secessionists', *South China Morning Post*, 1 November, <http://www.scmp.com/news/hong-kong/article/1074148/love-china-or-lump-it-lu-ping-tells-would-be-secessionists?page=all> (last accessed 28 October 2015).

Cheung, Mandy, Cindy Chow and Nellie Chow (n.d.), 'WTO and China's responses in the regulation of the traditional media', <http://newmedia.cityu.edu.hk/cyberlaw/gp13/intro.html> (last accessed 23 October 2015).

Cheung, Chi-wai (2012), 'Changes of representations of "gambling" in Hong Kong Films', in *Pop Hong Kong: Reading Hong Kong Popular Culture 2000–2010*, Hong Kong: Hong Kong Educational Publishing Company, pp. 146–54.

China.com (2006), 'Grand opening event of *Pirates of the Caribbean 2*: Chow Yun-fat playing a pirate captain as a guest star' [*jialebi haidao shengda kaimu, Zhou Runfa kechuan haidaotou*], 29 June, <http://fun.china.com/zh_cn/movie/news/205/20060629/13436047.html> (last accessed 9 August 2006).

Chinese Canadian Military Museum (n.d.), 'Chinese Canadian history', <http://www.ccmms.ca/chinese-canadian-history/> [last accessed 9 June 2015].

Chow, Yun-fat (1988), *12 Fun 10 Fun Chuen* [*shi'er fen shi fencun*], LP, Cinepoly Record Co. Ltd, Hong Kong.

Chow Yun-fat Goes Hollywood [2001] (2002), Jeffrey Schwaz (dir.), documentary, *The Replacement Killers* DVD special edition extra features, United States: Columbia Pictures, 2002.

Chu, Yingchi (2003), *Hong Kong Cinema, Coloniser, Motherland and Self*, London: Routledge Curzon.

Chu, Yiu-wai [1998] (2004a), 'Who am I? Postcolonial Hong Kong cinema in the age of global capitalism', in Esther M. K. Cheung and Chu Yiu-wai (eds), *Between Home and World: A Reader in Hong Kong Cinema*, Oxford: Oxford University Press, pp. 39–58.

Chu, Yiu-wai (2004b), 'Introduction: the politics of home, memory and diaspora', in Esther M. K. Cheung and Chu Yiu-wai (eds), *Between Home and World, A Reader in Hong Kong Cinema*, Oxford: Oxford University Press, pp. 112–26.

Chu, Yiu-wai (2005), 'Hybridity and (G)local Identity in Postcolonial Hong Kong Cinema', in Sheldon H. Lu and Emilie Yeh Yueh-yu (eds), *Chinese-Language Film: Historiography, Poetics, Politics*, Honolulu: University of Hawaii Press, pp. 312–28.

Chua, Lam, Shi Nansun, Lai Kit, Shu Kei, Sek Kei, Li Cheuk-to, Roger Garcia, and Kam Ping-hing [1987] (2000), 'Looking back at 1986', translated by Leong Mo-ling, in Li Cheuk-to (ed.), *The 24th HK International Film Festival: Hong Kong Cinema '79–'89*, combined edition, Hong Kong: Leisure and Cultural Services Department, pp. 92–103.

Churchill, Bonnie (1999), 'Beauty and the bugs: "Anna and the King"', CNN, 14 December, <http://archives.cnn.com/1999/SHOWBIZ/Movies/12/14/anna.king/index.html> (last accessed 15 October 2015).

Ciecko, Anne T. (1997), 'Transnational action: John Woo, Hong Kong, Hollywood', in Sheldon Lu Hsiao-peng (ed.), *Transnational Chinese Cinemas: Identity, Nationhood, Gender*, Honolulu: University of Hawaii Press, pp. 221–37.

Codell, Julie F. (2007), 'World cinema: joining local and global', in Julie F. Codell (ed.), *Genre, Gender, Race and World Cinema: An Anthology*, Malden: Blackwell Publishing, pp. 359–68.

Cohen, David S. (2005), 'Chow down for "Pirates 3" sequel skedded for summer 2007', *Variety*, 6 July, <http://www.variety.com/article/VR1117925539.html> (last accessed 18 November 2006).

Coker, Cheo Hodari (1997), 'Cover story: Mister Fat goes to Hollywood', *Los Angeles Times*, home edition, 13 July, p. 8.

Corliss, Richard (2000), 'Year of the Tiger', *Time*, 3 December <http://content.time.com/time/magazine/article/0,9171,90548-1,00.html> (last accessed 4 July 2016).

Curtin, Michael (2003), 'Television and trustworthiness in Hong Kong', in Lisa Parks and Shanti Kumar (eds), *Planet TV–A Global Television Reader*, London: New York University Press, pp. 243–61.

Curtin, Michael (2007), *Playing to the World's Biggest Audience: The Globalization of Chinese Film and TV*, Berkeley, University of California Press.

D'Alessandro, Anthony (2006), 'In the pipeline', *Variety*, 9 July, <http://www.variety.com/article/VR1117946443.html> (last accessed 18 November 2006).

Da, Wen (2005), 'Exploring Chow's brand new pirate image in the sequels of *Pirates of the Caribbean*' [*Zhou Runfa shengui qihang xuji haidao xin xingxiang baoguang*], *People's Daily*, 17 January, <http://ent.people.com.cn/GB/1082/3125475.html> (last accessed 22 August 2006).

Davis, Darrell William and Emilie Yeh Yueh-yu (2008), *East Asian Screen Industries*, London: British Film Institute.

De, Yu (1984), 'What are you defending for?' [*nimen weihu shenme*], *City Entertainment*, no. 144, p. 3.

Denzin, Norman K. (2002), *Reading Race: Hollywood and the Cinema of Racial Violence*, London: Sage Publications.

Desser, David (2005), 'Hong Kong film and the new cinephilia', in Meaghan Morris, Siu Leung Li and Stephen Chan Ching-kiu (eds), *Hong Kong Connections: Transnational Imagination in Action Cinema*, Durham: Duke University Press, pp. 205–21.

Desser, David (2006), 'Diaspora and national identity: exporting "China" through the Hong Kong cinema', in Elizabeth Ezra and Terry Rowden (eds), *Transnational Cinema: The Film Reader*, New York: Routledge, pp. 143–56.

Di, Di (2000), 'Chow Yun-fat and Zhang Ziyi are competing for Oscar' [*Zhou Runfa Zhang Ziyi jiaozhu aosika*], *Southern Metropolis Daily*, 1 August, n.p.

Director's Commentary on The Corruptor (1999), DVD extra features, DVD, United States: New Line Cinema.

Director's Commentary on The Replacement Killers (2002), DVD extra features, DVD, special edition, United States: Columbia Pictures.

Dyer, Richard [1979] (1998), *Stars*, new edition, London: British Film Institute.

Dyer, Richard [1986] (2004), *Heavenly Bodies: Film Stars and Society*, 2nd edition, London: Routledge.

Ebert, Roger (2003), 'Bulletproof monk', *Chicago Sun-Times*, 16 April, <http://rogerebert. suntimes.com/apps/pbcs.dll/article?AID=/20030416/REVIEWS/304160301/1023> (last accessed 21 October 2015).

Elliott, Dorinda (1999), 'The royal treatment', *Newsweek International*, 16 August, <http://abesapien.tripod.com/articles/anna_newsweek1.html> (last accessed 3 November 2015).

Ellis, John (1991), 'Stars as a cinematic phenomenon', in Jeremy G. Butler (ed.), *Star Texts, Image and Performance in Film and Television*, Detroit: Wayne State University Press, pp. 300–15.

Entgroup (2010), *China Film Industry Report 2009–2010*, <http://english.entgroup.cn/ report_detail.aspx?id=15> (last accessed 17 September 2015).

Entgroup (2015), *China Film Industry Report 2014–2015 (In Brief)*, <http://english.entgroup. cn/report_detail.aspx?id=29> (last accessed 17 September 2015).

Epstein, Rebecca L. (2007), 'Sharon Stone in a gap turtleneck', in Sean Redmond and Su Holmes (eds), *Stardom and Celebrity*, Los Angeles: Sage Publications, pp. 206–18.

Er, Dong (2003), 'Chow Yun-fat's new film lost box office but won charisma in America' [*Zhou Runfa xinpian meiguo shu piaofang ying meili*], SouthCN.com, 21 April, <http:// www.southcn.com/ent/celeb/zhourunfa/news/200312310555.htm> (last accessed 21 October 2015).

Evans, Jessica (2005), 'Introduction – Celebrity: what's the media got to do with it?', in Jessica Evans and David Hesmondhalgh (eds), *Understanding Media: Inside Celebrity*, Maidenhead: Open University Press, pp. 1–10.

Featherstone, Mike and Andrew Wernick (1995), 'Introduction', in Mike Featherstone and Andrew Wernick (eds), *Images of Aging: Cultural Representations of Later Life*, London: Routledge, pp. 1–15.

Feng, Lici (1982), 'Two pities – *The Postman Strikes Back* and *Bin Mei*' [*liang zhong wanxi – xunchengma yu bin mei*], *City Entertainment*, no. 88, p. 40.

Fleming, Michael (2005), '"Autumn" in China, Zhang to direct Chow, Gong in "Remembrance"', *Variety*, 5 August, <http://www.variety.com/article/VR1117927035. html> (last accessed 27 October 2006).

Fong, Leslie (1980), '*The Good, the Bad, and the Ugly*: Catch this splendid act', *Strait Times*, 9 August, <http://www.templeofchow.com/tvb/gall_manneto1.html> (last accessed 18 February 2007).

Ford, Stacilee (2008), *Mabel Cheung Yuen-ting's An Autumn's Tale*, Hong Kong: Hong Kong University Press.

Fore, Steve (1997), 'Jackie Chan and the cultural dynamics of global entertainment', in Sheldon Lu Hsiao-peng (ed.), *Transnational Chinese Cinemas: Identity, Nationhood, Gender*, Honolulu: University of Hawaii Press, pp. 239–62.

Fore, Steve (2004), 'Home, migration, identity: Hong Kong film workers join the Chinese diaspora', in Esther M. K. Cheung and Chu Yiu-wai (eds), *Between Home and World: A Reader in Hong Kong Cinema*, Oxford: Oxford University Press, pp. 85–99.

'From the (under)ground up: the making of *The Corruptor*' (1999), documentary, DVD extra features, DVD, United States: New Line Home Video.

Fu, Poshek (2000), 'The 1960s: modernity, youth culture, and Hong Kong Cantonese cinema', in Poshek Fu and David Desser (eds), *The Cinema of Hong Kong: History, Arts, Identity*, Cambridge: Cambridge University Press, pp. 71–89.

Gao, Siya (1985), 'The hat of "reality" is too big' [*xianshi de maozi tai da*], *City Entertainment*, no. 153, pp. 8–9.

Garcia, Roger [1981] (2000), 'The static image' in Li Cheuk-to (ed.), *The 24th HK International Film Festival: Hong Kong Cinema '79–'89*, combined edition, Hong Kong, Leisure and Cultural Services Department, pp. 27–32.

Ginn, Jay and Sara Arber (1999), 'Ageing and cultural stereotypes of older women', in Julia Johnson and Robert Slater (eds), *Ageing and Later Life*, London: Sage Publications, pp. 60–7.

Gledhill, Christine (1991), 'Introduction', in Christine Gledhill (ed.), *Stardom, Industry of Desire*, London: Routledge, pp. vii–xx.

Graham, Bob (1999), '"Anna's" long journey: Foster is luminous, but romantic epic bogs down when Chow leaps into action', *San Francisco Chronicle*, 17 December, C-1.

Gott, Merryn and Sharon Hinchliff (2003), 'Sex and ageing: a gendered issue', in Sara Arber, Kate Davidson and Jay Ginn (eds), *Gender and Ageing: Changing Roles and Relationships*, Maidenhead: Open University Press, pp. 63–78.

Gu, Zhenhuang (1990a), 'Obtain British citizenship shortly: the benefit of a British passport' [*juyingquan bujiu daoshou: yingguo huzhao dailai de haochu*], *Ming Pao Weekly*, no. 1155, pp. 88–9.

Gu, Zhenhuang (1990b), 'From the Christmas in Shanghai to the idea of "reverse-migration"' (*cong shanghai de shengdanjie dao fanxiang yimin de sikao*), *Ming Po Weekly*, no. 1104, pp. 86–7.

Guangdong TV Station (2006), '*Pirates of the Caribbean 2* blows the wind from China: Chow Yun-fat joins the cast' [*jialebi haidao 2 chui zhongguo feng*], QQ.com, 23 May, <http://ent.qq.com/a/20060523/000229.htm> (last accessed 9 August 2006).

Guo, Xiaoqin (2003), *State and Society in China's Democratic Transition: Confucianism, Leninism, and Economic Development*, New York: Routledge.

Guy Laroche (1987a), advertisement, *Ming Pao Weekly*, no. 933, p. 22; no. 995, p. 9; no. 996, p. 3; no. 997, p. 11; no. 998, p. 3.

Guy Laroche (1987b), advertisement, *Ming Pao Weekly*, no. 960, p. 12; no. 983, p. 7; no. 984, p. 20; no. 988, p. 11.

Guy Laroche (1987c), advertisement, *Ming Pao Weekly*, no. 964, p. 5.

Guy Laroche (1987d), advertisement, *Ming Pao Weekly*, no. 971, p. 3; no. 972, p. 3; no. 973, p. 5; no. 974, p. 3; no. 975, p. 3; no. 977, p. 3, and no. 979, p. 5.

Hafez, Kai (2007), *The Myth of Media Globalization*, translated by Alex Skinner, Cambridge: Polity Press.

He, Xiaoxin (2015), '*Ah-Long* partners reunited' [*Ah Lang tie sanjiao jijie*], Sina.com, 18 August, <http://dailynews.sina.com/gb/ent/film/sinacn/20150818/09376858535.html> (last accessed 20 September 2015).

Hearn, Jeff (1995), 'Imaging the ageing of men', in Mike Featherstone and Andrew Wernick (eds), *Images of Aging: Cultural Representations of Later Life*, London: Routledge, pp. 97–115.

Hepworth, Mike (1999), 'Old age in crime fiction', in Julia Johnson and Robert Slater (eds), *Ageing and Later Life*, London: Sage Publications, pp. 32–7.

Higbee, Will and Song Hwee Lim (2010), 'Concepts of transnational cinema: towards a critical transnationalism in film studies', *Transnational Cinemas*, vol. 1, issue 1, pp. 7–21.

Higson, Andrew (2004), 'Film acting and independent cinema', in Pamela Robertson Wojcik (ed.), *Movie Acting: The Film Reader*, London: Routledge, pp. 145–64.

Hjort, Mette (2010), 'On the plurality of cinematic transnationalism', in Nataša Ďurovičová and Kathleen Newman (eds), *World Cinemas: Transnational Perspectives*, New York: Routledge, pp. 12–33.

Holden, Stephen (1999), 'Anna and the King: what? no singing? is a puzzlement!', *New York Times*, 17 December, <http://www.nytimes.com/library/film/121799anna-film-review.html> (last accessed 15 October 2015).

Holmes, Su and Sean Redmond (2010), 'A journal in celebrity studies', *Celebrity Studies*, vol. 1, issue 1, pp. 1–10.

Holmlund, Chris (2002), *Impossible Bodies: Femininity and Masculinity at the Movies*, London: Routledge.

Hong, Jinyu and Ling Ni (1997), *Reporting Hong Kong's Return from the Newspapers around the World* [*quanqiu baokan lun huigui*], Hong Kong: Hong Kong Honour Publishing Company.

Hong Kong Economic Times (1999), 'Fat Gor is expecting the millennium with his new look of bald head and tiger fist' [*fa ge guangtou huzhua* Look *ying xinxi*], 2 November, C02.

Hong Kong Film Archive (n.d.a), *The Eighth Happiness*, <http://ipac.hkfa.lcsd.gov.hk/ipac/cclib/search/showBib.jsp?f=e&id=6553715948805> (last accessed 13 October 2015).

Hong Kong Film Archive (n.d.b), *God of Gamblers*, <http://ipac.hkfa.lcsd.gov.hk/ipac/cclib/search/showBib.jsp?f=e&id=65537112921605> (last accessed 13 October 2015).

Hong Kong Film Archive (n.d.c), *Now You See Love, Now You Don't*, <http://ipac.hkfa.lcsd.gov.hk/ipac/cclib/search/showBib.jsp?f=e&id=6553748972805> (last accessed 13 October 2015).

Hong Kong Film Archive (n.d.d), *Hard Boiled*, <http://ipac.hkfa.lcsd.gov.hk/ipac/cclib/search/showBib.jsp?f=e&id=65537106726405> (last accessed 13 October 2015).

Hong Kong Film Archive (n.d.e), *Full Contact*, <http://ipac.hkfa.lcsd.gov.hk/ipac/cclib/search/showBib.jsp?f=e&id=6553763718405> (last accessed 13 October 2015).

Hong Kong Legislative Council Police Tactical Unit (2002), *Government Policies on Frontier Closed Area*, CB (2)1713/01-02 (06) [*lifahui bao'an shiwu weiyuanhui 'bianjing jinqu zhengce' CB (2)1713/01-02 (06) hao wenjian*], <http://www.legco.gov.hk/yr01-02/chinese/panels/se/papers/se0502cb2-1713-6c.pdf> (last accessed 30 January 2015).

Hu, Chunhui, Li Gucheng and Ren, Shaoling (1998), *Hong Kong's Position and Role in the Strait Relationship during the Post-97 Era* [*jiuqi hou xianggang zai liang'an guanxi zhong de diwei yu zuoyong*], Hong Kong: Chu Hai College of High Education.

Huang, Zhi (1985), 'New Wave and *Woo Viet*: a special publication for the re-screening of *The Story of Woo Viet*' [*xinchao cangsang hua Hu Yue, Hu Yue de gushi chongying tekan*], *City Entertainment*, no. 178, pp. 25–8.

Hunt, Leon (2003), *Kung Fu Cult Masters*, London: Wallflower Press.
Imdb (n.d.), 'Trivia of *Pirates of Caribbean: At World's End*', <http://www.imdb.com/title/tt0449088/trivia?ref_=tt_ql_2> (last accessed 23 October 2015).
Iritani, Evelyn and Marla Matzer (1998), 'Fox gives up on Thailand for "King" remake', *Los Angeles Times*, home edition, 11 November, p. 1.
Jameson, Fredric (2010), 'Globalization and hybridization', in Nataša Ďurovičová and Kathleen Newman (eds), *World Cinemas: Transnational Perspectives*, New York: Routledge, pp. 315–19.
Jancovich, Mark (2004), '"Charlton Heston is an axiom": spectacle and performance in the development of the blockbuster', in Andy Willis (ed.), *Film Stars: Hollywood and Beyond*, Manchester: Manchester University Press, pp. 51–70.
Jenkins, Henry (2000), 'Reception theory and audience research: the mystery of the vampire's kiss', in Christine Gledhill and Linda Williams (eds), *Reinventing Film Studies*, London: Arnold, pp. 162–82.
Ji, Si (1988), 'Chow Yun-fat complains Hong Kong lacks good screenwriters' [*Zhou Runfa zeguai xianggang meiyou hao bianju*], *Cinemart*, no. 226, pp. 24–5.
Jia, Leilei (2003), 'Sword and heart: *Crouching Tiger, Hidden Dragon*'s double texts' [*jian yu xin – wohucanglong de shuangchong wenben*], in China Film Yearbook Press (ed.), *China Film Yearbook 2002*, Beijing: China Film Yearbook Press, pp. 237–43.
Keys Secondary School Textbook of Chinese [*qisi zhongguo yuwen*] (2003), level 1, no. 2, Hong Kong: Keys Press.
King, Barry (1987), 'The star and the commodity: notes towards a performance theory of stardom', *Cultural Studies*, vol. 1, no. 2, pp. 145–61.
King, Barry [1985] (1991), 'Articulating stardom', in Jeremy G. Butler (ed.), *Star Texts: Image and Performance in Film and Television*, Detroit: Wayne State University Press, pp. 125–54.
King, Geoff (2002), *Film Comedy*, London: Wallflower Press.
Kirby, Michael (1995), 'On acting and not-acting', in Phillip B. Zarrilli (ed.), *Acting (Re)considered: Theories and Practices*, London: Routledge, pp. 43–58.
Koehler, Robert (2003), 'Bulletproof monk', *Variety*, 14 April, <http://www.variety.com/review/VE1117920496.html?categoryid=31&cs=1&p=0> (last accessed 21 October 2015).
Kracauer, Siegfried (2004), 'Remarks on the actor', in Pamela Robertson Wojcik (ed.), *Movie Acting: The Film Reader*, London: Routledge, pp. 19–27.
Krämer, Peter and Alan Lovell (1999), 'Introduction', in Alan Lovell and Peter Krämer (eds), *Screen Acting*, London: Routledge, pp. 1–19.
Krutnik, Frank (2003), 'Introduction', in Frank Krutnik (ed.), *Hollywood Comedians: The Reader*, London: Routledge, pp. 1–18.
Kwong, Peter (2002), *New Chinatown, Contemporary Chinese Community in America* [*xin tangrenjie: dangdai meiguo huaren shequ*], Beijing: World Affairs Press.
Lamb, David (2000), 'World perspective; media; Thai movie ban shows respect for King supersedes freedoms', *Los Angeles Times*, home edition, 12 February, A2.
LaSalle, Mick (2003), 'Chow's "*Bulletproof Monk*" has few comedic holes', *Chronicle Movie Critic*, 16 April, D-1.
Lau, Jenny Kwok Wah (1998), 'Besides fists and blood: Hong Kong comedy and its master of the eighties', *Cinema Journal*, vol. 37, no. 2, pp. 18–34.
Law, Anna O. (2010), *The Immigration Battle in American Courts*, Cambridge: Cambridge University Press.
Law, Kar (1991), 'The state and trend of the Hong Kong film market in the 1980s' [*bashi niandai xianggang dianying shichang zhuangkuang yu chaoliu zoushi*], in Hong Kong Urban Council (ed.), *The 15th Hong Kong International Film Festival: Hong Kong Cinema in the*

Eighties – A Comparative Study with Western Cinema, Hong Kong: Hong Kong Urban Council, pp. 30–8.

Lee, Paul S. N. (1991), 'The absorption and indigenization of foreign media cultures: Hong Kong as a cultural meeting point of East and West', in Hong Kong Urban Council (ed.), *The 15th Hong Kong International Film Festival: Hong Kong Cinema in the Eighties – A Comparative Study with Western Cinema*, Hong Kong, Urban Council, pp. 80–6.

Legge, James (trans.) (1861), *The Analects of Confucius*, in *The Chinese Classics*, vol. 1, Chinese Text Project, <http://ctext.org/analects/li-ren?searchu=son&searchmode=showall#result> (last accessed 28 October 2015).

Leung, Noong-kong [1981] (2000), 'Notes on the Hong Kong cinema', in Hong Kong Leisure and Cultural Services Department (ed.), *The 24th Hong Kong International Film Festival: Hong Kong Cinema '79–'89*, combined edition, Hong Kong: Leisure and Cultural Services Department, pp. 33–9.

Levy, Emanuel (1999), 'Anna and the King: romantic epic-adventure', *Variety*, 29 November, <http://www.variety.com/review/VE1117759803.html?categoryid=31&cs=1&p=0> (last accessed 15 October 2015).

Li, Cheuk-to (1982), 'General criticism on four Ann Hui's films II' [*zonglun Xu Anhua de si bu dianying (zhong)*], *City Entertainment*, no. 96, pp. 25–7.

Li, Feng (2009), '*Confucius* finished the filming' [*dianying kongzi shaqing*], *China Online*, 3 September, <http://gb.cri.cn/27564/2009/09/03/4212s2611334.htm> (last accessed 28 October 2015).

Li, Huazeng (2006), 'Zhang Yimou started shooting the most expensive film, paired Gong Li and Chow Yun-fat' [*Zhang Yimou kaipai zui 'gui' dianying, cuohe Gong Li Zhou Runfa*], 15 June, <http://www.cq.xinhuanet.com/2006-06/15/content_7272127.htm> (last accessed 23 October 2015).

Li, Lu (2010), 'A prophet of melancholies: commemorating Cao Yu's centenary' [*kumen de xianzhi: ji'nian Cao Yu bainian dancheng*], <http://www.people.com.cn/GB/198221/1988 19/204159/12915567.html> (last accessed 23 October 2015).

Li, Ziyu (1992), 'Chow Yun-fat has become a part-time advertisement star' [*Zhou Runfa yishi jianzhi guanggao mingxing*], *Cinemart*, no. 269, pp. 22–3.

Liang, Kuan [1981] (2002), 'The story of the small box – watching long-length TV serials' [*xiao xiangzi de gushi – kankan dianshi chang pian ju*], in Wu Junxiong and Zhang Zhiwei (eds), *Reading Hong Kong Popular Cultures 1970–2000*, Hong Kong: Oxford University Press (China), pp. 120–7.

Liang, Liang (1992), 'Hong Kong Cinema under the shadow of "97"' [*jiuqi yinying xia de xianggang dianying*], *City Entertainment*, no. 341, pp. 62–5.

Liang, Ning (2004), 'Chow Yun-fat will play a pirate in the sequels of *Pirates of the Caribbean*' [*Zhou Runfa jiepai shenggui qihang xuji, yan hai shang xiaoxiong*], CRI Online, 18 December, <http://gb.chinabroadcast.cn/6851/2004/12/18/1326@395566.htm> (last accessed 26 August 2006).

Lin, Bin (1990), 'Chow Yun-fat: from box office poison to box office guarantee' [*Zhou Runfa: you piaofang duyao dao piaofang baozheng*], in *Cinemart*, no. 240, pp. 36–7.

Lin, Guan (2000), 'Martial arts and light body skills in front the eyes' [*wuda zhashi qinggong xian yan qian*], *Ta Kung Pao*, 15 July, C08.

Liu, Guojun (2000), 'Exceeding naturalness: strength of style – exploring the notion of performance in Hong Kong cinema' [*sheng zi ziran, gui zai fengge – xianggang dianying biaoyan guannian tansuo*], in Cai Hong Kong, Song Jialing and Liu Guiqing (eds), *80 Years of Hong Kong Cinema*, Beijing: Beijing Broadcasting Institute Press, pp. 105–14.

Lo, Kwai-cheung [2001] (2004), 'Double negations: Hong Kong cultural identity in

Hollywood's transnational representations', in Esther M. K. Cheung and Chu Yiu-wai (eds), *Between Home and World, A Reader in Hong Kong Cinema*, Oxford: Oxford University Press, pp. 59–84.

Lo, Wai Luk (1999), 'A child without a mother, an adult without a motherland: a study of Ann Hui's films', in Provisional Urban Council of Hong Kong (ed.), *The 23rd Hong Kong International Film Festival: Hong Kong New Wave, The Twenty Years After*, Hong Kong, Provisional Urban Council of Hong Kong, pp. 65–71.

Louie, Kam (2002), *Theorising Chinese Masculinity: Society and Gender in China*. Cambridge: Cambridge University Press.

Lu, Sheldon H. (2005a), 'Hong Kong diaspora film and transnational television drama: from homecoming to exile to flexible citizenship', in Sheldon H. Lu and Emilie Yeh Yueh-yu (eds), *Chinese-Language Film: Historiography, Poetics, Politics*, Honolulu: University of Hawaii Press, pp. 298–311.

Lu, Sheldon H. (2005b), 'Crouching tiger, hidden dragon, bouncing angels: Hollywood, Taiwan, Hong Kong, and transnational cinema', in Sheldon H. Lu and Emilie Yeh Yueh-yu (eds), *Chinese-Language Film: Historiography Poetics, Politics*, Honolulu: University of Hawaii Press, pp. 220–33.

Lu, Sheldon H. (2014), 'Genealogies of four critical paradigms in Chinese-language film studies', in Audrey Yue and Olivia Khoo (eds), *Sinophone Cinemas*, Basingstoke: Palgrave Macmillan, pp. 13–25.

Luo, Jianming (1984), '*Love in a Fallen City*: from novel to film' [*qing cheng zhi lian: cong xiaoshuo dao dianying*], *City Entertainment*, no. 142, pp. 34–5.

Luo, Weiming, Tian Shi and Lin Sange (1991), 'Shining star' [*shanliang zhi xing*], *City Entertainment*, no. 320, pp. 30–4.

Lusted, David [1984] (1991), 'The glut of the personality', in Christine Gledhill (ed.), *Stardom, Industry of Desire*, London: Routledge, pp. 253–61.

Ma, Hui (1985), 'Special interview: the impression of Chow Yun-fat' [*renwu zhuanfang: yinxiang Zhou Runfa*], *City Entertainment*, no. 177, pp 19–20.

Ma, Junxiong (1988), 'Recording 97: making history' [*jilu jiuqi: chuangzao lishi*], in Hong Kong Urban Council (ed.), *The 12th Hong Kong International Film Festival: Changes in Hong Kong Society through Cinema*, Hong Kong: Hong Kong Urban Council, pp. 93–5.

Ma, Laurence J. C. (2003), 'Space, place, and transnationalism in the Chinese diaspora', in Laurence J. C. Ma and Carolyn Cartier (eds), *The Chinese Diaspora: Space, Place, Mobility, and Identity*, Oxford: Rowman & Littlefield, pp. 1–49.

Ma, Sheng-mei (2005), 'Kung Fu films in diaspora: death of the bamboo hero', in Laikwan Pang and Day Wong (eds), *Masculinities and Hong Kong Cinema*, Hong Kong: Hong Kong University Press, pp. 101–18.

Marchetti, Gina (1991), 'Ethnicity, the cinema and cultural studies', in Lester D. Friedman (ed.), *Unspeakable Images: Ethnicity and the American Cinema*, Urbana: University of Illinois Press, pp. 277–307.

Marchetti, Gina (2001), 'Hollywood's construction, deconstruction, and reconstruction of the "Orient"', in Roger Garcia (ed.), *Out of the Shadows: Asians in American Cinema*, Milano: Edizioni Olivares, pp. 35–57.

Marshall, P. David (2006a), 'Induction', in P. David Marshall (ed.), *The Celebrity Culture Reader*, New York: Routledge, pp. 1–20.

Marshall, P. David (2006b), 'Introduction to Part Two: The textual and the extra-textual dimensions of the public persona', in P. David Marshall (ed.), *The Celebrity Culture Reader*, New York: Routledge, pp. 179–80.

Martin, Michael F. (2007), *CRS Report for Congress: Hong Kong: Ten Years After the*

Handover, United States Foreign Affairs, Defense, and Trade Division: Congressional Research Service.

McCabe, Kristen (2012), 'Chinese immigrants in the United States', Migration Policy Institute, <http://www.migrationpolicy.org/article/chinese-immigrants-united-states-1/> (last accessed 15 October 2015).

McCarthy, Todd (2000), 'Review: *Crouching Tiger, Hidden Dragon*', *Variety*, 18 May, <http://www.variety.com/review/VE1117780997.html?categoryid=31&cs=1&p=0> (last accessed 21 October 2015).

McDonald, Paul (1998), 'Reconceptualising stardom', a supplementary chapter in Richard Dyer, *Stars*, London: BFI Publishing, pp. 177–200.

McDonald, Paul (2000), *The Star System: Hollywood Production of Popular Identities*, London: Wallflower Press.

Ming Pao (2000), '*Crouching Tiger, Hidden Dragon* has to win the box office' [*wohucanglong piaofang xu sheng bu xu bai*], 2 July, C07.

Ming Pao Weekly (1987), 'Events of the week' [*yi zhou dashi*], no. 967, 24 May, p. 87.

Minois, Georges (1999), 'History of old age in Western culture and society', in Julia Johnson and Robert Slater (eds), *Ageing and Later Life*, London: Sage Publications, pp. 327–31.

Mo, Jianwei (2002), 'Hong Kong film industry and film policy' [*xianggang dianying gongye yu zhengce*], *Media Digest*, December, <http://www.rthk.org.hk/mediadigest/20021216_76_55191.html> (last accessed 3 November 2015).

Mohamedbhai, Goolam (2012), 'Confucius institutes: China's global presence', *Inside Higher Ed*, 2 September, <https://www.insidehighered.com/blogs/world-view/confucius-institutes-china%E2%80%99s-global-presence> (last accessed 28 October 2015).

Morris, Larry A. (1997), *The Male Heterosexual, Lust in His Loins, Sin in His Soul?* London: Sage Publications.

Moseley, Rachel (2000), *Growing Up with Audrey Hepburn, Text, Audience, Resonance*, Manchester: Manchester University Press.

NetEast (2003), '*Bullet Proof Monk* performed poorly in box office, but Chow Yun-fat received positive criticism' [*fangdan wuseng piaofang cha Zhou Runfa zhao huo haoping*], 21 April, <http://ent.163.com/edit/030421/030421_161659.html> (last accessed 21 October 2015).

New York Times (2000), '*Crouching Tiger, Hidden Dragon*: fans, be prepared for heart and feminism', 9 October, http://www.nytimes.com/2000/10/09/arts/09TIGE.html> (last accessed 21 October 2015).

Ni, Zifang (2009), 'Hu Mei comments on the cast: Chow wins for his charisma' [*Hu Mei tan kongzi xuanjue, Zhou Runfa yi qizhi qusheng*], *Qilu Evening News*, 31 March, <http://yule.sohu.com/20090331/n263106966.shtml> (last accessed 28 October 2015).

Nowell-Smith, Geoffrey (2000), 'How films mean, or, from aesthetics to semiotics and halfway back again', in Christine Gledhill and Linda Williams (eds), *Reinventing Film Studies*, London: Arnold, pp. 8–17.

Ong, Aihwa (1999), *Flexible Citizenship: The Cultural Logics of Transnationality*, Durham: Duke University Press.

Original poster of *The Hunter, The Butterfly and The Crocodile* (1976), collection from Hong Kong Film Archive.

Original promotion booklet for *The Last Affair* (1983), collection from Hong Kong Film Archive.

Original promotion booklet for *Love in a Fallen City* (1984), collection from Hong Kong Film Archive.

Original promotion leaflets for *Story of Woo Viet* (1981), collection from Hong Kong Film Archive.

Original promotion leaflets for *Their Private Lives* (1978), collection from Hong Kong Film Archive.

Original theatrical trailer for *The Replacement Killers* (1998), video clip, United States: Columbia Pictures.

Pan, Bingchang (1987), 'The Chow Yun-fat I know' [*wo suo renshi de Zhou Runfa*], *Cinemart*, no. 212, pp. 22–3.

Pan, Bingchang (1989), 'Chow Yun-fat: gained the fame and fortune, lost the freedom' [*Zhou Runfa suiran you ming you li, que shiqu zizhu, ziyou, ziwo*], in *Cinemart*, no. 230, pp. 22–3.

Pang, Bei and Zheng Xiang (2005), *Romantic Heroic Icon: Chow Yun-fat's Private Album* [*langman yingxiong ouxiang: Zhou Runfa sijia xiangce*], Beijing: The Writers Publishing House, <http://book.sina.com.cn/nzt/ent/zhourenfasijiaxiangce.shtml> (last accessed 5 May 2006).

Pang, Laikwan (2005), 'The diversity of masculinities in Hong Kong cinema', in Laikwan Pang and Day Wong (eds), *Masculinities and Hong Kong Cinema*, Hong Kong: Hong Kong University Press, pp. 1–14.

Parker-Pope, Tara (2008), 'The midlife crisis goes global', *New York Times*, 30 January, <http://well.blogs.nytimes.com/2008/01/30/the-midlife-crisis-goes-global/> (last accessed 21 October 2015).

Pearson, Roberta E. (2004), '"Bright particular star': Patrick Stewart, Jean-Luc Picard, and Cult Television", in Sara Gwenllian-Jones and Roberta E. Pearson (eds), *Cult Television*, Minneapolis: University of Minnesota Press, pp. 61–80.

Perkins, Tessa (2000), 'Who (and what) is it for?', in Christine Gledhill and Linda Williams (eds), *Reinventing Film Studies*, London: Arnold, pp. 76–95.

Poy, Vivienne and Huhua Cao (2011), *The China Challenge: Sino-Canadian Relations in the 21st Century*, Ottawa: University of Ottawa Press.

Price, John (2012), *Orienting Canada: Race, Empire, and the Transpacific*, Vancouver: UBC Press.

Qi, Fuhui (1984), 'Delicate relationship of a (love) triangle' [*weimiao de sanjiao guanxi*], *City Entertainment*, no. 149, p. 22.

Qiao, Chu (1991), 'Shining star: a history of Hong Kong people – Chow Yun-fat' [*shanliang zhi xing: xianggangren de yiduan lishi – Zhou Runfa*], *City Entertainment*, no. 310, pp. 20–5.

Redmond, Sean and Su Holmes (2007a), 'Introduction: what's in a reader?', in Sean Redmond and Su Holmes (eds), *Stardom and Celebrity: A Reader*, Los Angeles: Sage Publications, pp. 1–11.

Redmond, Sean and Su Holmes (2007b), 'Introduction: consuming fame/becoming famous? Celebrity and its audience', in Sean Redmond and Su Holmes (eds), *Stardom and Celebrity: A Reader*, London: Sage Publications, pp. 308–12.

Ronald, Skeldon (1994), 'Hong Kong in an international migration system', in Ronald Skeldon (ed.), *Reluctant Exiles? Migration from Hong Kong and the New Overseas Chinese*, Hong Kong: Hong Kong University Press, pp. 21–51.

Rojeck, Chris (2001), *Celebrity*, London: Reaktion Books.

Rosen, Stanley (2006), 'Hollywood and the Great Wall', *Los Angeles Times*, 18 June, <http://articles.latimes.com/2006/jun/18/opinion/op-rosen18> (last accessed 23 October 2015).

Salaff, Janet W. and Wong Siu-lun (1997), 'Globalization of Hong Kong's people: international migration and the family', in Gerard A. Postiglione and James T. H. Tang (eds), *Hong Kong's Reunion with China: The Global Dimensions*, New York: M.E. Sharpe, pp. 200–21.

Sandell, Jillian [1994] (2001), 'A better tomorrow? American masochism and Hong Kong action films', *Bright Lights Film Journal*, issue 13, <http://www.brightlightsfilm.com/31/hk_better1.html> (last accessed 3 November 2015).

Seidman, Steve (1991), *Romantic Longings: Love in America, 1830–1980*, New York: Routledge.

Sek, Kei (1985), 'The city and the village', in Hong Kong Urban Council (ed.), *The 9th Hong Kong International Film Festival: The Traditions of Hong Kong Comedy*, Hong Kong: Hong Kong Urban Council, pp. 27–35.

Sek, Kei (1988), 'The social psychology of Hong Kong cinema', in Hong Kong Urban Council (ed.), *The 12th Hong Kong International Film Festival: Changes in Hong Kong Society Through Cinema*, Hong Kong: Hong Kong Urban Council, pp. 10–20.

Sek, Kei [1991] (1999a), 'Achievement and crisis: Hong Kong Cinema in the'80s', in Hong Kong Urban Council (ed.), *The 15th Hong Kong International Film Festival: Hong Kong Cinema in the Eighties – A Comparative Study with Western Cinema*, revised edition, Hong Kong: Hong Kong Urban Council, pp. 54–63.

Sek, Kei [1981] (1999b), '*The Story of Woo Viet* (I) – the extremity of escape, profusion of sadness' [*Hu Yue de gushi (yi) – taowang juejing, beige kangkai*], in *The Collected Film Criticism: The Approach of New Wave Cinema I*, vol. 1, Hong Kong: Ciwenhua Tang/Subculture Ltd, 1999), pp. 41–2.

Sek, Kei [1985] (1999c), '*The Story of Woo Viet* (II) – the product of '81: song of the exile' [*Hu Yue de gushi (er): bayi zuopin: piaoling zhi ge*], in *The Collected Film Criticism: The Approach of New Wave Cinema I*, vol. 1, Hong Kong: Ci Wenhua Tang/Subculture Ltd, pp. 45–6.

Sek, Kei [1984] (1999d), '*Love in a Fallen City* – too much dialogue; too little narrative' [*qing cheng zhi Lian – duibai tai duo, juqing tai shao*], in *The Collected Film Criticism: The Approach of New Wave Cinema I*, vol. 1, Hong Kong: Ci Wenhua Tang/Subculture Ltd, pp. 59–60.

Sek, Kei [1982] (1999e), '*The Postman Strikes Back* – a unique style and excellent duel' [*xunchengma – bieju fengwei, juedou chuse*], in *The Collected Film Criticism: The Approach of New Wave Cinema II*, vol. 2, Hong Kong: Ci Wenhua Tang/Subculture Ltd, pp. 169–70.

Sek, Kei [1985] (1999f), 'Review *Women* again – agile techniques' [*zai tan nüren xin – shoufa lingmin*], in *The Collected Film Criticism: From Prosperity to Crisis*, vol. 4, Hong Kong: Ci Wenhua Tang/Subculture Ltd, pp. 7–8.

Sek, Kei [1986] (1999g), '*The Lunatics* – a real picture of the society, great techniques' [*dianlao zhengzhuan shehui xieshi, shoufa keguan*], in *The Collected Film Criticism: From Prosperity to Crisis*, vol. 3, Hong Kong: Ci Wenhua Tang/Subculture Ltd, 1999, pp. 175–6.

Sek, Kei [1986] (1999h), 'The counter promotion of the protest – the lunatics and the issue of mental illness' [*kangyi de fan xuanchuan – dianlao zhengzhuan yu jingshen wenti*], in *The Collected Film Criticism: From Prosperity to Crisis*, vol. 3, Hong Kong: Ci Wenhua Tang/Subculture Ltd, pp. 177–8.

Sek, Kei [1991] (1999i), 'Scribble on *Once a Thief*' [*zongheng sihai zatan*], in *The Collected Film Criticism: From Prosperity to Crisis*, vol. 4, Hong Kong: Ci Wenhua Tang/Subculture Ltd, pp. 35–7.

Sek, Kei [1988] (1999j), '*The Diary of a Big Man* – the politics of bigamous comedies' [*dazhangfu riji: qiren xiju de zhengzhixing*], in *The Collected Film Criticism: Style and Features of Eight Celebrated Filmmakers*, vol. 6, Hong Kong: Ci Wenhua Tang/Subculture Ltd, pp. 105–6.

Sek, Kei (2000), 'Following King Hu's footsteps by adding love and desire – rethinking *Crouching Tiger, Hidden Dragon*' [*jicheng Hu Jinquan zengtian qing yu yu – zaitan wohucanglong*], *Ming Pao*, 10 July, C06.

Sek, Kei, Law Kar, Shu Kei, Lam Chiu-wing, Li Cheuk-to and Bryan Chang [1988] (2000), 'A Review of the 1987 Hong Kong cinema', translated by Maria Ho, in Li Cheuk-to (ed.),

The 24th HK International Film Festival: Hong Kong Cinema '79–'89, combined edition, Hong Kong: Leisure and Cultural Services Department, pp. 104–11.

Shan, Zong (2006), 'Producer of *Curse of the Golden Flower*, Zhang Weiping, denies the report of Chow Yun-fat's arrogance' [*Zhou Runfa huangjinjia shua dapai? Zhang Weiping: mei zhe hui shi*], Sina.com, 28 April, <http://ent.sina.com.cn/m/c/2006-04-28/01181067570.html> (last accessed 16 June 2006).

Short, Stephen (1999), 'I felt like Sisyphus', *Time Asia*, vol. 154, no. 25, <http://www.time.com/time/asia/magazine/99/1227/cinema.tennant.html> (last accessed 16 September 2009).

Sichuan Daily (2006), '*Golden Flower* starts filming: Chow Yun-fat's salary is calculated in Hollywood model' [*huangjinjia zhengshi kaipai: Zhou Runfa haolaiwu moshi jixin*], Sina.com, 22 February, <http://ent.sina.com.cn/m/c/2006-02-22/1043993587.html> (last accessed 16 August 2006).

Silverstone, Roger (1994), *Television and Everyday Life*, London: Routledge.

Sina.com (2006a), '*Pirates of the Caribbean 3* starts filming in Singapore: Fat Gor presents a pirate image' [*jialebi haidao 3 xinjiapo kaipai, fa ge yi haidao xingxiang shiren*], 15 July, <http://vshow.sina.com.cn/news/2006-07-15/2643340.html> (last accessed 6 November 2006).

Sina.com (2006b), 'Co-starring with Chow Yun-fat, Rolling Stone guitarist becomes the guest star of "Pirates"' [*gunshi jitashou kechuan haidao yu Zhou Runfa yan duishouxi*], 3 July, <http://ent.sina.com.cn/m/f/2006-07-03/02111143621.html> (last accessed 27 October 2006).

Sina.com (2006c), *The First News Briefing of Curse of the Golden Flower* [*huangjinjia shou kai fabuhui, Zhang, Zhou, Gong san dawan jushou*], video clip, 11 March, <http://ent.sina.com.cn/m/c/2006-03-11/17321012884.html> (last accessed 15 July 2006).

Sina.com (2006d), *Guo Degang Hosts the News Briefing of Curse of the Golden Flower* [*Guo Degang gaoxiao lingxian huangjinjia fabuhui*], video clip, 17 April, <http://ent.sina.com.cn/m/c/2006-04-17/17381052637.html> (last accessed 15 July 2006).

Sing Tao Daily (2000), 'Ang Lee: one film: one adventure' [*Li An: yi bu dianying: yi ci maoxian*], 29 June, A35.

Skeldon, Ronald (1994), 'Hong Kong in an international migration system', in Ronald Skeldon (ed.), *Reluctant Exiles? Migration from Hong Kong and the New Overseas Chinese*, Hong Kong: Hong Kong University Press, pp. 21–51.

Skeldon, Ronald (2004), 'China: from exceptional case to global participant', *Migration Policy Institute*, <http://www.migrationpolicy.org/article/china-exceptional-case-global-participant> (last accessed 15 October 2015).

Sky News (2007), 'What men spend on mid-life crisis', 2 September, <http://news.sky.com/story/538114/what-men-spend-on-mid-life-crisis> (last accessed 21 October 2015).

Smith, R. J. (1995), 'The coolest actor in the world', *Los Angeles Times*, home edition, 12 March, p. 10.

Soennichsen, John Robert (2011), *The Chinese Exclusion Act of 1882*, Santa Barbara: Greenwood.

Solvil et Titus (1988), advertisement, video clip, Hong Kong, <https://www.youtube.com/watch?v=rwapAq_Wvl4> (accessed 12 October 2015).

Solvil et Titus (1992), advertisement, video clip, Hong Kong, <https://www.youtube.com/watch?v=7DbsjRuFbv8> (last accessed 12 October 2015).

Solvil et Titus (1994), advertisement, video clip, Hong Kong, <http://www.youtube.com/watch?v=OtQpHpMn4Fk&feature=related> (accessed 12 October 2015).

Song, Fangcan (2004), 'After a two-year relaxing holiday, Chow Yun-fat is going to play a

Chinese pirate' [*jieshu liangnian youchang jiaqi hou fuchu, Zhou Runfa jiang banyan zhongguo haidao*], Chinanews.com, 16 December, <http://www.chinanews.com.cn/news/2004/2004-12-16/26/517607.shtml> (last accessed 29 August 2006).

Song, Lin (2004), 'When Chow Yun-fat met Carol Cheng: *The Good, the Bad, and the Ugly*' [*dang Zhou Runfa yudao Zheng Yuling: wang zhong ren*], CRI Online, 20 December <http://gb.cri.cn/6851/2004/12/20/113@397001.htm> (last accessed 26 February 2007).

Song, Weijie (2007), 'Space, swordsmen, and utopia: the dualistic imagination in Jin Yong's narratives', in Ann Huss and Jianmei Liu (eds), *The Jin Yong Phenomenon: Chinese Martial Arts Fiction and Modern Chinese Literary History*, New York: Cambria Press, pp. 155–78.

Squires, Sally (1999), 'Midlife without a crisis', *Washington Post*, 9 April, Z20.

Stacey, Jackie (1991), 'Feminine fascinations, forms of identification in star–audience relations', in Christine Gledhill (ed.), *Stardom, Industry of Desire*, London: Routledge, pp. 141–65.

Staiger, Janet (2000), *Perverse Spectators: The Practices of Film Reception*, New York: New York University Press.

Staiger, Janet (2005), *Media Reception Studies*, New York: New York University Press.

Steinmetz, Devora (1991), *From Father to Son: Kinship, Conflict and Continuity in Genesis*, Louisville: Westminster/John Knox Press.

Stokes, Lisa Odham and Michael Hoover (1999), *City on Fire: Hong Kong Cinema*, London: Verso.

Stringer, Julian (2003a), 'Introduction', in Julian Stringer (ed.), *Movie Blockbusters*, London: Routledge, pp. 1–14.

Stringer, Julian (2003b), 'Scrambling Hollywood: Asian stars/Asian American star cultures', in Thomas Austin and Martin Barker (eds), *Contemporary Hollywood Stardom*, London: Arnold, pp. 229–42.

Stringer, Julian (2004), '"Your tender smiles give me strength": paradigms of masculinity in John Woo's *A Better Tomorrow* and *The Killer*', in Esther M. K. Cheung and Chu Yiu-wai (eds), *Between Home and World, A Reader in Hong Kong Cinema*, Oxford: Oxford University Press, pp. 437–58.

Studlar, Gaylyn (2000), '"Chi-Chi Cinderella": Audrey Hepburn as couture countermodel', in David Desser and Garth S. Jowett (eds), *Hollywood Goes Shopping*, Minneapolis: University of Minnesota Press, pp. 159–78.

Sun, Linlin (2009a), 'Confucius's descendent visited the crew of *Confucius* and highly praised Chow's image as perfectly incorporating both the look and characteristics of Confucius' [*Kongzi houren tanban kongzi, sheng zan Zhou Runfa shenxingjianbei*], xinhuanet, 7 June, <http://ent.news.cn/2009-06/07/content_11500723.htm> (last accessed 28 October 2015).

Sun, Linlin (2009b), 'Hu Mei comments on the cast of *Confucius*: Chow Yun-fat has both of the *De* [ethics, morals and virtues] and *Yi* [arts and skills]' [*Hu Mei tan kongzi xuanjue biaozhun: Zhou Runfa fuhe deyishuangxin*], 17 March, <http://news.xinhuanet.com/ent/2009-03/17/content_11022770.htm> (last accessed 28 October 2015).

Ta Kung Pao (1999), 'Fat Gor is going to Beijing next week for *Crouching Tiger, Hidden Dragon*, which breaks the replacement rumour' [*fa ge xiazhou fujing paixi, wohucanglong yijue chuanwen bugongzipo*], 17 July, D08.

Tasker, Yvonne (1995), *Spectacular Bodies, Gender, Genre and the Action Cinema*, London: Routledge.

Tasker, Yvonne (2006), 'Fists of fury: discourses of race and masculinity in the martial arts cinema', in Dimitris Eleftheriotis and Gary Needham (eds), *Asian Cinemas: A Reader & Guide*, Edinburgh: Edinburgh University Press, pp. 437–56.

Tempest, Rone (1998), '98: year in review/Cover story: rolling with the punches', *Los Angeles Times*, home edition, 27 December, p. 5.

Teo, Stephen (1997), *Hong Kong Cinema, The Extra Dimensions*, London: British Film Institute.

Travers, Peter (2009), '*Crouching Tiger, Hidden Dragon*', *Rolling Stone*, <http://www.rollingstone.com/movies/reviews/crouching-tiger-hidden-dragon-20001210> (last accessed 21 October 2015).

Turner, Graeme (2004), *Understanding Celebrity*, London: Sage Publications.

TVB (1980), *Family Feelings [qinqing]* promotion booklet, Hong Kong: TVB.

TVB (1981a), *The Fate [huo fenghuang]*, promotion booklet, Hong Kong: TVB.

TVB (1981b), *The Good Old Times [eyu tan]*, promotion booklet, Hong Kong: TVB.

US Citizenship and Immigration Services (n.d.), *Immigration Legal History: Legislation from 1981–1996*, <http://www.nps.gov/elis/learn/education/upload/Legislation-1981-1996.pdf> (last accessed 5 November 2015).

US Bureau of Labor Statistics (2014), 'Employed persons by detailed industry and age, 2013 annual averages', 25 April, <http://www.bls.gov/cps/industry_age.htm> (last accessed 10 September 2015).

US Department of State (n.d.), *United States–Hong Kong Policy Act of 1992*, <http://hongkong.usconsulate.gov/ushk_pa_1992.html> (last accessed 7 July 2013).

University of Hong Kong (2015a), 'Ethnic identity Chinese citizen (per roll)' [*shenfen leibie rentong – zhongguoren-an ci jisuan*], *Public Opinion Programme*, 23 June, <https://www.hkupop.hku.hk/chinese/popexpress/ethnic/eidentity/poll/eid_poll_chart.html> (last accessed 17 September 2015).

University of Hong Kong (2015b), *People's Confidence in HK's Future-half-yearly Average* [*shimin dui xianggang qiantu xinxin – ban nian jie*], *Public Opinion Programme*, 25 June, <https://www.hkupop.hku.hk/chinese/popexpress/trust/conhkfuture/halfyr/hk_halfyr_chart.html> (last accessed 17 September 2015).

Variety (2005), 'Chow down for "Pirates"', 6 July, <http://www.variety.com/article/VR1117925557.html> (last accessed 18 November 2006).

Wada, Shuichi (1995), 'The status and image of the elderly in Japan: understanding the paternalistic ideology', in Mike Featherstone and Andrew Wernick (eds), *Images of Aging: Cultural Representations of Later Life*, London: Routledge, pp. 48–60.

Wang, Haizhou (2000), 'Ringo Lam's world "on fire"' [*Lin Lingdong de fengyun shijie*], in Cai Hongsheng, Song Jialiang and Liu Guiqing (eds), *80 Years of Hong Kong Film*, Beijing: Beijing Broadcasting Institute Press, pp. 183–95.

Wang, Simeng (2010), 'CCTV6 Confucius Premiere: Chow Yun-fat Kowtow to Confucius Descendant' [*CCTV6 kongzi shouyingli Zhou Runfa xianchang guibai Kongzi houren*], 4 January, <http://dailynews.sina.com/gb/ent/film/sinacn/file/20100114/20011113147.html> (last accessed 28 October 2015).

Wang, Yiman (2007), 'A star is dead: a legend is born: practising Leslie Cheung's posthumous fandom', in Sean Redmond and Su Holmes (eds), *Stardom and Celebrity: A Reader*, London: Sage Publications, pp. 326–40.

Watts, Jonathan (2012), 'Chinese professor calls Hong Kong residents "dogs of British imperialists"', *The Guardian*, 24 January, <http://www.guardian.co.uk/world/2012/jan/24/chinese-professor-hong-kong-dogs> (last accessed 28 October 2015).

Wen Wei Po (2000), 'Ang Lee's first martial arts film' [*Li An de di yi bu wuxia pian*], 21 February, n.p.

Weng, Haiyun (1990), 'Yun-fat successfully quit smoking: spending time on building models' [*fa zai jieyan chenggong, qi moxing duri*], *Ming Pao Weekly*, no. 1118, pp. 32–3.

Williams, Tony (1997), 'Space, place and spectacle: the crisis cinema of John Woo', *Cinema Journal*, vol. 36, no. 2, pp. 67–84.

Willis, Andy (2004a), 'Introduction', in Andy Willis (ed.), *Film Stars: Hollywood and Beyond*, Manchester: Manchester University Press, pp. 1–7.

Willis, Andy (2004b), 'Cynthia Rothrock: from the ghetto of exploitation', in Andy Willis (ed.), *Film Stars: Hollywood and Beyond*, Manchester: Manchester University Press, pp. 174–88.

Wilson, Rob (2005), 'Spectral critiques: tracking "uncanny" filmic paths towards a bio-poetics of trans-Pacific globalization', in Meaghan Morris, Siu Leung Li and Stephen Chan Ching-kiu (eds), *Hong Kong Connections: Transnational Imagination in Action Cinema*, Durham: Duke University Press, pp. 249–68.

Wojcik, Pamela Robertson (2004a), 'Character and type', in Pamela Robertson Wojcik (ed.), *Movie Acting, The Film Reader*, London: Routledge, pp. 165–7.

Wojcik, Pamela Robertson (2004b), 'Introduction', in Pamela Robertson Wojcik (ed.), *Movie Acting, The Film Reader*, London: Routledge, 2004, pp. 1–13.

Wojcik, Pamela Robertson (2004c), 'Typecasting', in Pamela Robertson Wojcik (ed.), *Movie Acting, The Film Reader*, London: Routledge, pp. 169–89.

Wong, Joseph Wai-chung and Joseph W. Yu (1978), *Television News and Television Industry in Hong Kong*, Hong Kong: Communications Studies, CUHK.

Xiao, Yang (2015), '*Office* in cinema soon: Sylvia Chang revealed that Chow Yun-fat's salary is calculated on the basis of hourly rate' [*huali shangbanzu jiang ying, Zhang Aijia bao Zhou Runfa paixi an xiaoshi shoufei*], People.com, 19 August, <http://media.people.com. cn/n/2015/0819/c40606-27483110.html> (last accessed 20 September 2015).

Xiao, Miao (2000), '*Crouching Tiger, Hidden Dragon* wants to touch audience's soul' [*wohucanglong xiang gei guanzhong yi ge zhendong*], *People's Daily*, overseas edition, 29 July, p. i.

Xiao, Shuang (2006), 'Leading box office for three weeks, "Caribbean" becomes the richest pirate' [*piaofang yi lianxu san zhou guanjun, jialebi chengwei zui fuyou haidao*], *Sohu.com*, 25 July, <http://yule.sohu.com/20060725/n244443859.shtml> (last accessed 18 November 2006).

Xiao, Ying (1987), 'Chow Yun-fat on dotted line' [*xuxian shang de Zhou Runfa*], *City Entertainment*, no. 226, pp. 3–5.

Ximen, Yi (2000), 'Radiating the imaginativeness and keeping the balance between the emotion and rationality – *Crouching Tiger, Hidden Dragon*' [*lingqi feiyang, qingli bingzhong*], *Ta Kung Pao*, 7 July, D08.

Yang, Huilan (1994), 'Chow Yun-fat has something to say' [*Zhou Runfa you hua yao shuo*], *City Entertainment*, no. 407, pp. 45–9.

Yang, Huilan (1995), 'Shining Star: say goodbye to Chow Yun-fat with a smile' [*shanliang zhi xing: dai xiao hua bie Zhou Runfa*], *City Entertainment*, no. 417, pp. 22–8.

Yao, Yao [1978] (2002), 'Sound, colour, art: a review of the development of Hong Kong Mass Culture' [*sheng, se, yi: huigu xianggang dazhong wenhua de fazhan*], in Wu Junxiong and Zhang Zhiwei (eds), *Reading Hong Kong Popular Cultures 1970–2000*, Hong Kong: Oxford University Press (China), pp. 7–18.

Ye, Huilan (2005), 'Chow Yun-fat's new bearded image in *Pirates of the Caribbean 2*' [*Zhou Runfa jialebi haidao 2 zhong xuhu zaoxing baoguang*], Sina.com, 17 January, <http://ent.sina.com.cn/m/f/2005-01-17/0844632211.html> (last accessed 22 August 2006).

Yi, Lian (2006), *Victory and Loneliness: Chow Yun-Fat's Hero Essence* [*feiyang yu luomo: Zhou Runfa de yingxiong bense*], Beijing: Orient Press.

Yu, Jia'ao (2000), 'A comparison of the blockbusters in this summer' [*shuqi dapian duizhao ji*], *Beijing Youth Daily*, 24 June, p. 12.

Yu, Sabrina (2012), 'Vulnerable Chinese stars: from *Xizi* to film worker', in Yingjin Zhang (ed.), *A Companion to Chinese Cinema*, Chichester: Wiley-Blackwell, pp. 218–38.

Zarrilli, Phillip B. (1995), 'Introduction: theories of and meditations on acting', in Phillip B. Zarrilli (ed.), *Acting (Re)considered: Theories and Practices*, London: Routledge, pp. 7–21.

Zhang, Bingliang (1987), 'The emergence of the new middle class and its impact on politics' [*xin zhongchan jieji de maoqi yu zhengzhi yingxiang*], *Ming Pao Monthly*, vol. 22, no. 1, pp. 10–15.

Zhang, Yingjin (2003), *Screening China: Critical Interventions, Cinematic Reconfigurations, and the Transnational Imaginary in Contemporary Chinese Cinema*, Ann Arbor: University of Michigan Press.

Zhang, Yu (1990), 'The most expensive passport' [*zuigui de huzhao*], *Ming Pao Weekly*, no. 1137, p. 135.

Zhao, Gang (2011), 'It is a wrap up of Jade Emperor's scenes in *Monkey King*: Chow Yun-fat's screen image disclosed' [*danao tiangong Yudi xifen shaqing, Zhou Runfa zaoxing baoguang*], People.com, 16 February, <http://ent.people.com.cn/GB/13934286.html> (last accessed 28 October 2015).

Zheng, Yongnian (2010), *The Chinese Communist Party as Emperor: Culture, Reproduction and Transformation*, Oxon: Routledge.

Zhong, Baoxian (2004), *Hundred Years of Hong Kong Film and Television Industry* [*xianggang yingshiye bainian*], Hong Kong: Joint Publishing.

Zhong, Baoxian 2012), 'Test time after ten years into the "gold rush": the phenomenon of Hong Kong filmmakers drifting to the north' [*'taojin shi nian' zoujin kaoyan shike – tan xianggang dianyingren de beipiao xianxiang*], in *Today*, issue 99, pp. 1–15.

Zhou, Chengzhen (1982), 'Criteria for judging acting quality' [*pinglun yanji de biaozhun*], *City Entertainment*, no. 98, pp. 38–9.

Zhu, Tongman (2011). 'The 130 million *The Assassins* starts filming in October: Chow Yun-fat plays Cao Cao' ['*Tongquetai*' *shiyue kaiji touzi 1.3yi Zhou Runfa yan Cao Cao*], 13 September <http://yule.sohu.com/20110913/n319140548.shtml> (last accessed on 4 July 2016).

Zi, Teng (2003), '2003 Chinese year in Hollywood' [*2003 haolaiwu huaren nian*], *Xinmin Evening News*, 21 February, p. 35.

Index